THE TINY HOUSE HANDBOOK

Charlie Wing

RSMeans WILEY

For the next generation…
in hopes they restore
us to sanity

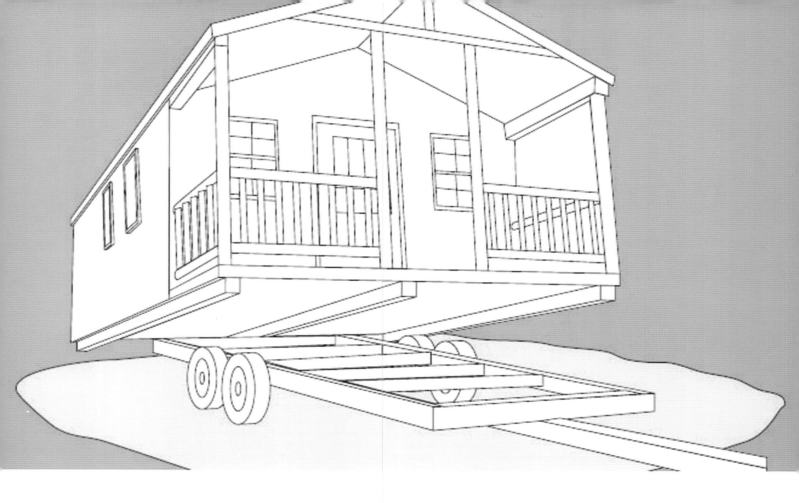

41" 78³/₈" 32⁵/₈"

THE
TINY
HOUSE
HANDBOOK

CHARLIE WING

WILEY

Published by John Wiley & Sons, Inc., Hoboken, New Jersey

Published simultaneously in Canada

For general information about our other products and services, please contact our Customer Care Department within the United States at (800) 762-2974, outside the United States at (317) 572-3993 or fax (317) 572-4002.

Wiley publishes in a variety of print and electronic formats and by print-on-demand. Some material included with standard print versions of this book may not be included in e-books or in print-on-demand. If this book refers to media such as a CD or DVD that is not included in the version you purchased, you may download this material at http://booksupport.wiley.com. For more information about Wiley products, visit www.wiley.com.

Library of Congress Cataloging-in-Publication Data:

Names: Wing, Charles, 1939- author.
Title: The tiny house handbook / Charlie Wing.
Description: Hoboken, NJ : Wiley, [2020] | Includes index.
Identifiers: LCCN 2020031687 (print) | LCCN 2020031688 (ebook) | ISBN 9781119581871 (paperback) | ISBN 9781119581895 (adobe pdf) | ISBN 9781119581864 (epub)
Subjects: LCSH: Small houses—Design and construction—Handbooks, manuals, etc. | House construction—Handbooks, manuals, etc. | House construction—Pictorial works.
Classification: LCC NA7533 .W56 2020 (print) | LCC NA7533 (ebook) | DDC 728/.37—dc23
LC record available at https://lccn.loc.gov/2020031687
LC ebook record available at https://lccn.loc.gov/2020031688

Cover Design: Wiley
Cover Illustrations: Courtesy of Charlie Wing

Printed in the United States of America

SKY10020949_090320

CONTENTS

INTRODUCTION

The idea of living in a tiny house is not new. Outside of the developed world, most of the world's people live in shelters no larger than those now defined in the US as "tiny" (less than 400 square feet). We have all read of and seen photographs of the Eskimo igloo, Native American teepee, Bedouin Arab tent, Gypsy vardo, Mongolian yurt, and Aboriginal dome. These are not temporary shelters, nor are they what Americans call "starter homes." Rather, they are, and have been for millennia, the standard homes for their cultures.

For reasons this book does not address, the average new home in the US has grown to 2,400 square feet of living space, four bedrooms, three bathrooms, and a two-car garage. While many, and probably most, Americans aspire to ownership of these McMansions, an increasing number are questioning, "What if a person gets everything and it's not enough?"

The tiny house movement is not just about tiny houses. It's about lifestyle; it's about less is more; it's about a smaller footprint but a larger life.

There are already many books on the tiny house philosophy and lifestyle. Most contain photos of tiny homes on wheels parked in dramatic settings and a myriad of clever ideas for the utilization of small spaces. Few, however, offer much guidance on how to proceed from present situation (usually a house that no longer fits or no home at all) to a tiny home fulfilling one's dream.

The Tiny House Handbook leads you through the full process from discovery (just what is a tiny home?) to the regulatory minefield of codes and zoning, to cost estimates, to design, to the actual construction (yes, you can build it yourself).

ACKNOWLEDGMENTS

Thirty years ago I had the idea of compiling a massive amount of information on residential construction into a *Visual Handbook of Building and Remodeling*. Two things the project required were: 1) my residence for a month in the Washington DC libraries of virtually every building trade association in the nation, and 2) someone to convince a publisher that such a project could be profitable.

This project, *The Tiny House Handbook*, was researched without my ever having to leave home. Thanks to the internet I was able to "pick the brains" of dozens of tiny home pioneers through their books, blogs, and articles. So, although too many to enumerate, let me acknowledge their unknowing contributions.

The second requirement, a person to sell the idea to a publisher, was fulfilled by Ray Wolf, my agent both then and now. I think it fair to say at least a dozen of my subsequent books, including *The Tiny House Handbook*, would have never seen the light of day without his powers of persuasion.

This project required a third element. Because tiny homes are an evolving phenomenon, I needed a insider, an observer, and a player in the trenches. That person has, and continues to be, Corinne Watson, founder and president of *Tiny Homes of Maine*. Thank you, Corinne.

Finally, and perhaps mostly, I have to thank the one who makes me glad to wake every morning, my soulmate, Barbara Rogerson.

THE AUTHOR

Charlie Wing is a nationally recognized home building/improvement/repair expert. He has written or co-written more than 20 books on these topics, including Home Depot's *Decorative Painting, Tiling, and Plumbing 1-2-3* books, *Better Homes & Gardens' Complete Guide to Home Repair*, Taunton Press's *The Visual Handbook of Building and Remodeling* and *The Visual Handbook of Energy Conservation*, Reader's Digest's *The Big Book of Small Household Repairs*, and many others, including *Ortho's Home Improvement Encyclopedia* and *How to Build Additions*.

An MIT PhD, Charlie has been a guest more than 400 times on home improvement radio and television shows, including on the Discovery Channel, PBS, and NBC's *Today Show*. He developed and hosted a national PBS series on home remodeling for energy efficiency. He was founding and technical editor for *Smart Homeowner* magazine from 2001 to 2004.

Author's Note

My love affair with tiny houses began in 1972. I was teaching physics at Bowdoin College and was asked to lead a senior seminar on any subject I knew nothing about. Bowdoin was experimenting with the notion of students learning to learn through emulation of the teacher in exploring a new subject.

One subject I knew nothing about was how buildings, in particular houses, worked or didn't work from the viewpoint of physics. I admit to having chosen the subject selfishly. The 1794 Maine farmhouse I had recently purchased was a preservationist's dream—as free of insulation, weatherstripping, and mechanical systems as the day it was born. Situated at the very top of a bare hill, on a windy night the best it could do was lower the speed of the infiltrating wind.

The seminar proved popular, not only among the Bowdoin students (they called the course "Hammer and Nails"), but also among a growing number of auditing back-to-the-land hippies wanting to construct their own shelters.

From a personal standpoint the course was a great success, for it resulted in an overwhelming urge to build my own energy-efficient passive solar house. Hearing of my desire, two of the graduating seniors asked if they could help. Both Jan Pierson and Steve Alcaide had scored an A on the final exam, and both were strong as bulls. How could I refuse?

The employment agreement was, for the summer: a room in the farmhouse, board, and the minimum wage at the time of $2.75/hour.

On the agreed starting date the two young men arrived on motorcycles. Behind each was a large duffel bag—and an enthusiastic young lady. I was, they informed me, getting four workers for the price of two. How could I refuse?

But, as so often happens, reality soon raised its head. That evening I held a crew meeting and presented several issues. First, my family of four plus the crew of four made eight people in just three bedrooms. Second, a rainy May had extended Maine's mud season, keeping the mile-long cowpath to the building site impassable. Third, not unexpected, and yet not insignificant, none of the crew had any prior carpentry experience.

The following morning the crew proposed a solution. If I supplied the materials, they would learn carpentry by building without pay a small cabin on site. There they would sleep and cook their own meals. At the end of summer I would have a guest house or writing shack for the cost of materials alone. The looks on their young faces reminded me of my dog's upon presentation of the retrieved ball. The energy generated among the four could have powered a small town. How could I refuse? Off they went on the motorcycles. Over his shoulder one yelled, "We're gonna do a charette!" (Look it up.)

In late afternoon they returned with a rough sketch for a 12' by 20' solar shed with two sleeping lofts. Over the next four days I produced foundation, framing, and sheathing drawings accurate to 1/8" inch while they measured, cut, and numbered every piece in my workshop. The following Monday they loaded all onto my farm tractor and trailer and plowed their way through the mud to the building site. One week later they moved into the shell of their tiny home.

The little house on its foundation of telephone poles and containing a compressed but complete kitchen, tiny wood stove, and two sleeping lofts, has now been continually occupied by single and couple tenants for forty-eight years.

Four years later found me at Cornerstones School in Brunswick, Maine, where adults from around the US and Canada would attend 3-week workshops on designing and building their own passive solar homes. Mornings, 9 to 12, would be spent in the classroom. Afternoons, 1 to 5, the students would practice construction skills.

The classroom portion consisted of fifteen lectures based on the fifteen chapters in *From the Ground Up*, the owner-builder text I had lately coauthored with John Cole. But what about the construction skills? How could forty students saw wood and pound nails for fifteen days without creating an immense heap of scrap?

Then I remembered the little 12' × 20' house. What could be more instructive, satisfying, and economical than constructing actual tiny houses that could later be sold for the cost of the materials? Over the next few years Cornerstones students completed a dozen. Construction took place in the Cornerstones parking lot in the heart of town. Upon completion, a pair of forklifts volunteered by the local lumberyard would load the completed building onto a flatbed trailer for delivery to its purchaser.

With each iteration the design improved and the public's interest increased. Local newspapers and then television newscasts carried brief stories. It being summer in Vacationland, the national media noticed. One class completed a tiny house in a 96-hour building bee during the annual *Maine Arts Festival* on the Bowdoin campus. The event was recorded and aired in a 20-minute segment on the PBS *MacNeil/Lehrer Report*. Another PBS series, *A House for all Seasons,* produced a segment comparing the tiny house to a "land yacht." *Country Living* magazine, not willing to wait, spent a fortune at the local nursery transforming the

Cornerstones parking lot into a forest setting for the little house. The cover banner on the magazine read, "Build This House for $5,000!" (They later reported sales for the building plans set a record.)

I purchased the last of the tiny houses and moved it to its present site on an ocean cove in nearby Harpswell, Maine. I lived in it for a year. The annual property tax including the oceanfront site was $120. The winter heating bill totalled one-half cord of hardwood.

I miss that tiny house. I'm going to build another.

From the back door, south-west reading and thinking corner. Sleeping loft overhead. Corner of 36" × 80" writing desk at bottom right.

From the kitchen/dining area, looking at sleeping loft, Jotul 602 wood stove, wall-hinged writing desk over couch (in working/down position).

From the woodstove, looking toward kitchen/dining area (kitchen is behind bookcase). Second sleeping loft over dining area has been removed.

From the driveway. A 6' × 20' extension to the rear added—at the request of a lady occupant—a bathroom and a walk-in closet. Total floor area is now 360 square feet.

1 TINY HOUSES

Shelter accounts for the largest expense in most homeowners' budgets. Monthly and annual payments go to mortgage principle and interest, property taxes, insurance, water, sewer, maintenance and repair, lighting, and fuels for cooking, heating, and cooling. Phew!

Of course, the smaller the home, the less the expense. The wealthy have always afforded large homes, even mansions, but while the housing trend of the recent past has been toward mini-mansions for all, incomes have not kept pace. The disparity in income between the wealthy and the rest of the population has never been greater.

In response there has been a surge in interest in smaller, even "tiny" houses. Of what does the market for tiny houses consist?

- young couples looking for starter homes
- renters finding it impossible to accumulate a $50,000 downpayment
- empty nesters no longer needing four bedrooms
- the elderly desiring to live in on-property accessory dwellings in lieu of assisted living facilities
- and, of course, the homeless

In this first chapter we will introduce—or should we say, "reintroduce"—the outlandish idea of living on less in less space, even a *tiny* space.

TINY HOUSES
A Tiny House at Walden Pond

With all the recurring interest in tiny houses, no one ever promoted the idea more eloquently than Henry David Thoreau. As chronicled in his classic, *Walden*, Thoreau constructed and lived in for a period of two years and two months a simple 10' x 15' cabin on the shore of Walden Pond in Concord, Massachusetts. Here, condensed, are his thoughts on shelter:

If one designs to construct a dwelling-house, it behooves him to exercise a little Yankee shrewdness, lest after all he find himself in a workhouse, a labyrinth without a clue, a museum, an almshouse, a prison, or a splendid mausoleum instead. Consider first how slight a shelter is absolutely necessary...I used to see a large box by the railroad, six feet long by three wide, in which the laborers locked up their tools at night; and it suggested to me that every man who was hard pushed might get such a one for a dollar, and, having bored a few auger holes in it, to admit the air at least, get into it when it rained and at night, and hook down the lid, and so have freedom in his love, and in his soul be free. This did not appear the worst, nor by any means a despicable alternative. You could sit up as late as you pleased, and, whenever you got up, go abroad without any landlord or house-lord dogging you for rent. Many a man is harassed to death to pay the rent of a larger and more luxurious box who would not have frozen to death in such a box as this...

Though the birds of the air have their nests, and the foxes their holes... in modern civilized society not more than one half the families own a shelter. In the large towns and cities, where civilization especially prevails, the number of those who own a shelter is a very small fraction of the whole. The rest pay an annual (rent that)... now helps to keep them poor as long as they live...

It is evident that... the civilized man hires his shelter commonly because he cannot afford to own

Replica of Thoreau's cabin on Walden Pond
Source: RhythmicQuietude at en.wikipedia https://commons.wikimedia.org/wiki/File:Replica_of_Thoreau%27s_cabin_near_Walden_Pond_and_his_statue.jpg licensed under CC BY-SA 3.0.

it; nor can he, in the long run, any better afford to hire...

Most men appear never to have considered what a house is, and are actually though needlessly poor all their lives because they think that they must have such a one as their neighbors have. There is some of the same fitness in a man's building his own house that there is in a bird's building its own nest. But alas! we do like cowbirds and cuckoos, which lay their eggs in nests which other birds have built, and cheer no traveller with their chattering and unmusical notes. Shall we forever resign the pleasure of construction to the carpenter? I never in all my walks came across a man engaged in so simple and natural an occupation as building his house. Where is this division of labor to end? and what object does it finally serve? No doubt another may also think for me; but it is not therefore desirable that he should do so to the exclusion of my thinking for myself...

I have thus (built) a tight shingled and plastered house, ten feet wide by fifteen long, and eight-feet posts, with a garret and a closet, a large window on each side, two trap doors, one door at the end, and a brick fireplace opposite... I had three chairs in my house; one for solitude, two for friendship, three for society. When visitors came in larger and unexpected numbers there was but the third chair for them all, but they generally economized the room by standing up. It is surprising how many great men and women a small house will contain…

My "best" room, however, my withdrawing room, always ready for company, on whose carpet the sun rarely fell, was the pine wood behind my house. Thither in summer days, when distinguished guests came, I took them, and a priceless domestic swept the floor and dusted the furniture and kept the things in order.

Should not every apartment in which man dwells be lofty enough to create some obscurity overhead, where flickering shadows may play at evening about the rafters? These forms are more agreeable to the fancy and imagination than… the most expensive furniture…My dwelling was small, and I could hardly entertain an echo in it; but it seemed larger for being a single apartment and remote from neighbors. All the attractions of a house were concentrated in one room; it was kitchen, chamber, parlor, and keeping-room; and whatever satisfaction parent or child, master or servant, derive from living in a house, I enjoyed it all…

I sometimes dream of a larger…house, standing in a golden age, of enduring materials, and without gingerbread work, which shall still consist of only one room, a vast, rude, substantial, primitive hall, without ceiling or plastering, with bare rafters and purlins supporting a sort of lower heaven over one's head…such a shelter as you would be glad to reach in a tempestuous night, containing all the essentials of a house, and nothing for house-keeping; where you can see all the treasures of the house at one view, and everything hangs upon its peg, that a man should use; at once kitchen, pantry, parlor, chamber, storehouse, and garret; where you can see so necessary a thing,

as a barrel or a ladder, so convenient a thing as a cupboard, and hear the pot boil, and pay your respects to the fire that cooks your dinner, and the oven that bakes your bread, and the necessary furniture and utensils are the chief ornaments.

Thoreau's Floor Plan?

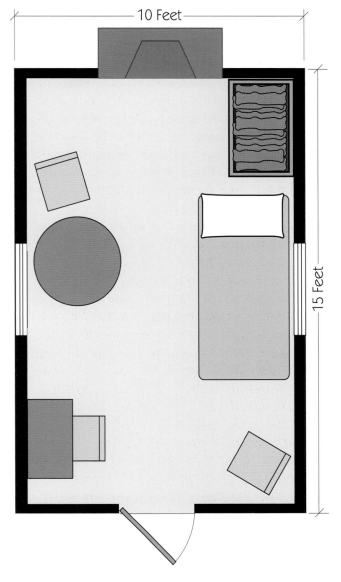

10 Feet

15 Feet

TINY HOUSES
What Is a Tiny House?

By Definition

From Thoreau's *Walden*, published in 1854, we find the idea of living in smaller spaces is not new. Search online book stores today and you will find dozens, if not hundreds, of titles referencing small homes, modest mansions, and not-so-big homes. The first title to contain the term *tiny house*, however, was *Tiny Houses: or How to Get Away From It All* by architect Lester Walker (1987).

But the most credit for promoting tiny houses as serious solutions to a growing housing problem should be given to Jay Shafer. Shafer wrote his first tiny house article in 1997. That same year he founded the Tumbleweed Tiny House Company, building tiny houses on wheels. The tiny trailered homes (maximum width 8'-6") created interest from multiple perspectives:

On Wheels

Most people, when hearing the term *tiny house*, picture a conventional but narrow house built on a trailer. The appeal is not only in its less-is-more statement, but the suggestion of total independence.

While the freedom to **go** anywhere is true, the freedom to **stay** is more complex. Most zoning considers tiny homes on wheels akin to recreational vehicles and campers which are not subject to real estate taxes. They are thus considered squatters and are generally limited to stays of several months maximum.

And like RVs, tiny homes on wheels have to provide for—at least temporarily—their own electricity, water, and sewage. Like perpetual motion, **total** shelter freedom is still an elusive dream.

- Like mobile homes and RVs, they were on wheels, but they were constructed of wood and actually looked like houses.

- Being on wheels they also fed our desire for freedom. "Hasta la vista, I'm out of here!"

- Having your home, like a turtle, "on your back" meant changing jobs would no longer require selling the old and buying new.

In 2007 Jay and his tiny home appeared on the *Oprah Winfrey Show*.

Finally, in 2017, the *International Residential Code* officially recognized tiny homes as "houses that are 400 square feet in area or less." In consultation with Jay and others the IRC added *Appendix Q*, allowing space-saving exceptions for stairs and sleeping lofts and egress (in case of fire) from roof windows.

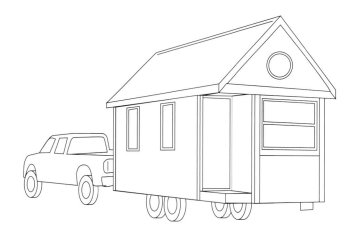

Delivered on Skids

One solution to the where-to-stay dilemma is the built-to-be-moved tiny house on skids. Small structures sheathed in structural plywood are rigid enough without supporting beams, so the skids serve primarily as runners allowing the structure to be moved across the ground.

And while tiny homes on wheels are limited to widths of 8'6" and height above ground of 13'6", structures up to 12' wide may be transported on a truck or trailer (loaded height limit 14') with a routine permit.

Inexpensive and widely available "Amish sheds" in widths to 12' and lengths to 32' provide examples. An Amish shed with upgraded doors, windows, sheathing, and siding could provide the starting point for a tiny home on a foundation.

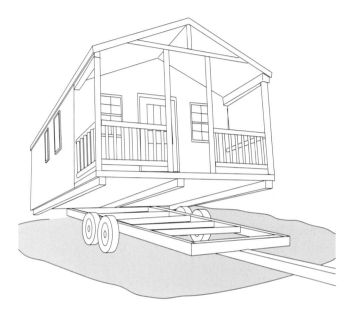

Built on Site

Why not build a tiny home the conventional way on a permanent foundation? In the past half century, with the emphasis on bigger is better, most communities imposed minimum size requirements in their zoning. This had little to do with health or safety but everything to do with maintaining property values and the real estate tax base.

Well over ninety percent of US communities base their building standards on the *International Residential Code (IRC)*. With the formal adoption in 2018 of *IRC Appendix Q,* dealing with homes 400 square feet in area or less, there are now few if any logical reasons to outlaw tiny homes. Imposing a size limit may not be against the law, but it is increasingly difficult to defend.

1 TINY HOUSES
How Big Is Big Enough?

US House Sizes, 1920–2015

The average size of houses in the US remained at a near constant 200 sq.ft. per occupant until the end of WWII when millions of young GIs returned looking for homes in which to start their families. The response of the building industry was tract housing: thousands of 800 sq.ft. homes in developments such as the "Levittowns." But as incomes increased, the size of one's home became a status symbol. From a single bathroom and no garage, the norm grew to 4 bedrooms, 2½ baths, and a 2-car garage. Family room, media room, playroom, and a bedroom for every child added up to over 1,000 sq.ft. per occupant.

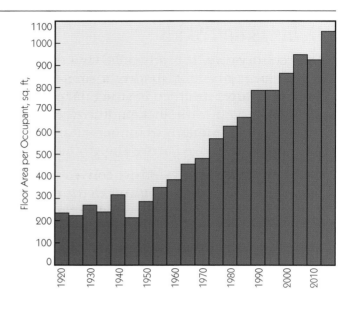

Shelter Sizes Around the World

Although homeowners in Australia, Canada, and the US apparently think bigger is better, the 2009 map below shows the feeling is not universal. Homeowners in Hong Kong, one of the wealthiest countries in the world, get by with (almost) tiny homes of 484 sq.ft. and a thoroughly Thoreauvian space per occupant of just 150 sq.ft.

New Life for an Old Idea: The ADU

What Is an ADU?

An accessory dwelling unit (ADU) is a compact independent dwelling sharing a single-family lot with a larger primary dwelling. While tiny, it contains its own bathroom, kitchen, living, and sleeping areas.

As illustrated, the ADU can be created within the existing primary dwelling, converted from a garage, added as an extension to the existing dwelling, or built on or delivered to the site.

Why an ADU?

The ADU offers a host of housing solutions:

• Older homeowners would rather age in place than be shipped off to a prohibitively expensive assisted living or nursing facility. Grandma and Grandpa can enjoy their last years at home and in the old neighborhood while their children take over the family residence.

• Young singles and couples, often saddled with college debt, can live for little or nothing while saving up for the downpayment on their first home.

• When family members no longer require the ADU, it can provide rental income to the homeowners, possibly paying the mortgage.

• In this age of decreasing housing availability and increasing cost, cities and towns are beginning to view ADUs as solutions without changing the physical character of neighborhoods.

• Finally, the great unspoken issue with tiny homes is **where to put them**. Even when zoning permits, the costs of land and site services usually equal or exceed the cost of the building itself. With an ADU the cost for the site is zero, and the costs of extending the already existing site services is minimal.

Options for ADUs

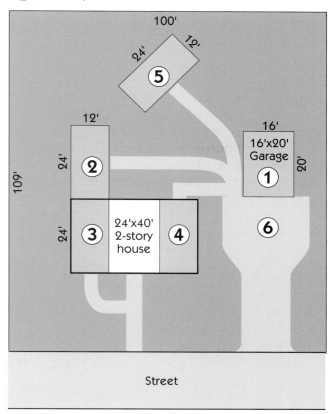

OPTIONS

(1) A single-car 16' x 20', 1-story garage makes a perfect, groundfloor accessible apartment.

(2) A 12' x 24' groundfloor addition is accessible and private, and adds just 30% to the house footprint.

(3) A 12' x 24' apartment within the house first floor requires only 15% of the original house floor area.

(4) A 12' x 24' apartment in a walkout basement makes a perfect, groundfloor accessible apartment.

(5) A 12' x 24' (or up to 400 sq.ft.) tiny house is totally private and can be placed anywhere.

(6) An additional parking space can usually be created for an ADU just by widening the original driveway.

NOTES

2 LEGAL ASPECTS

You are excited; you are motivated; you are ready to begin a life based on need, not greed, in a shelter that sustains you, not drains you. This book is designed to provide the information you need to realize your dream, but first a dose of reality.

While 90% of the world's 7,800,000,000 people live in just 200 square feet per person, the average allocation for Americans has bloated to 832 square feet. Why so big? Because, like so many other aspects of the American way, we could. The size of one's home has become a status symbol. The towns we live in speak to who we are. This has been going on since the end of World War II—long enough for *minimum lot size* and *minimum house size* to creep into our zoning ordinances. The reality is that you will have a difficult time obtaining a building permit for your tiny home in affluent residential areas.

But there is often an out. Even the affluent like to have family nearby. There is an equally long history of zoning allowances for accessory dwelling units, so-called "granny flats." Very often the size minimum, if there is one, falls within the 400 square foot "tiny house" range.

Then there are the building codes. Your house may be tiny, but it still must meet building, electrical, and plumbing codes. But relax. These codes are not designed to stop you. They are designed solely to keep you safe and healthy. Embrace them.

2 LEGAL ASPECTS
Zoning and Building Codes

Assuming you have prepared mentally and emotionally for the tiny house lifestyle, and assuming you have the financial resources or credit to fund your project, what legal hurdles remain to be cleared? Principally, they fall under two headings: *Zoning* and *Building Codes*.

Zoning

A town zoning ordinance specifies how its land may be used. The ordinance is enforced by an appointed planning board of 3 to 7 residents. Items in the ordinance usually include:

- *Use zones*, for example: agricultural, commercial, residential, conservation

- *Minimum lot size*, for example 2 acres for residential

- *Minimum setbacks* of buildings from property lines, for example 20 feet

- *Minimum habitable area* of residential buildings, for example 800 sq.ft.

- *Maximum building heights*, either in feet or floors, above grade

- *Activities permitted and forbidden*

- *Offstreet parking requirements*

- *Accessory Dwelling Unit (ADU) regulations*

In most jurisdictions the zoning ordinance is posted online. It may also be available for purchase. After choosing a geographic area for your site your first step is to become familiar with each candidate town's zoning ordinance with an eye to spotting possible roadblocks to your tiny house plans.

If the tiny home of your dreams is on wheels, chances are great you will encounter a problem right away. Although your tiny home is an actual wood-framed house built on a trailer it is, strictly speaking, neither a house as commonly defined nor a trailer. The closest legally recognized category is a camper trailer, and most zoning ordinances forbid the permanent occupation of camper trailers on residential lots. This is, one hopes, a temporary issue because tiny houses, on or off wheels, offer affordable solutions in a time of increasing housing shortages. If you find your town's ordinance is not favorable to tiny homes, then request they update it to include them. Contact your local tiny home manufacturer if you need help. In the meantime you will probably be able to park your tiny home on wheels in back of a friend's or relative's home—at least until someone complains—or in a designated mobile home or tiny home park.

Provided, however, your vision of a tiny home is one sitting on a foundation in a permanent location, familiarize yourself with the zoning ordinances of each of your target towns. Then schedule appointments with a building code official in each. IMPORTANT: These are human beings performing an important service for the good of the town and its citizens. Treating them with respect for their public service and their knowledge (many are retired builders, plumbers, or electricians) will usually result in their respecting you and your project in return. You are not there to demand their approval; you are there to request their guidance in realizing your dream.

Your first meeting will be for gathering information prior to purchasing land and drawing plans. Once you feel the official is engaged and at least somewhat encouraging, ask if they could help by supplying the answers to a list of specific zoning questions. Assuming the answer is yes, complete a copy of the survey form on the facing page.

Town Zoning Survey

Town _____

Phone _____ Hours _____

Address_____

_____

Code Officer _____

Phone _____ Hours _____

Zoning Head _____

Phone _____ Hours _____

Min. Lot Size _____

Residence sq.ft. min. _____ max. _____

Allowed Housing Types:

☐ Manufactured

☐ Mobilehome

☐ Recreational Vehicle

☐ Camper Trailer

☐ Moveable (on wheels)

☐ Moveable (on skids)

Permanent foundation required? (Y/N) _____

Allowed Foundation Types

☐ Masonry full basement

☐ Masonry crawl space

☐ Slab on grade

☐ Concrete grade beam

☐ All-weather wood. full or crawl

☐ Concrete piers

☐ Pressure-treated wood posts

Detached ADU allowed? (Y/N) _____

Permanent foundation required? (Y/N) _____

Aesthetic compatibility required? (Y/N) _____

Square footage: min. _____ **max.** _____

Percent of main: min. _____ **max.** _____

Occupancy:

☐ Family only

☐ Rentals allowed

Once you have found town and code officials receptive to at least the concept of a tiny house, you need to find your spot. Sticking only to totally legal possibilities, they are:

- an already approved development specifically for tiny houses

- a building site meeting all zoning requirements

- an existing residential property which could host an ADU (see page 7).

Once you have acquired your legal site, the next step is to design and draw up plans for your tiny house on that site. You might get away with hand-drawn sketches in a few sparsely populated rural areas, but the approval process—not to mention the construction process—will be much easier if the plans are drawn to standard architectural conventions and scales (see Chapter 6).

Of course detailed architectural plans include such things as:

- sizes of floor joists and roof rafters

- stairway dimensions

- minimum clearances for doorways, halls, and plumbing fixtures

- locations and ratings of electrical receptacles

All of these are regulated by building codes, which we address next.

 **LEGAL ASPECTS**

Building Codes

Local building codes are usually based on the International Residential Code (IRC). Both states and local jurisdictions are free to modify the IRC, but until a local code enforcement official states otherwise, consider the IRC your bible.

How do you make sure your tiny house design meets the Code? Here are the possible ways:

- Have it built by a tiny home manufacturer (expensive, but the simplest way).

- Have it designed by a local architect (adds 10–15% to the project cost).

- Follow this book's directions, then pay to have your plans reviewed by an architect.

- Provided your local code enforcement officer really likes you, follow the directions in this book, meeting often with him or her to guide your progress.

Permits and Variances

Before building you will have to obtain permits. In a small town the permits may be issued by a single code enforcement officer. In heavily populated cities and towns you or your builder will have to present your plans to the planning board for approval. Often you will need to resubmit your plans after making changes requested by the board members.

Sometimes the board will turn down your application because it fails to meet a fundamental zoning requirement. In the case of a tiny home, this will most likely be size. If the planning board refuses to grant your application a variance, your final option would be an appearance at the separate zoning board of appeals. If determined to prevail you should at this point consider hiring a real estate attorney to help you present your case.

The IRC Minimum Size

With the exception of *IRC Appendix Q*, any tiny house (no larger than 400 sq.ft. habitable area) has to conform to the same IRC requirements as any other one- and two-family dwelling. Since size is of such critical importance, it bears listing the IRC main body regulations regarding size:

R304.1 Minimum area. *Habitable rooms shall have a floor area of not less than 70 square feet.*

R304.2 Minimum dimensions. *Habitable rooms shall be not less than 7 feet in any horizontal dimension.*

      Exception: *Kitchens.*

R304.3 Height effect on room area. *Portions of a room with a sloping ceiling measuring less than 5 feet or a furred ceiling measuring less than 7 feet from the finished floor to the finished ceiling shall not be considered as contributing to the minimum required habitable area for that room.*

R306.1 Toilet facilities. *Every dwelling unit shall be provided with a water closet, lavatory, and a bathtub or shower.*

R306.2 Kitchen. *Each dwelling unit shall be provided with a kitchen area, and every kitchen area shall be provided with a sink.*

NOTE: The minimum area of a bathroom containing the three fixtures listed in R306.1 and conforming to the minimum fixture clearances shown on page 35 is 18 square feet.

Since R306.2 refers to a kitchen area, not a separate kitchen, the kitchen may be part of the minimum habitable room of R304.1. Thus the minimum total area of a dwelling can be as little as 70 + 18 = 88 square feet!

IRC Appendix Q

IRC Appendix Q: Tiny Houses

The provisions contained in this appendix are not mandatory unless specifically referenced in the adopting ordinance.

User note:

About this appendix: *Appendix Q relaxes various requirements in the body of the code as they apply to houses that are 400 square feet in area or less. Attention is specifically paid to features such as compact stairs, including stair handrails and headroom, ladders, reduced ceiling heights in lofts and guard and emergency escape and rescue opening requirements at lofts.*

GENERAL

AQ101.1 Scope. This appendix shall be applicable to *tiny houses* used as single *dwelling units*. *Tiny houses* shall comply with this code except as otherwise stated in this appendix.

DEFINITIONS

AQ102.1 General. The following words and terms shall, for the purposes of this appendix, have the meanings shown herein. Refer to Chapter 2 of this Code for general definitions.

EGRESS ROOF ACCESS WINDOW. A *skylight* or roof window designed and installed to satisfy the emergency escape and rescue opening requirements of Section R310.2.

LANDING PLATFORM. A landing provided as the top step of a stairway accessing a *loft*.

LOFT. A floor level located more than 30 inches above the main floor, open to the main floor on one or more sides with a ceiling height of less than 6 feet 8 inches and used as a living or sleeping space.

TINY HOUSE. A *dwelling* that is 400 square feet or less in floor area excluding *lofts*.

CEILING HEIGHT

AQ103.1 Minimum ceiling height. *Habitable space* and hallways in *tiny houses* shall have a ceiling height of not less than 6 feet 8 inches. Bathrooms, toilet rooms and kitchens shall have a ceiling height of not less than 6 feet 4 inches. Obstructions including, but not limited to, beams, girders, ducts and lighting, shall not extend below these minimum ceiling heights.

LOFTS

AQ104.1 Minimum Loft Area & Dimensions *Lofts* used as a sleeping or living space shall meet the minimum area and dimension requirements of Sections AQ104.1.1 through AQ104.1.3.

AQ 104.1.1 Minimum area. *Lofts* shall have a floor area of not less than 35 square feet.

AQ 104.1.2 Minimum dimensions. *Lofts* shall be not less than 5 feet in any horizontal dimension.

AQ 104.1.3 Height effect on loft area. Portions of a *loft* with a sloped ceiling measuring less than 3 feet from the finished floor to the finished ceiling shall not be considered as contributing to the minimum required area for the loft

> **Exception:** Under gable roofs with a minimum slope of 6 units vertical in 12 units horizontal (50 percent slope) portions of a *loft* with a sloped ceiling measuring less than 16 inches from the finished floor to the finished ceiling shall not be considered as contributing to the minimum required area for the *loft*.

AQ104.2 Loft Access. The access to and primary egress from *lofts* shall be of any type described in Sections AQ104.2.1 through AQ104.2.4.

AQ 104.2.1 Stairways. Stairways accessing *lofts* shall comply with this code or with Sections AQ104.2.1.1 through AQ104.2.1.5.

AQ 104.2.1.1 Width. Stairways accessing a *loft* shall not be less than 17 inches in clear width at or above the handrail. The width below the handrail shall be not less than 20 inches.

AQ 104.2.1.2 Headroom. The headroom in stairways accessing a *loft* shall be not less than 6 feet 2 inches, as measured vertically, from a sloped line connecting the tread or platform nosings in the middle of their width.

AQ 104.2.1.3 Treads and risers. Risers for stairs accessing a *loft* shall be not less than 7 inches and not more than 12 inches in height. Tread depth and riser height shall be calculated in accordance with one of the following formulas:

1. The tread depth shall be 20 inches minus four-thirds of the riser height.

2. The riser height shall be 15 inches minus three-fourths of the tread depth.

AQ 104.2.1.4 Landing platforms. The top tread and riser of stairways accessing *lofts* shall be constructed as a *landing platform* where the *loft* ceiling height is less than 6 feet 2 inches where the stairway meets the loft. The *landing platform* shall be 18 inches to 22 inches in depth measured from the nosing of the landing platform to the edge of the *loft*, and 16 to 18 inches in height measured from the *landing platform* to the *loft* floor.

AQ 104.2.1.5 Handrails. Handrails shall comply with Section R311.7.8.

AQ 104.2.1.6 Stairway guards. Guards at open sides of stairways shall comply with Section R312.1.

AQ 104.2.2 Ladders. Ladders accessing *lofts* shall comply with Sections AQ104.2.1 and AQ104.2.2

AQ 104.2.2.1 Size and capacity. Ladders accessing *lofts* shall have a rung width of not less than 12 inches, and 10- to 14-inch spacing between rungs. Ladders shall be capable of supporting a 200-lb load on any rung. Rung spacing shall be uniform within $^3/_8$ inch.

AQ 104.2.2.2 Incline. Ladders shall be installed at 70 to 80 degrees from horizontal.

AQ 104.2.3 Alternating tread devices. Alternating tread devices accessing *lofts* shall comply with Sections R311.7.11.1 and R311.7.11.2. The clear width at and below the handrails shall be not less than 20 inches.

AQ 104.2.4 Ships ladders. Ships ladders accessing *lofts* shall comply with Sections R311.7.12.1 and R311.7.12.2. The clear width at and below the handrails shall be not less than 20 inches.

AQ 104.2.5 Loft guards. *Loft* guards shall be located along the open side of *lofts*. *Loft* guards shall be not less than 36 inches in height or one-half of the clear height to the ceiling, whichever is less.

EMERGENCY ESCAPE & RESCUE OPENINGS

AQ105.1 General. *Tiny houses* shall meet the requirements of Section R310 for emergency escape and rescue openings. **Exception:** *Egress roof access windows* in *lofts* used as sleeping rooms shall be deemed to meet the requirements of Section R310 where installed such that the bottom of the opening is not more than 44 inches above the *loft* floor, provided the egress roof access window complies with the minimum opening area requirements of Section R310.2.1,

Highway Width & Height Limits

As shown on the map and in the illustrations below, there is good reason tiny homes on wheels are limited to 13' 6" in height and 8' 6" in width. However, with state-issued permits, much larger tiny homes on skids can be transported from point of assembly to building site. Low clearances, restricted routes, and state permitting agency phone numbers and websites are all listed in the *Rand McNally Deluxe Motor Carrier's Road Atlas* (available on Amazon).

Maximum Unpermitted Highway Height Limits

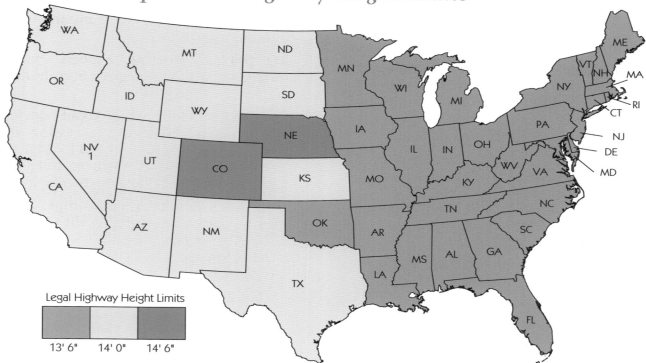

Legend: Legal Highway Height Limits — 13' 6" | 14' 0" | 14' 6"

Example (Maine) DOT Size Limits for Drop-Deck Trailers

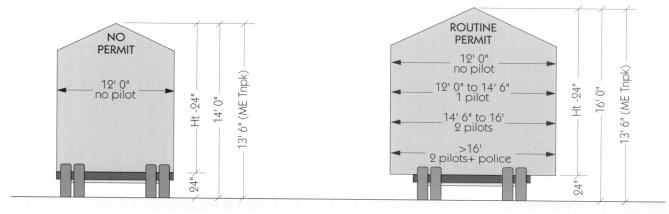

NO PERMIT
12' 0" no pilot
Ht - 24"
14' 0"
24"
13' 6" (ME Tnpk)

ROUTINE PERMIT
12' 0" no pilot
12' 0" to 14' 6" 1 pilot
14' 6" to 16' 2 pilots
>16' 2 pilots+ police
Ht -24"
16' 0"
24"
13' 6" (ME Tnpk)

NOTES

3 COSTS

As a general statement it is certainly fair to say, "Tiny houses cost less than big houses." Still, the costs of your tiny house project must be scrutinized and analyzed carefully and objectively lest you run out of money before completion.

If you have no prior building experience, two surprises await you. First, the smaller the house, the greater the cost per square foot. All houses have certain minimal elements in common: toilet, shower or tub, lavatory, refrigerator, cook stove, kitchen sink, water heater, heating system, cooling system, and electrical service equipment. The smaller the house, the fewer square feet this minimum cost is spread over.

The second surprise is that, in the case of a tiny house, the cost of the house may be less than half the cost of the total project. Due to the usual zoning requirement of a minimum lot size, in a residential area the cost of the bare site will likely exceed $100,000. To that must be added the costs of site improvements: potable water, sewage disposal, electric service, road or driveway, and landscaping.

"To be forewarned is to be forearmed." This chapter is your warning. Think outside the box. Consider all your options. Consider an accessory dwelling unit (ADU), a tiny dwelling (apartment, addition, or tiny house) accessory to an existing primary dwelling: cost of land = $0.00, cost of site services = $?.?? (but minimal since shared).

3 Building Cost Breakdown

The stack of boxes at right illustrates a rough breakdown of the costs of building the average house. Adapted from data in Table 1 of the National Association of Home Builders' *Single Family Price and Cost Breakdowns, 2015 National Results*, it includes the costs of permits, inspections, landscaping, and driveways as well as the physical structure.

Since the average house surveyed contained 2,802 sq.ft., the numbers must be considered but rough approximations to those for a tiny (less than 400 sq.ft.) house. Percentages for painting, flooring, trim, drywall, insulation, wiring and lighting, siding, roofing, windows, sheathing, framing, and foundation would be comparable, but tiny house driveways, landscaping, cabinets and countertops, appliances, doors, and plumbing fixtures would represent a greater percentage of the whole cost.

To get dollar costs for each item, multiply the percentages shown by the average total cost of the homes in the survey, $289,000.

Also realize that the average figures include both much higher and much lower costs depending on the nature of the construction. The all-granite kitchen and bath countertops in a luxury home would cost at least five times as much as laminated plastic equivalents in the more economical home. Similarly full-thickness hard maple strip flooring would cost five times as much as the perfectly serviceable painted plywood chosen by a do-it-yourselfer on a tight budget.

One of the best tools the do-it-yourselfer can buy is a residential construction estimating book. A one-year-old copy of the *Craftsman National Construction Estimator* can be had on Amazon for about $30.

Where Does the Money Go?

Percentage	Item
2%	Sheathing
2%	Insulation
2%	Deck and Stairs
2%	Driveway
2%	Appliances
3%	Roofing
3%	Cabinets and Countertops
3%	Trim
3%	Landscaping
4%	Painting
4%	Drywall
4%	HVAC
4%	Permits and Inspections
5%	Wiring and Lighting
5%	Siding
5%	Flooring
6%	Plumbing and Fixtures
6%	Windows and Doors
7%	Foundation
14%	Framing
14%	Other miscellaneous

Savings by Doing It Yourself

Using the data from the same National Association of Home Builders' *Single Family Price and Cost Breakdowns, 2015 National Results* and assuming the cost of each material item consists of equal parts material and labor, results in the graph at right.

In addition to the use of less expensive materials, two ways for an owner to save significant money are to:

- assume the role of the general contractor in hiring and directing subcontractors, ordering materials, and securing permits and inspections.
- alternatively, perform every task as a do-it-yourselfer.

The first option saves about 20% in the general contractor's overhead and general expenses, real estate marketing and commissions, and profit.

The much more labor- and required-skills-intensive option of doing it entirely one's self saves the entire cost of labor for a total of about 50%.

Before entertaining either cost-saving option one is urged to perform an honest assessment of their knowledge, skills, dedication, and available time. Experience teaching hundreds of aspiring DIY homebuilders has taught the author three rules of thumb. The total person hours required to build a house are approximately:

- for the experienced builder, 1 hr./sq.ft.
- for an average "handyman," 2 hr./sq.ft.
- for a complete novice, at least 3 hr./sq.ft.

Complete novices would be wise to first volunteer at their local Habitat for Humanity, where they would both pick up skills and get a better sense of the tasks they face.

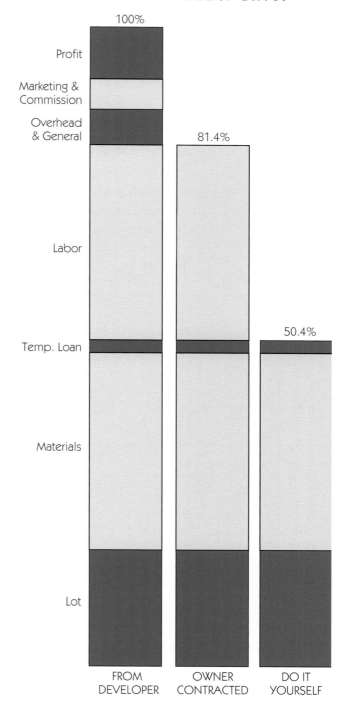

How Much Can a DIYer Save?

COSTS
Square Foot Construction Cost

The top curve in the graph below was generated by averaging current (2018) prices of new homes not including site over a size range of 100 sq.ft. to 2,000 sq.ft. and dividing the prices by the home's square footage. Of course the data points displayed a lot of scatter, so the smooth curves represent the best fit. The green and blue curves were then generated by applying the percentage savings expected from owner contracting (green) and doing it all one's self (blue).

The graphs demonstrate what should be intuitive: the smaller the house, the more expensive per square foot. The reason for this phenomenon is that kitchens, baths, heating and cooling systems, and so on are common to all homes, but are not strictly proportional to size.

The magnitude of the differences is seen in the two examples shown. The average contracted 200-sq.ft. house costs $300 per sq.ft., while the 1,800-sq.ft. home costs about half as much per sq.ft., $163.

Again, applying the savings from supplying labor, the owner-contractor (green curve) and the total do-it-yourselfer (blue curve) can reduce those numbers by approximately twenty and fifty percent.

Contracted vs Do-It-Yourself Costs/Sq.Ft. as a Function of Size

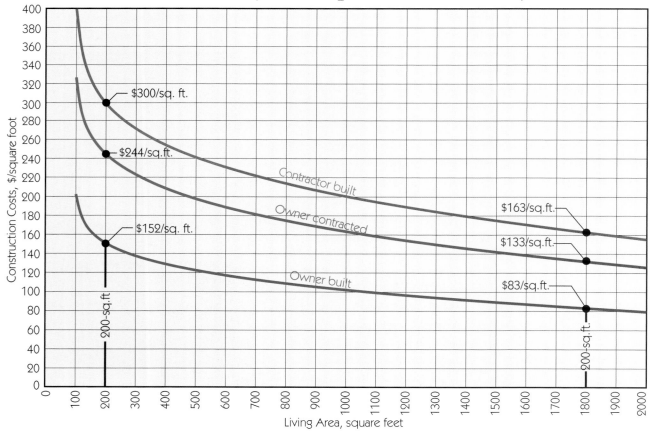

Total Construction Cost

Of course the bottom line when building or buying a home is not cost per square foot but total cost. Total cost is simply cost per square foot × total square feet. The graph below is the result of performing this multiplication on the curves on the previous page.

Using the same two example homes, 1,800 and 200 square feet, we get $293,400 and $60,000 for the fully contracted versions. For the total do-it-yourself versions of the same homes we project $149,400 and $30,400—plenty of incentive for the prospective small-home DIYer!

If $30,400 doesn't align with what you have heard, seen on television, or read in a magazine, remember: the figures in these graphs represent *average* figures for *average* construction. The use of less expensive grades and recycled or donated materials and appliances can lower these costs substantially.

Contracted vs Do-It-Yourself Total Cost as a Function of Size

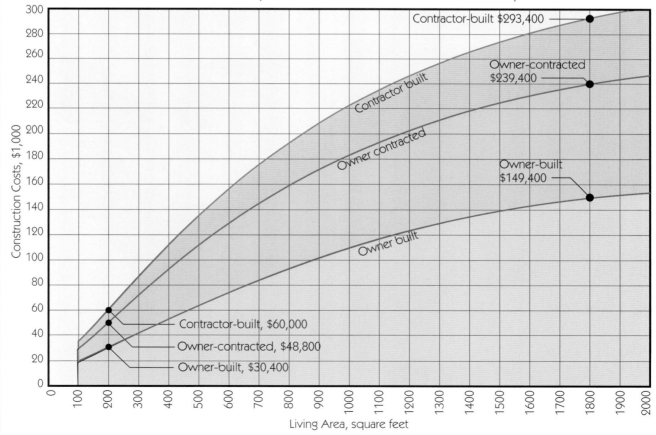

The cost figures in the previous charts are for the building alone, not including the site and site services. Unless your planned tiny home is on wheels and you plan an eternal road trip, or your home will be an "accessory dwelling unit" sharing the site with an existing home, sooner or later you will have to purchase or rent a site on which to place the structure.

The map below displays the extraordinary range of prices of land in dollars per acre, from about $15,000 in rural areas such as New Hampshire, West Virginia, and Oklahoma, to over $400,000 in sunny California.

The numbers are not prices *per lot* but prices *per acre*, so you have to multiply by the size of the lot. Minimum lot size is specified in zoning ordinances and usually varies by zone. In rural and very affluent areas minimum lot sizes can be three or more acres, while densely populated areas may be zoned ¼ acre minimum.

Prices also vary widely within states. Lots within metropolitan areas are much more expensive than those in less developed areas. Lesson: do your homework! Websites such as *Zillow.com* allow unlimited research on your computer or mobile device.

2018 Residential Building Site Costs, $1,000 per Acre

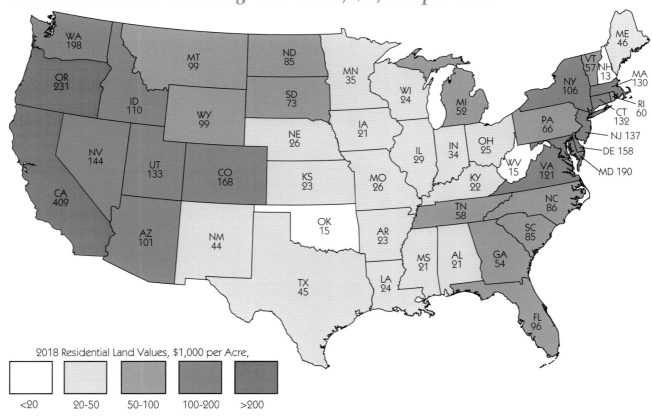

2018 Residential Land Values, $1,000 per Acre,

| <20 | 20-50 | 50-100 | 100-200 | >200 |

More Added Costs: Site Services

Site services are all those things added to a lot to make the building/lot combination habitable. If the lot is in a development it may already have most or all services already. If not, here are the things you may have to add (see illustration below):

1. Public Water. If a public water main runs in front of your lot, you will be required to connect to it for a fee.

2. Well. If public water is not available you will need to drill a well or haul water.

3. Public Sewage. If a public sewer line runs past your lot, you will be required to connect to it even if the lot contains a private system.

4. Septic System. Unless public sewage is available or you use a composting toilet to eliminate "black waste" you will need a septic tank and leach field or a holding tank.

5. Electric Service. Unless you go off grid with a solar system, you will connect to the power line. Extending the existing line more than one or two poles is extremely expensive.

6. Driveway. You will probably want a solid, low-maintenance driveway. A 3-inch-thick asphalt drive costs about $10 per sq.ft.

7. Landscaping. Grading for drainage, a layer of topsoil, and a few shade trees are the minimal starting point.

Building Site Services

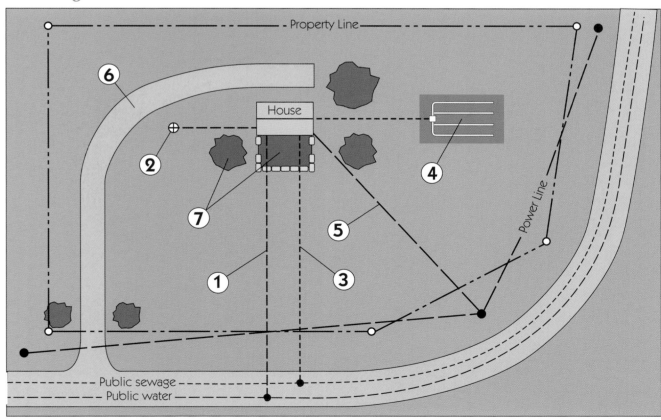

Added Costs: Impact Fees?

Impact fees comprise a fairly recent addition to the cost of building a home. In areas experiencing rapid growth, counties, cities, and towns are having to improve and expand roads, extend water and sewer lines, expand water and sewage treatment plants, add fire stations, develop parks and recreational facilities, and build additional schools.

The map shows where impact fees are most often assessed and the average fees imposed per home. It is not surprising to see the most and the highest fees occurring in the western, southwestern, and southeastern states where the population growth rate is greatest.

Depending on the state, fees may be charged for any or all of these categories:

- Schools
- Roads
- Water
- Sewage
- Storm water drainage
- Police
- Fire
- Library
- Parks

Average Residential Building Impact Fees by State

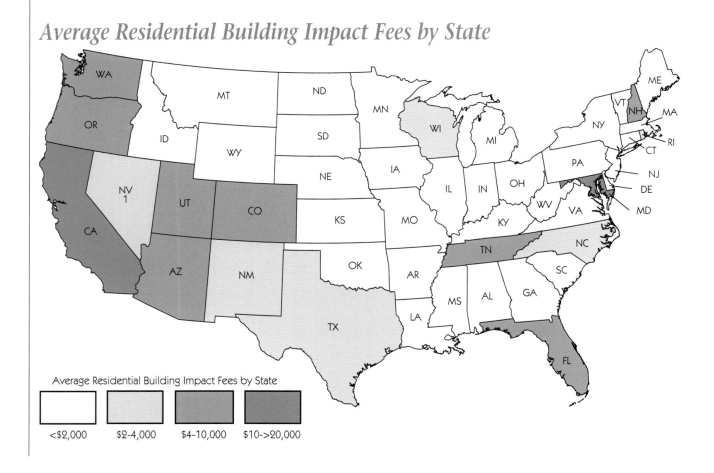

Average Residential Building Impact Fees by State

| <$2,000 | $2-4,000 | $4-10,000 | $10->20,000 |

4 DESIGN

Oh boy, let the fun begin!

When was the last time someone said to you, "Go ahead, pick anything you want." Of course the understanding was not **anything**, but anything within reason—in your case within your budget. But, hey! You get to pick what **you** want, not what someone else thinks you should have.

Designing is the most fun part of creating your tiny house. It is also the most important because it can:

- be the first time you have ever defined your life
- be the most creative thing you have ever done
- bring all your previous dreams together in a single entity
- bring partners closer through the shared project.

Designing is also a serious matter requiring hours and hours of imagination, research, and discipline.

Carpenters have a saying, "Measure twice; cut once." In other words, cut a board too short and you'll have to throw it in the scrap pile. To that let me add, "Design twice (or more); build once." If your stair design fails to meet the rather stringent requirements of the building code, you chance having to: purchase the expensive materials, build the stairs, tear down the stairs, throw away much of the material, purchase more material, and build the stairs a second time.

Design twice; build once.

4 DESIGN
The Process

Where to Begin

Since you are reading this book, you are probably in one of these categories:

- an empty-nester single or couple whose children have abandoned the 4-bedroom, 2½-bath home that now feels like an empty warehouse

- a young prechild couple wishing to begin owning a home, but not able to come up with the $50,000 downpayment on a $250,000 mortgage

- a single man or woman who just wants a simple, small, secure, low-maintenance shelter

- an older couple wishing to transfer ownership of the family home to their children while staying on the property in separate quarters in lieu of moving into an assisted living facility

- a member of an organization wishing to create low-cost shelters for homeless individuals and couples.

Regardless of your purpose, the starting point should be the same. Following the architectural dictate "Form follows function," the place to start is the compilation of a list of all the things you wish your tiny home to be or do for you.

Don't be hasty. This is the most important step in the whole process of creating a tiny home that works. Some of your decisions will be irreversible once the concrete is poured or the rafters raised. If you are a couple, some of your decisions will require compromise. And speaking of compromise, there will probably be a few things that just won't fit into your 400-square foot maximum envelope. Regardless, this tiny home will be yours—all yours!

A Scrapbook

If you haven't already, invest $20 in a large 3-ring binder and at least 100 clear plastic sleeves. The sleeves will hold brochures, pages from home magazines, photos you have taken, sketches with dimensions, and screen shots from your research on the internet.

In addition to books and magazines, visit open houses and tiny home manufacturers. Especially valuable will be boat and RV shows because boats and RVs are the ultimate tiny homes, and manufacturers have invested millions in perfecting the utilization of small spaces.

And seek out existing tiny home owners. Most are proudly invested in the tiny home movement and will gladly share their experiences, both good and bad.

The Program

On the following page is an example program. Due to space constraints it is necessarily shorter than yours will be, but it contains all of the basic elements to be considered.

The program shown is for a semi-retired couple (actually the author and his wife!) who desire a simple existence six months of the year (May 1 through November 1) close to, but not on, the ocean in Midcoast Maine.

Having lived in both a 30-foot cruising boat and a 29-foot RV, they like the ideas of self-sufficiency (off-grid electric system), gray-waste-only plumbing (composting toilet and no septic system), and integration of outdoor spaces (attached sunspace, deck, and gardens). Looking to the future they want everything to be at ground level.

Follow us as we progress from program to finished drawings on the following pages.

The Program

LOCATION

Geographic location: Within 20 miles of Brunswick, ME

Use type (urban, suburban, village, rural): village or rural

The land

- vegetation (open, wooded, mixed) mixed
- topography (flat, hilly, mountainous) either flat or hilly
- water (marsh, lake, river, ocean) ocean
- access to water (private, public, view) view

BUDGET

Site purchase: $40,000

Site improvements (road, water, electricity, sewage, clearing & landscaping): $25,000

Construction including design and permits: $75,000

Appliances: $3,000

Maximum total of above: $125,000

FABRICATION

transportable 12' wide on skids (preferred) or on-site

EXTERIOR

Roofline gable   Siding vinyl or fiber cement (no maintenance)

INTERIOR SPACES

Entry: on S or W side with coat hooks and basket for shoes/boots

Kitchen: minimal, no disposal or dishwasher, all gas appliances, possible skylight

Dining: in kitchen or living room, or between kitchen and living room

Living: max. seating for 4, Jotul or VT Casting propane stove, TV, ocean view

Bedroom 1: queen-size bed, patio door to outside, cross ventilation, morning sun, large hanging closet, adjacent to bath, privacy, television

Bedroom 2: none-pullout couch in living room if possible

Bathroom(s): shower, compost toilet, openable window, next to bedroom

Workroom: desk for writing and art table. Can be in BR or LR

EXTERIOR SPACES (may be added and financed later)

Porch: just a roof over entrance door

Deck: large deck off BR, LR, or K, seating, planters, afternoon shade

Patio: flower and herb garden with paved paths, bird feeders, and bird bath

Sunspace: plan for future 4-season sunspace/greenhouse off K, BR or LR

4 Activity Space Analysis

Aside from what goes on in our minds, our lives consist of activities: sleeping, reading, listening to music, cooking, eating, making love, bathing, working and so on. As regards the home, all of these activities occur within spaces: big spaces, small spaces, public spaces, private spaces. Once the wish-list program has been established, architect and clients perform an activity space analysis identifying a space for each activity. Each space is assigned a required floor area, a preferred orientation and a degree of privacy.

Area

Before you even begin, remember you are designing a *tiny* (≤400 sq.ft.) house, so each activity area should be of the minimum square-footage required to perform the activity comfortably.

An average new home contains about 2,400 sq.ft. As a rule of thumb kitchens occupy between 10% and 15% of the total living space. Following this rule, the kitchen of even the largest (400 sq.ft.) tiny house would measure between 40 and 60 sq.ft.

If you have trouble picturing such a small kitchen, visit a boat or RV show and imagine yourself preparing a meal in a few of the models on display. Naval architects and RV designers have perfected designs for living in small spaces. I think you will find the tiny galleys (kitchens) surprisingly workable.

In this era of the "McMansion" many homes contain, in addition to a living room, a great room, a music room, a media room, a library, and a game room. Prior to the McMansion all of these separate activities often took place in a single room. In fact, that is the reason it was called the "*living* room." Because activities usually occur at differing times, you will find

it possible to share spaces. Think of your living room as the stage in a play. With slight set changes the stage becomes a different space for each act or scene. Our example program lists an "art" space for the wife and a "writing" space for the husband. The art space could be the dining room table, while the writing space could be the wall-mounted, fold-down desk over the pullout couch shown on page 40.

Orientation

With each technological "advance" humans become more disconnected from the natural world. We have forgotten that, though more mentally evolved than most, we are still animals. For example, we try to ignore the ticking of our subconscious clocks synchronized to the diurnal motion of the sun. We did not always wake to alarm clocks or morning rushhour news programs. For hundreds of thousands of years we, like all the rest of the animals, were wakened by the rising sun. DNA is persistent, and brain researchers have established the not-surprising fact that people who rise with the sun are generally less stressed than those jarred awake by alarms.

What does this have to do with orientation? Regardless of the season, the sun rises in the east, passes due south at noon, and sets in the west. Since most of our daily activities occur on regular schedules, there is a strong correlation between our activities and the position of the sun in the sky. In our analysis, *orientation* specifies the location of the source of light, the sun. For example, if you prefer being woken by the sun rising in the east, the orientation of your bedroom should be *east*.

Privacy

Outside our homes we are on guard. Crossing the street, driving cars, even sitting at meetings, we are on guard in our alert public mode. Once home the ambience, comfort, and familiarity of our personal spaces allow a more trusting, intimate state. Actually, between boardroom and bedroom lies a whole spectrum of privacy. People for whom boardrooms and bedrooms are daily events know the difficulty of the transition. Time, space, and for some a bit of "mood enhancer" are required.

Nothing gives a greater feeling of privacy than sheer distance. If we arrange our spaces in order of privacy, the most private will be remote from the most public. Assign degrees of privacy, with 1 being most public and 3 most private. Entries and kitchens generally rate a 1; hallways, dining rooms, and living rooms a 2; and bedrooms and bathrooms a 3. Arranging spaces in order of privacy avoids the discomforting juxtaposition of incompatible activities.

Example Activity Analysis

From your program, compile a table of activities. First recall your typical day, from waking until falling asleep. In the first column list the significant activities that take place inside the home. Then, keeping in mind you are designing a *tiny* home, imagine the smallest area in square feet in which that activity could take place. Next, relate each activity to its time of day. Where is the sun? Enter the orientation of the activity space as the direction its windows, if any, should face to catch the sun. Finally, enter the desired degree of privacy for each activity on a scale of 1 to 3. If orientation or privacy of an activity are unimportant, leave the entry blank.

Activity Space Table Example

Activity	Area sq.ft.	Orientation N,S,E,W	Privacy 1,2,3
Enter	15	S or W	1
Cook	60	N or W	1
Eat	30	S or W	1
Sit/Talk	50	S or W	2
Entertain	85		2
Write	20	S	2
Paint	20		
Sleep	90	E	3
Bathe	30		3
Dress/Launder	25		3
TOTAL	425		

After completing the table, just for fun add the areas. The total area will probably exceed 400 sq.ft.. Don't be dismayed. A lot of activities can share the same physical spaces, provided they happen at different times.

At this point think generally rather than specifically about the details of your activity spaces. At this early stage you are groping toward a finished design much like an artist or sculptor with a rough sketch or lump of clay. Like the artist beginning to draw a figure, you can use circles and ellipses positioned to rough out the major features, positions, and masses of the body. Architects purposely call these circles *bubbles* because bubbles have a dreamlike quality and can be distorted into shapes fitting the available spaces while retaining their basic areas.

4 DESIGN
Space Bubbles

To construct your bubble diagram, first draw circles representing the relative areas of your activity spaces. The illustration at right contains circles representing areas of 20, 40, 60, 80, and 100 sq.ft. (each blue square represents 1 sq. ft.). To create your own circles, place tracing paper over the illustration and use the illustrated circles as guides. Label each of your circles with its activity, preferred orientation, and degree of privacy.

Now comes the exciting part. Create a rectangular board (a sheet of cardboard) with its four edges labeled *NORTH/2*, *EAST/3*, *SOUTH/2*, and *WEST/1* (below). Place each of your activity circles on the board according to its orientation and privacy coordinates. Does the board look anything like a floor plan? Probably not, but you are just beginning.

Scaled Area Circles

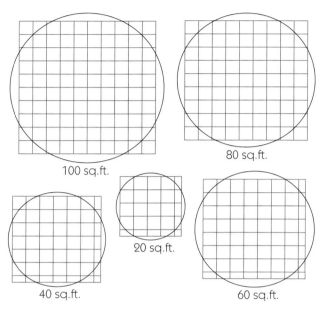

100 sq.ft.

80 sq.ft.

20 sq.ft.

40 sq.ft.

60 sq.ft.

Initial Bubble Diagram

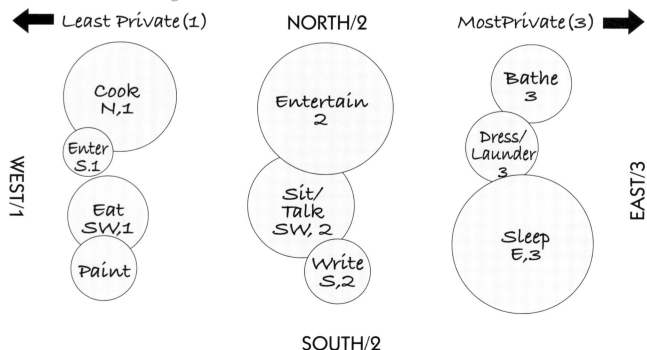

Least Private (1)   NORTH/2   Most Private (3)

WEST/1   EAST/3

Cook N,1

Enter S,1

Eat SW,1

Paint

Entertain 2

Sit/ Talk SW, 2

Write S,2

Bathe 3

Dress/ Launder 3

Sleep E,3

SOUTH/2

Second Bubble Diagram

Now identify activities which could take place in the *same* physical spaces and overlap their bubbles. For example, "entertain" requires a very large circle because entertaining guests may include the activities of sitting and talking in a group, eating, and watching television. As another example, writing never happens at the same time as entertaining, so it could take place in the same space as sitting and talking. Similarly, why couldn't painting take place at the dining table in the same space as eating?

And remember: the spaces don't have to be circles, so feel free to squeeze the circles into ellipses. (At this point you may elect to simply draw the ellipses on another board instead of cutting them out. Just be careful to retain their original areas.) Keep adjusting the shapes and overlaps until the collection of shapes fits into a rectangular area. Can you now visualize the rough outline of a rectangular building?

Replacing the *NORTH/2, EAST/3, SOUTH/2,* and *WEST/1* labels with the daily path of the sun helps in visualizing the building on a site.

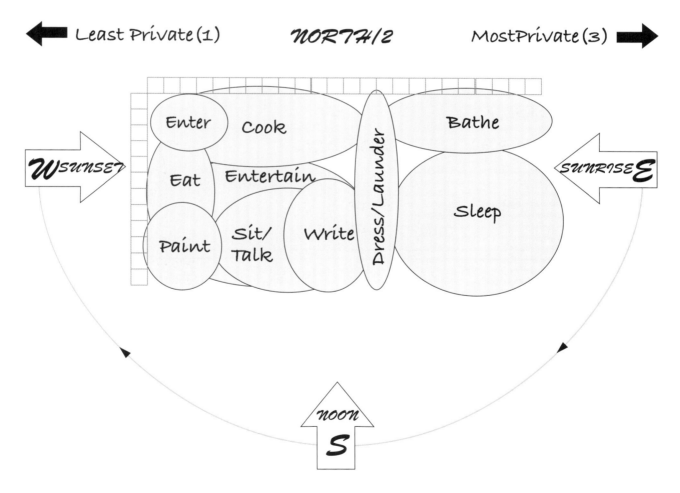

Squaring Up the Bubbles

Bubbles into Rectangles

The previous diagram shows strips of the original blue 1-sq.ft. grid overlaying the bubble diagram. Counting the squares we see that all of the bubbles appear to be contained within an area measuring 12' × 24' (288 sq.ft.). Of course we have yet to draw in furniture or appliances, and we haven't checked the dimensions of doorways and passageways. At 288 sq.ft. we still have plenty of latitude to add several feet in either direction and remain within the tiny house limit of 400 sq.ft. But we won't know for sure until we add the exact dimensions of all the planned furniture and appliances.

The diagram below constrains the enclosed space to exactly 12' × 24', Why *exactly*, and why only *even numbers* of feet? If you have built before, or if you wander the aisles of a home center, you know all sheet materials (plywood, oriented-strand board, particle board, sheetrock, etc.) measure 4' × 8'. Designing floors, wall, and ceilings to exact 2-foot increments minimizes both labor and material waste.

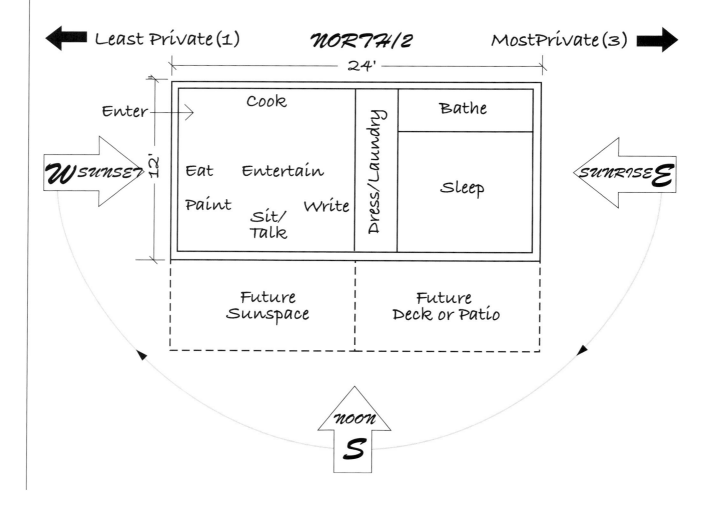

Fitting It All In

The final step, other than drawing the set of detailed plans, is to add the furnishings and appliances to scale. The most common scale is ¼ inch equals 1 foot (12 inches). Thus, everything in the plan is shown as $1/48$ the size of the real thing. This scale is perfect because even the largest tiny house (20' × 20' or 12' × 32') fits easily on a standard $8^1/_2$ × 11" sheet of paper.

You will probably find your preferences (a queen-sized bed, 4' × 8' shower, and a 3' × 8' dining table) just won't fit. If you can't live without these McMansion items, quit now! If, however, your goal is still living well in minimal space, consult the ¼-inch furnishings template on pages 36–37 and the catalog of special furnishings for tiny spaces on pages 38–39.

We managed to fit all of the basics with just three compromises: 1) a full-size instead of queen-size bed, 2) no lavatory sink (share the kitchen sink), 3) the wall-mounted, swing-down writing desk from page 40.

The plan is shown in more detail, on page 58.

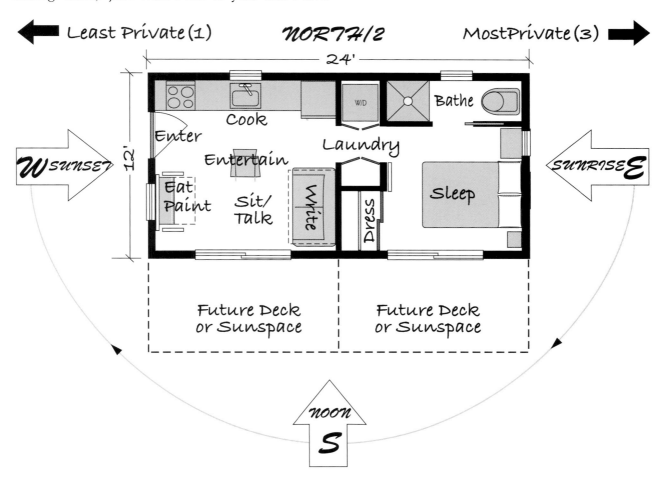

A Few Critical Dimensions

Exterior Doors

Standard exterior doors measure 36" wide × 80' high, although codes allow heights of 78" minimum. The top two illustrations show the IRC requirements for egress doors (at least one per dwelling). The bottom illustration shows a 2-riser exception for non-egress doors.

EGRESS DOOR: IN- OR OUT-SWINGING

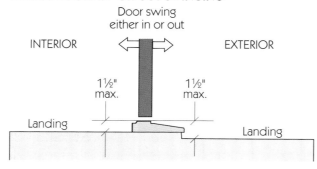

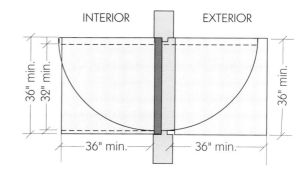

EGRESS DOOR: IN-SWINGING ONLY

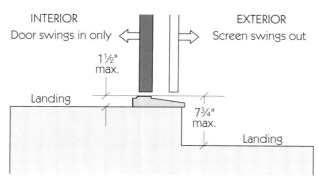

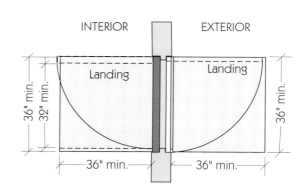

NON-EGRESS EXTERIOR DOOR

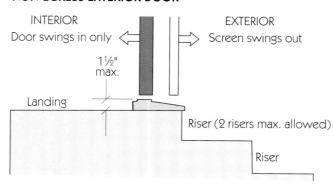

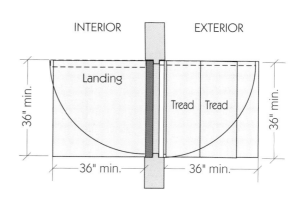

Minimum Bathroom Dimensions (IRC)

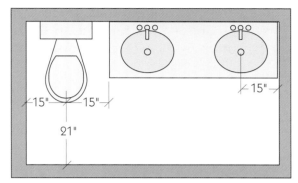

15" 15" 15"

21"

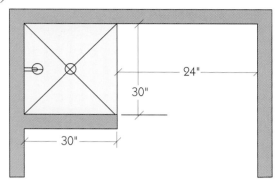

24"

30"

30"

Minimum Ceiling Heights (IRC Appendix Q)

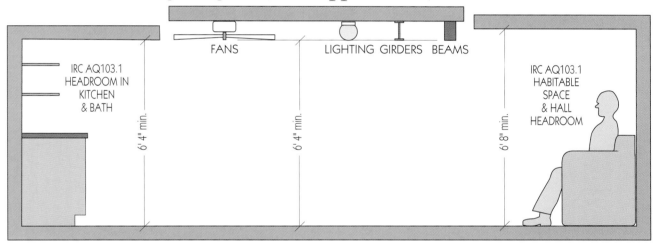

FANS   LIGHTING GIRDERS   BEAMS

IRC AQ103.1
HEADROOM IN
KITCHEN
& BATH

6' 4" min.

6' 4" min.

IRC AQ103.1
HABITABLE
SPACE
& HALL
HEADROOM

6' 8" min.

Window Heights for Views

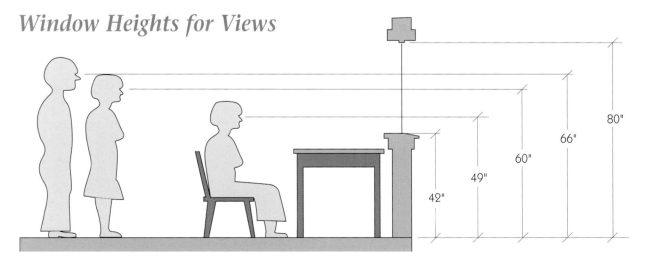

80"

66"

60"

49"

42"

Furniture and Appliances

Templates: All Drawn to ¹/₄" = 1' Scale

KITCHEN

Counter 25" Deep | Base cabinet 24" Deep | Wall cabinet 12" Deep | 0.7 cf Micro 17" x 13" | 1.2 cf Micro 21" x 16" | 1.6 cf Micro 22" x 19" | Apt. Range 20" x 24" | Range 30" x 24" | Dishwasher 24" x 25" | Stacked Wash/Dry 24" x 27"

3.1 cu.ft. 19" x 21" | 4.5 cu.ft. 22" x 23" | 7 cu.ft. Refridg. 22" x 30" | 10 cu.ft. Refridg. 24" x 30" | 14 cu.ft. Refridg. 26" x 30" | 20 cu.ft. Refridg. 30" x 32"

Double Sink 20" x 30" | Sink 12" x 18" | Bar sink 15" x 15"

HEAT & HOT WATER

4 gpm Tankless Elect. WH 18" x 5" | 6 gpm Tankless Gas WH 18" x 11" | 2.5 Gal. Elect. WH 12" Dia. | 12 Gal. Elect. WH 16" Dia. | 20 Gal. Elect. WH 18" Dia. | 40-Gal. H2O tank 18" high | 52-Gal. H2O tank 24" high | DV Gas Htr | Marine LP heater | Vt Castings LP heater | 22" x 14"

BATHROOM

Top 22" Deep | Base cabinet 20" Deep | IKEA base cabinet 12" Deep | 24x18 Vanity | 30x18 Vanity | IKEA lavatory 24" x 16" | IKEA lavatory 24" x 11" | Toilet 17" x 26" | Compost Toilet 21" x 16"

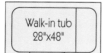

Standard Tub 30" x 60" | Walk-in tub 28"x48" | Shower 30x30r | Shower 32x32 | Shower 32x36 | Shower 36x36

BEDS

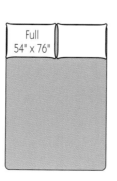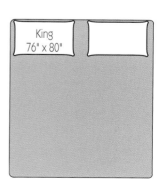

Bunk 30" x 75" | Twin 39" x 75" | Full 54" x 76" | Queen 60" x 80" | King 76" x 80"

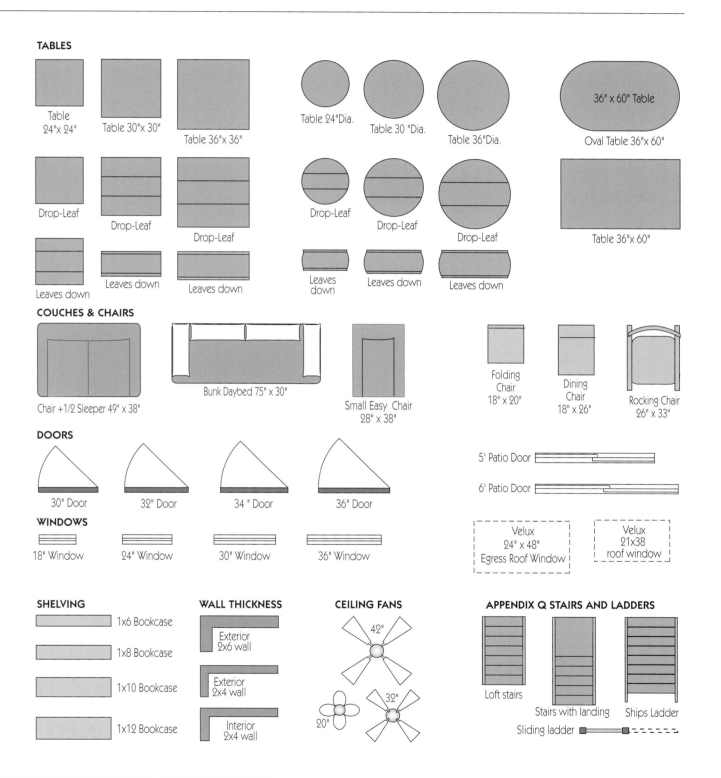

TABLES

Table 24"x 24"

Table 30"x 30"

Table 36"x 36"

Table 24"Dia.

Table 30 "Dia.

Table 36"Dia.

36" x 60" Table

Oval Table 36"x 60"

Drop-Leaf

Drop-Leaf

Drop-Leaf

Drop-Leaf

Drop-Leaf

Drop-Leaf

Table 36"x 60"

Leaves down

Leaves down

Leaves down

Leaves down

Leaves down

Leaves down

COUCHES & CHAIRS

Chair +1/2 Sleeper 49" x 38"

Bunk Daybed 75" x 30"

Small Easy Chair 28" x 38"

Folding Chair 18" x 20"

Dining Chair 18" x 26"

Rocking Chair 26" x 33"

DOORS

30" Door

32" Door

34 " Door

36" Door

5' Patio Door

6' Patio Door

WINDOWS

18" Window

24" Window

30" Window

36" Window

Velux 24" x 48" Egress Roof Window

Velux 21x38 roof window

SHELVING

1x6 Bookcase

1x8 Bookcase

1x10 Bookcase

1x12 Bookcase

WALL THICKNESS

Exterior 2x6 wall

Exterior 2x4 wall

Interior 2x4 wall

CEILING FANS

42"

32"

20"

APPENDIX Q STAIRS AND LADDERS

Loft stairs

Stairs with landing

Ships Ladder

Sliding ladder

Furnishings for Tiny Spaces

Bathroom Vanities and Fixtures

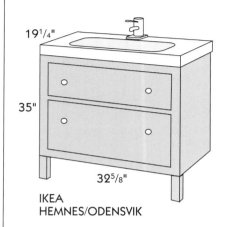

19¹/₄"

35"

32⁵/₈"

IKEA
HEMNES/ODENSVIK

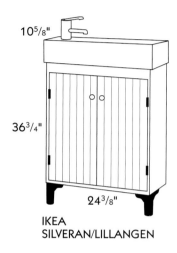

10⁵/₈"

36³/₄"

24³/₈"

IKEA
SILVERAN/LILLANGEN

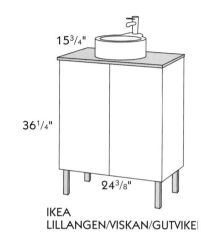

15³/₄"

36¹/₄"

24³/₈"

IKEA
LILLANGEN/VISKAN/GUTVIKEN

15³/₄"

34¹/₄"

32¹/₄"

IKEA
LILLANGEN/VISKAN/GUTVIKEN

15³/₄"

18¹/₈"

IKEA
FYNDIG

8"

17"

IKEA
FYNDIGNORRSJON

43¹/₂"

22³/₄"

28"

CYRANO CLAWFOOT TUB
BY BARCLAY

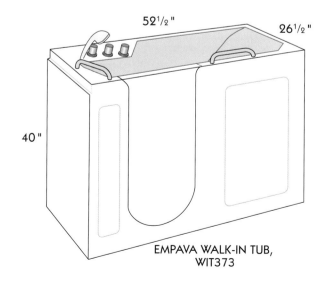

52¹/₂"

26¹/₂"

40"

EMPAVA WALK-IN TUB,
WIT373

Kitchen and Laundry Appliances

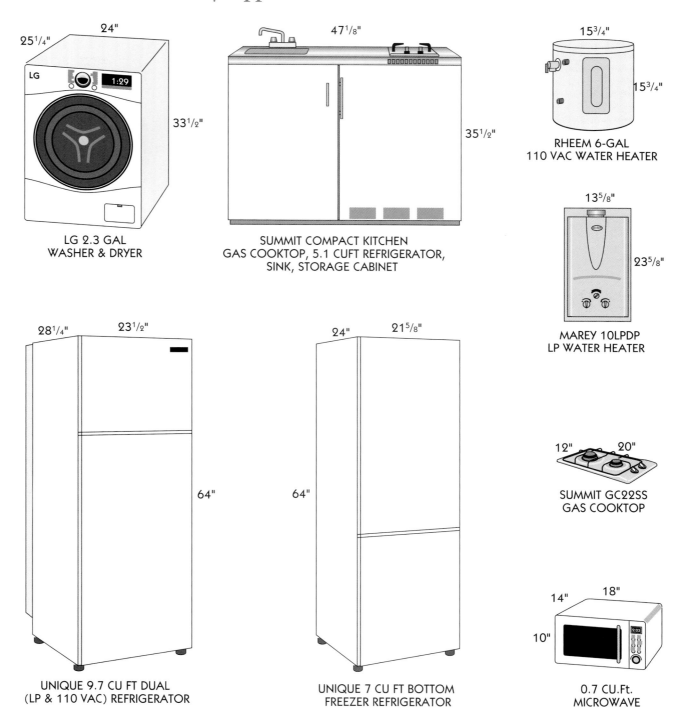

24"

25¹/₄"

33¹/₂"

LG 2.3 GAL
WASHER & DRYER

47¹/₈"

35¹/₂"

SUMMIT COMPACT KITCHEN
GAS COOKTOP, 5.1 CUFT REFRIGERATOR,
SINK, STORAGE CABINET

15³/₄"

15³/₄"

RHEEM 6-GAL
110 VAC WATER HEATER

13⁵/₈"

23⁵/₈"

MAREY 10LPDP
LP WATER HEATER

28¹/₄" **23¹/₂"**

64"

UNIQUE 9.7 CU FT DUAL
(LP & 110 VAC) REFRIGERATOR

24" **21⁵/₈"**

64"

UNIQUE 7 CU FT BOTTOM
FREEZER REFRIGERATOR

12" **20"**

SUMMIT GC22SS
GAS COOKTOP

14" **18"**

10"

0.7 CU.Ft.
MICROWAVE

IKEA Pullout Daybed with Storage

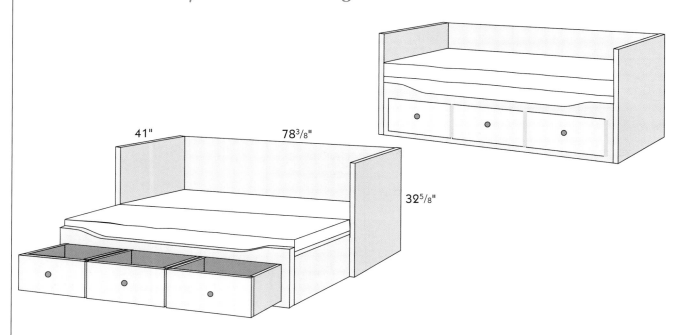

41" 78³/₈"

32⁵/₈"

DIY Fold-down Wall-hung Flush Door Desk

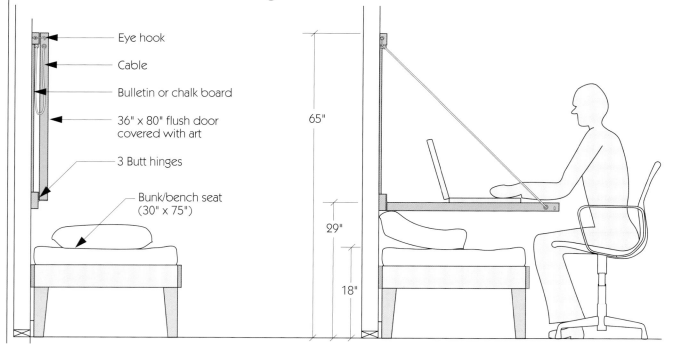

Eye hook

Cable

Bulletin or chalk board

36" x 80" flush door covered with art

3 Butt hinges

Bunk/bench seat (30" x 75")

65"

29"

18"

DIY Hinged Wall Pantry

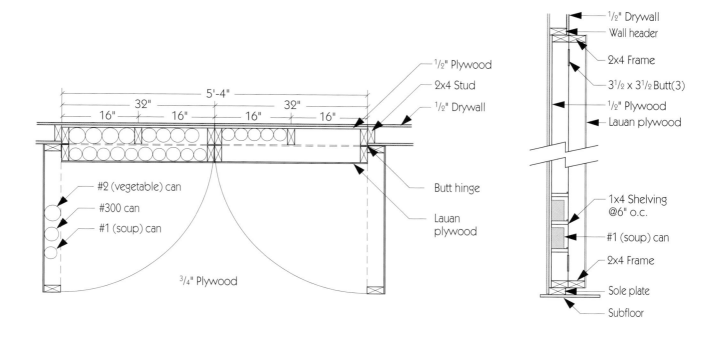

5'-4"

32" · 32"

16" · 16" · 16" · 16"

¹/₂" Plywood
2x4 Stud
¹/₂" Drywall

Butt hinge

Lauan plywood

#2 (vegetable) can
#300 can
#1 (soup) can

³/₄" Plywood

¹/₂" Drywall
Wall header
2x4 Frame
3¹/₂ x 3¹/₂ Butt(3)
¹/₂" Plywood
Lauan plywood

1x4 Shelving @6" o.c.
#1 (soup) can
2x4 Frame
Sole plate
Subfloor

DIY Fold-down Kitchen or Work Table

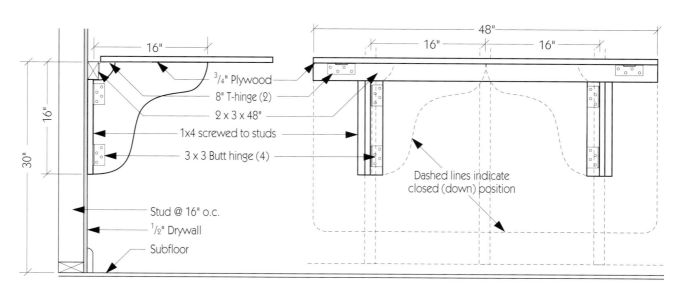

16"

48"

16" · 16"

16"

30"

³/₄" Plywood
8" T-hinge (2)
2 x 3 x 48"
1x4 screwed to studs
3 x 3 Butt hinge (4)

Dashed lines indicate closed (down) position

Stud @ 16" o.c.
¹/₂" Drywall
Subfloor

4

Designing the Exterior

Human constructs are less visually disturbing when emulating their natural surroundings. Blend your tiny home into the landscape with both color and form.

Desert and Prairie

The predominant colors are of sand and dry grass. Most architecture is of adobe. Paint your tiny home with earth tones.

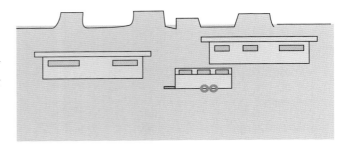

Mountains

Steep landforms and tall pointed trees set the stage. Nature's colors are gray for exposed rock and green and brown for the vegetation. Your tiny home should have a steep roof and color, if not the material, of the trees.

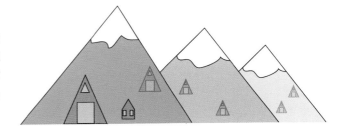

Forest

Trees, trees, everywhere large trees with dark green foliage and brown trunks. What could be more natural than a tiny log home constructed, or at least sided, from those very same trees. If not of logs, then at least painted or stained in the same color.

New England

New England is known for its many small towns centered on commons with imposing steepled churches. Church and houses are nearly always white, while barns and outbuildings are painted "barn red." Blend in!

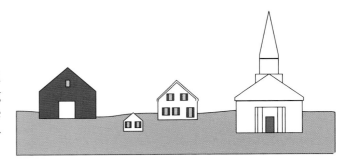

As with people, what's inside your home is more important than the exterior. However, consider these four exterior design principles. See if minor adjustments to window and door placements enhance your home's exterior appearance.

Symmetry

The overall building form and aperture pattern should work together. Symmetric form = symmetric window pattern; asymmetric form = asymmetric windows.

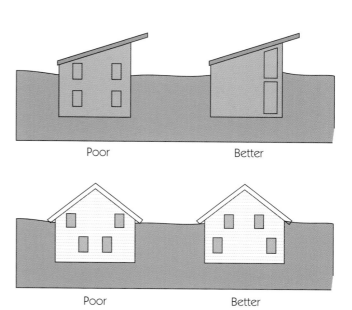

Poor   Better

Stability

The window group on the left appears to be top-heavy and, thus, unstable. The window group on the right, with its "feet" spread apart, is going nowhere—not in wind nor earthquake.

Poor   Better

Horizontal Alignment

The windows of the house on the left appear to be jumping up and down as if they can't decide where they should be. The convention is to align the tops of all windows and doors.

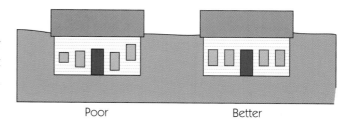

Poor   Better

Vertical Alignment

Windows are the significant visual masses in the otherwise blank canvas of a building's wall. The off-center group on the left create the illusion that the whole building is leaning.

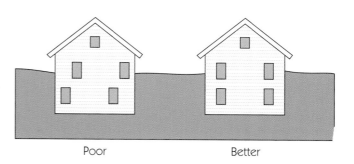

Poor   Better

Visual Element Variations

Each of the elevations below is based on the identical, basic 8-foot wide tiny home on wheels. We show twenty-four variations, all with the same type of siding and color scheme. Imagine your range of choices with different sidings and colors!

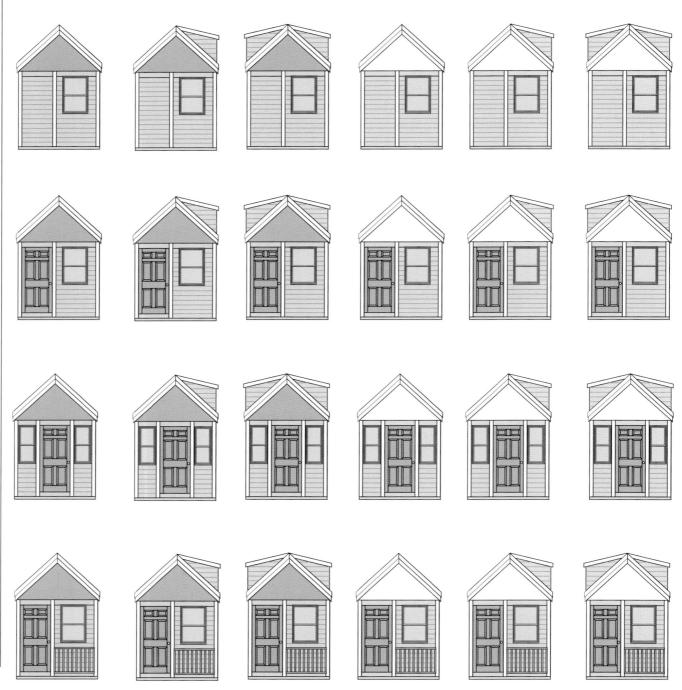

Increasing the building's width to 12 feet presents an even broader canvas for elevation design. The sixteen variations below, again with but a single type of siding and single color scheme, are just a small sample of the possible variations. Let your imagination go wild!

Notes

5 SOME FLOOR PLANS

Those wishing a home larger than *tiny* (over 400 square feet) can turn to books and magazines containing hundreds of architect-drawn designs ranging from about 800 to over 2,000 square feet in floor area. What the publications show are miniature floor plans and elevations (views of the exterior). For $500 to $1,000 one can purchase architect-stamped sets of plans, excluding, of course, the site plan because the site is unknown.

All is not lost, however. Amazon lists several books devoted exclusively to tiny house designs, and I urge you purchase them for your research library. Discovery of a single space-saving solution that works for you will justify your purchase.

And as stated in the "Author's Note" in the front of this book, I am planning a tiny house for my wife and myself. Much of the past year has been spent, in addition to writing this book, playing with a variety of designs including versions on wheels, on skids, and built on site. Twenty-one designs are presented, but they can easily become eighty-four. Each plan can be flipped front-to-back, side-to-side, and a combination of both, resulting in four plans from one.

Because we are post-child-raising seniors, most of the designs are single-story and contain but a single bedroom. Feel free to use as-they-are or to adapt any portion for your own design.

Plan 1: On Wheels 8' × 16'

LOFT LEVEL

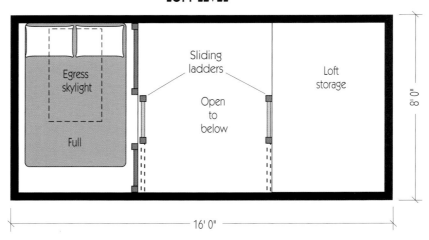

GROUND LEVEL

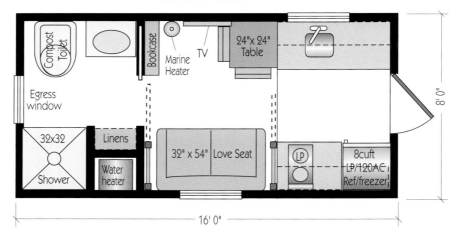

SCALE: 1/4" = 1' 0"

Plan 2: On Wheels 8' × 16'

LOFT LEVEL

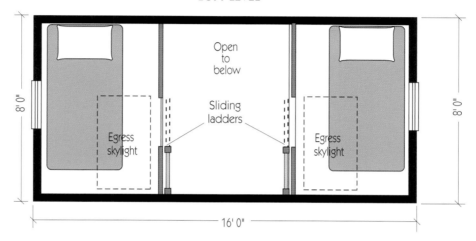

GROUND LEVEL

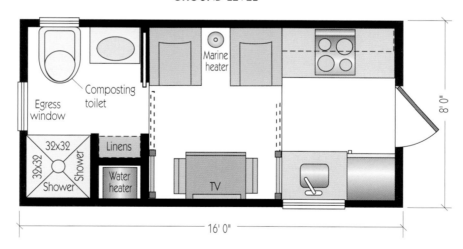

SCALE: 1/4" = 1' 0"

Plan 3: On Wheels 8' × 20'

GROUND LEVEL

LOFT LEVEL

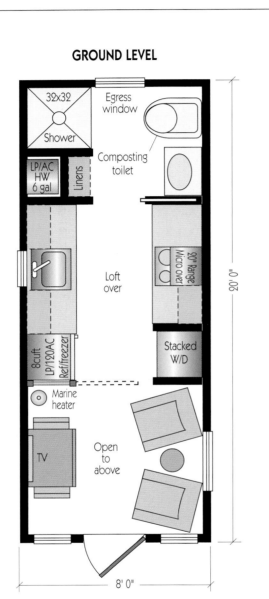

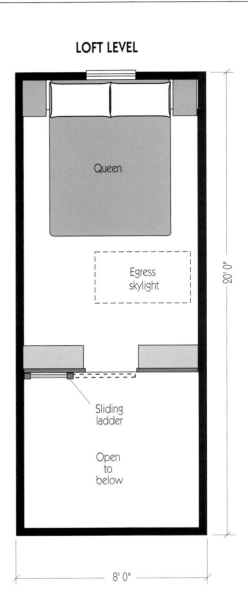

SCALE: 1/4" = 1' 0"

Plan 4: On Wheels 8′ × 20′

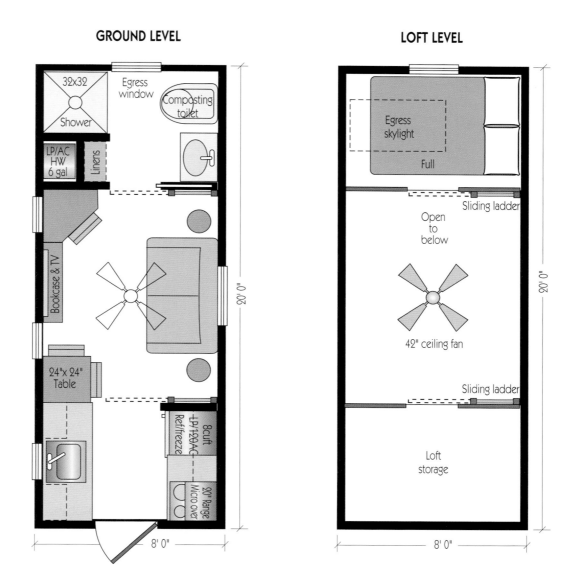

GROUND LEVEL

32x32 Shower

Egress window

Composting toilet

LP/AC HW 6 gal

Linens

Bookcase & TV

24"x 24" Table

Ref/freeze 8cuft LP/120AC

20" range Micro over

20' 0"

8' 0"

LOFT LEVEL

Egress skylight

Full

Sliding ladder

Open to below

42" ceiling fan

Sliding ladder

Loft storage

20' 0"

8' 0"

SCALE: 1/4" = 1' 0"

SOME FLOOR PLANS
Plan 5: On Wheels 8′ × 24′

GROUND LEVEL

32x32

Shower

Egress window

Composting toilet

LP/AC HW 6 gal

Ref/freezer 8 cu ft

LP/120AC

24″x 24″ Table

TV

36″

Bunk

Bunk

Egress window

24′ 0″

8′ 0″

UPPER LEVEL

Storage loft

Sliding ladder

42″ ceiling fan
Sliding ladder

Storage loft

24′ 0″

8′ 0″

SCALE: 1/4″ = 1′ 0″

Plan 6: On Wheels 8′ × 30′

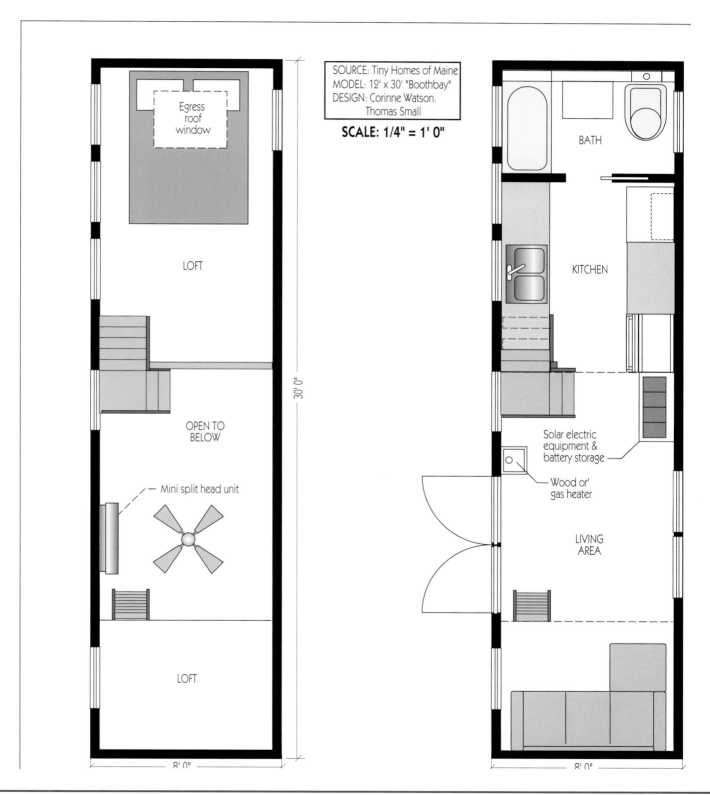

SOURCE: Tiny Homes of Maine
MODEL: 12′ × 30′ "Boothbay"
DESIGN: Corinne Watson.
　　　　 Thomas Small

SCALE: 1/4" = 1′ 0"

Egress roof window

LOFT

OPEN TO BELOW

Mini split head unit

LOFT

30′ 0"

8′ 0"

BATH

KITCHEN

Solar electric equipment & battery storage

Wood or' gas heater

LIVING AREA

8′ 0"

Plan 7: On Skids 12′ × 16′

GROUND LEVEL

- Egress window
- Compost Toilet
- 32x32 Shower
- LP/AC HW 6 gal
- Shelves Over
- Stacked W/D
- Pantry
- Closed above
- Storage
- 8cuft LP/120AC Ref/freezer
- Landing
- TV
- 30"x 30" Table
- Open above
- 36 x 60 Love Seat
- 20" Range Micro over
- DV Gas Htr
- 12′ 0″
- 16′ 0″

LOFT LEVEL

- Dresser
- Loft
- 24x48 Egress roof window
- Twin
- Twin
- Landing
- Open below
- 12′ 0″
- 16′ 0″

SCALE: 1/4″ = 1′ 0″

Plan 8: On Skids 12′ × 16′

GROUND LEVEL

LOFT LEVEL

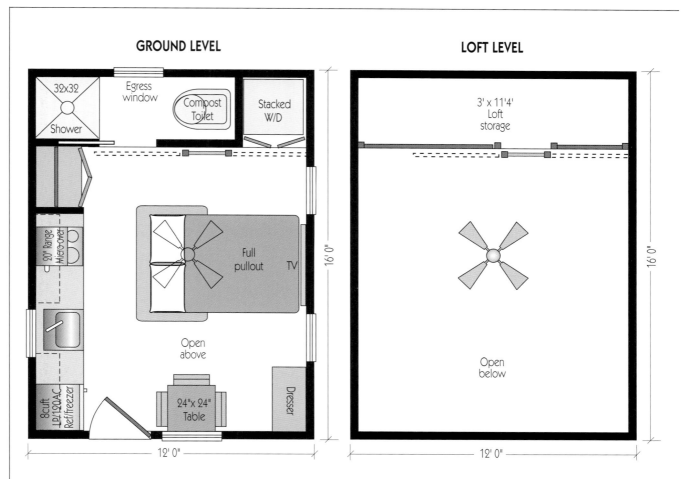

Ground level labels:
- 32x32 Shower
- Egress window
- Compost Toilet
- Stacked W/D
- 20" Range
- Micro-over
- 8cuft LP/120AC Ref/freezer
- Full pullout
- TV
- Open above
- 24"x 24" Table
- Dresser
- 12' 0"
- 16' 0"

Loft level labels:
- 3' x 11'4' Loft storage
- Open below
- 12' 0"
- 16' 0"

SCALE: 1/4" = 1' 0"

Plan 9: On Skids 12′ × 20′

GROUND LEVEL

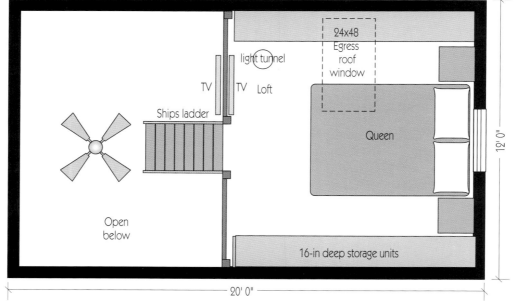

36 x 60 Love Seat

24x48 Hinged Desk
(Art on back)

V.t Castings
DV gas htr

Easy
Chair
26x30

TV
over

32x32
Shower

light tunnel

Compost
toilet

20" Range
Micro over

12 x 18
K Sink

8cuft
LP/120AC
Ref/freezer

Stacked
W/D

Ships ladder

Open
above

Hinged Pantry

Coat hooks

24 x48
Table

20' 0"

12' 0"

LOFT LEVEL

light tunnel

TV   TV   Loft

Ships ladder

Open
below

24x48
Egress
roof
window

Queen

16-in deep storage units

20' 0"

12' 0"

SCALE: 1/4" = 1'

Plan 10: On Skids 12′ × 20′

GROUND LEVEL

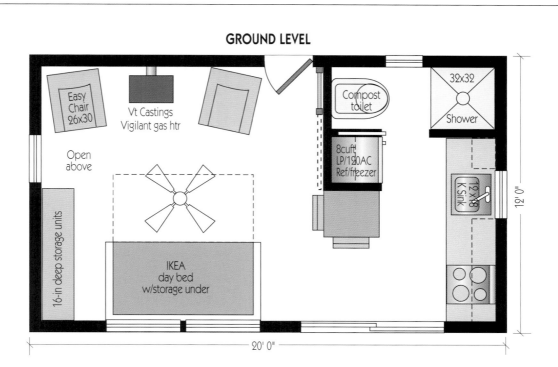

Easy Chair 26x30

Vt Castings Vigilant gas htr

Open above

16-in deep storage units

IKEA day bed w/storage under

Compost toilet

32x32 Shower

8cuft LP/120AC Ref/freezer

12x18 K Sink

20' 0"

12' 0"

LOFT LEVEL

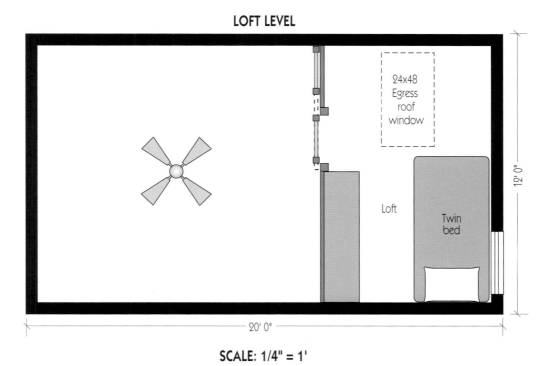

24x48 Egress roof window

Loft

Twin bed

20' 0"

12' 0"

SCALE: 1/4" = 1'

Plan 11: On Skids 12′ × 24′

GROUND LEVEL

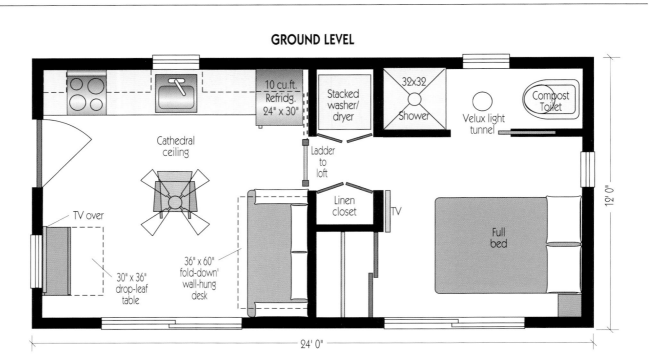

- 10 cu.ft. Refridg. 24" x 30"
- Stacked washer/dryer
- 32x32 Shower
- Velux light tunnel
- Compost Toilet
- Cathedral ceiling
- Ladder to loft
- Linen closet
- TV
- Full bed
- TV over
- 30" x 36" drop-leaf table
- 36" x 60" fold-down' wall-hung desk
- 24' 0"
- 12' 0"

LOFT LEVEL

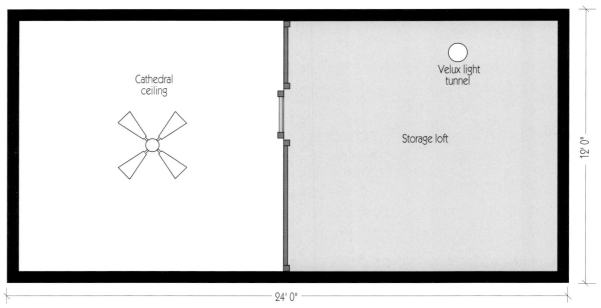

- Cathedral ceiling
- Velux light tunnel
- Storage loft
- 24' 0"
- 12' 0"

SCALE: 1/4" = 1'

Plan 12: On Skids 12' × 24'

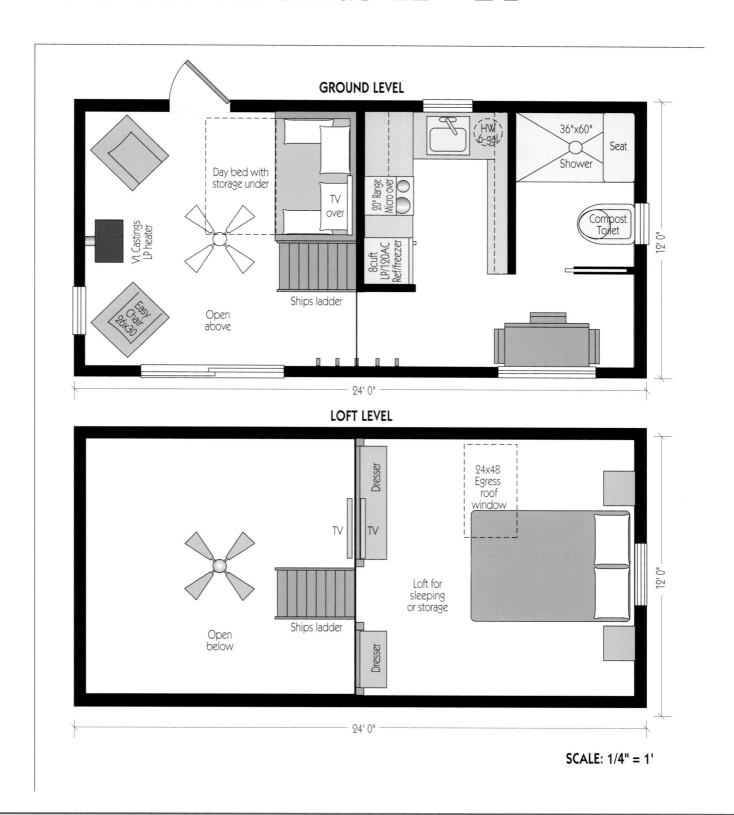

GROUND LEVEL

Day bed with storage under

TV over

Vt Castings LP heater

Easy Chair 26x30

Open above

Ships ladder

20" Range Micro over

8cuft LP/120AC Ref/freezer

HW 6-gal

36"x60"

Seat

Shower

Compost Toilet

24' 0"

12' 0"

LOFT LEVEL

Dresser

TV

TV

24x48 Egress roof window

Loft for sleeping or storage

Open below

Ships ladder

Dresser

24' 0"

12' 0"

SCALE: 1/4" = 1'

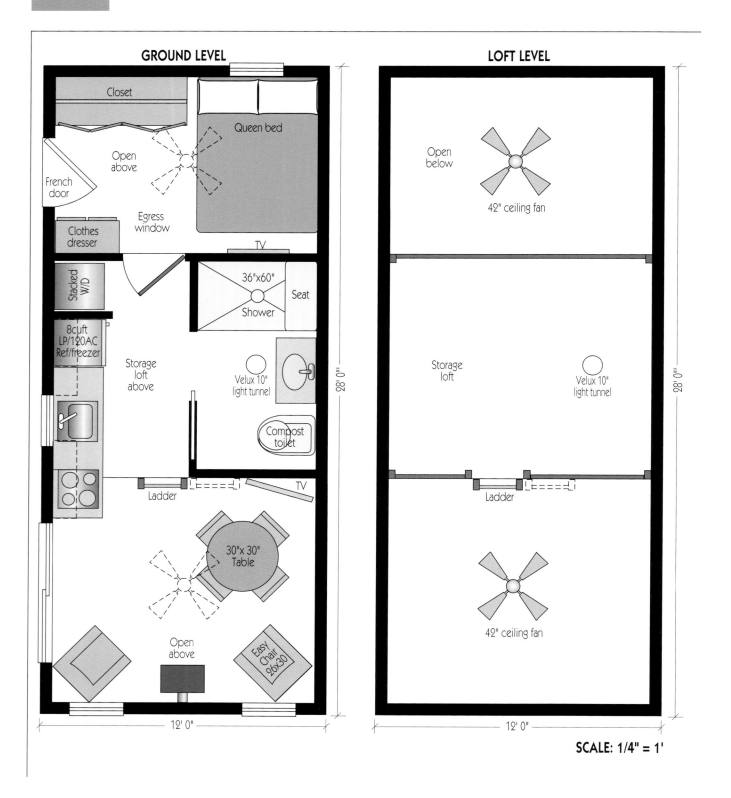

GROUND LEVEL

Closet

Queen bed

Open above

French door

Egress window

Clothes dresser

Stacked W/D

8cuft LP/120AC Ref/freezer

Storage loft above

TV

36"x60" Shower

Seat

Velux 10" light tunnel

Compost toilet

Ladder

TV

30"x 30" Table

Open above

Easy Chair 26x30

12' 0"

28' 0"

LOFT LEVEL

Open below

42" ceiling fan

Storage loft

Velux 10" light tunnel

Ladder

42" ceiling fan

12' 0"

28' 0"

SCALE: 1/4" = 1'

Plan 14: On Skids 12′ × 28′

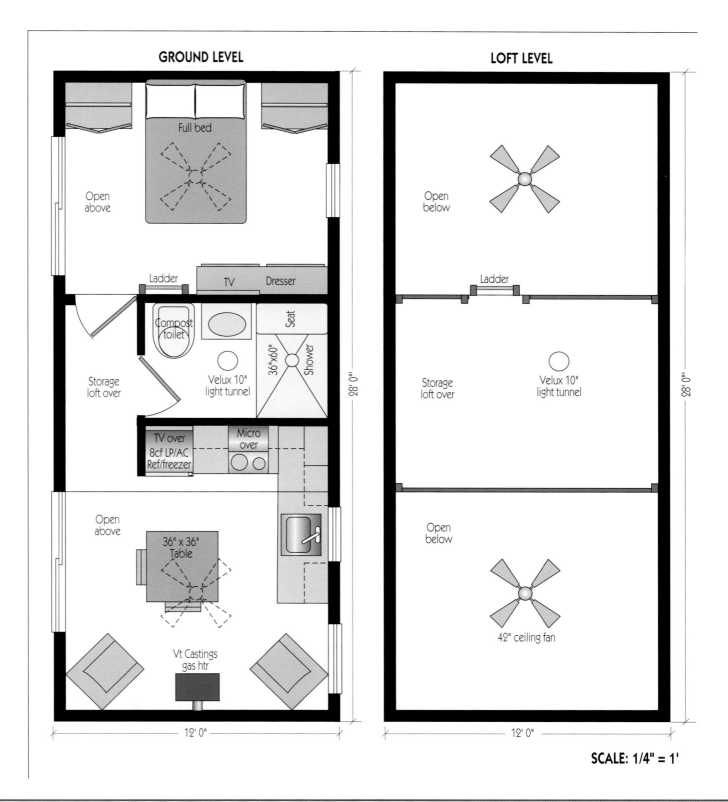

GROUND LEVEL

- Full bed
- Open above
- Ladder
- TV
- Dresser
- Compost toilet
- Seat
- 36"x60" Shower
- Velux 10" light tunnel
- Storage loft over
- TV over
- 8cf LP/AC Ref/freezer
- Micro over
- Open above
- 36" x 36" Table
- Vt Castings gas htr
- 28' 0"
- 12' 0"

LOFT LEVEL

- Open below
- Ladder
- Storage loft over
- Velux 10" light tunnel
- Open below
- 42" ceiling fan
- 28' 0"
- 12' 0"

SCALE: 1/4" = 1'

Plan 15: Site-Built 12′ × 20′

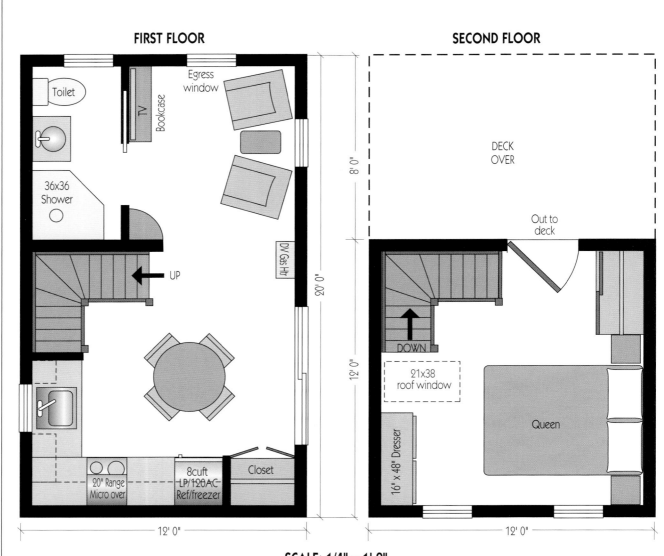

FIRST FLOOR

Toilet

Egress window

TV

Bookcase

36x36 Shower

DV Gas Htr

UP

20" Range Micro over

8cuft LP/120AC Ref/freezer

Closet

SECOND FLOOR

DECK OVER

Out to deck

DOWN

21x38 roof window

16" x 48" Dresser

Queen

8' 0"

20' 0"

12' 0"

12' 0"

12' 0"

SCALE: 1/4" = 1' 0"

Plan 16: Site-Built 20′×26′

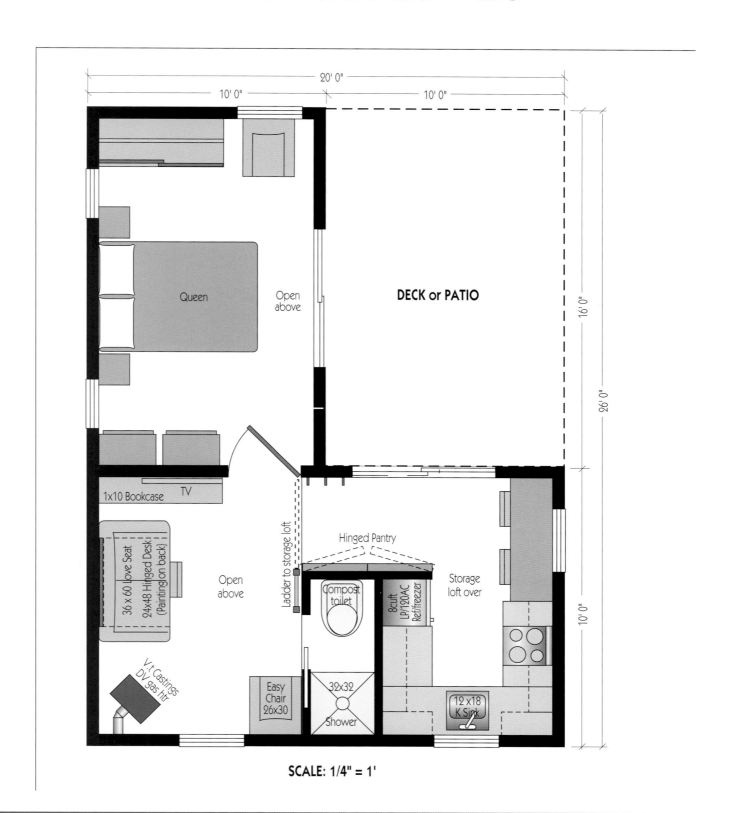

20' 0"

10' 0"   10' 0"

16' 0"

26' 0"

10' 0"

Queen

Open above

DECK or PATIO

1x10 Bookcase   TV

Open above

Ladder to storage loft

Hinged Pantry

Storage loft over

36 x 60 love Seat

24x48 Hinged Desk (Painting on back)

Compost toilet

8cuft LP/120AC Ref/freezer

V.t.Castings DV gas htr

Easy Chair 26x30

32x32

Shower

12 x 18 K Sink

SCALE: 1/4" = 1'

Plan 17: Site-Built 20′ × 32′

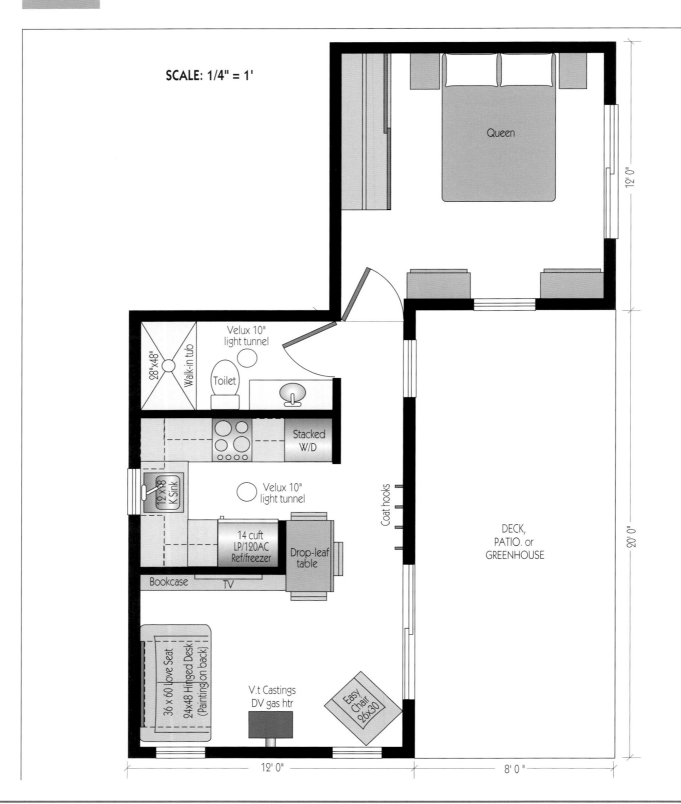

SCALE: 1/4" = 1'

Queen

12' 0"

20' 0"

Velux 10" light tunnel

28"x48" Walk-in tub

Toilet

Velux 10" light tunnel

Stacked W/D

12 x18 K Sink

Coat hooks

DECK, PATIO. or GREENHOUSE

14 cuft LP/120AC Ref/freezer

Drop-leaf table

Bookcase

TV

36 x 60 Love Seat
24x48 Hinged Desk (Painting on back)

V.t Castings DV gas htr

Easy Chair 26x30

12' 0"

8' 0 "

Plan 18: Site-Built 14′×28′

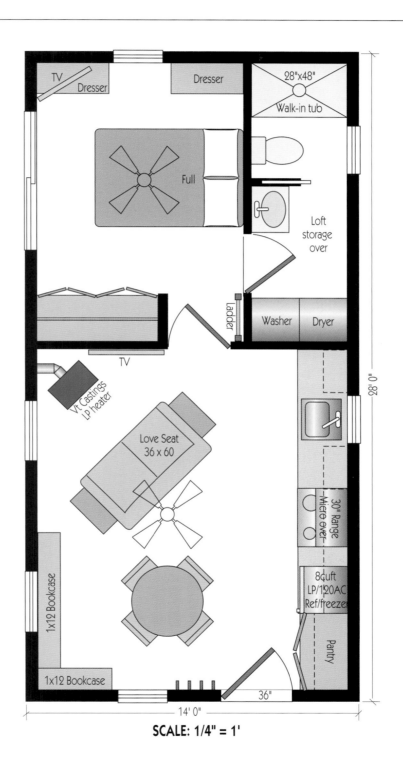

TV
Dresser
Dresser
28"x48"
Walk-in tub
Full
Loft storage over
Ladder
Washer
Dryer
TV
Vt Castings LP heater
Love Seat 36 x 60
30" Range
Micro over
1x12 Bookcase
8 cuft LP/120AC Ref/freezer
Pantry
1x12 Bookcase
36"
28' 0"
14' 0"

SCALE: 1/4" = 1'

SOME FLOOR PLANS
Plan 19: Site-Built 16′ × 24′

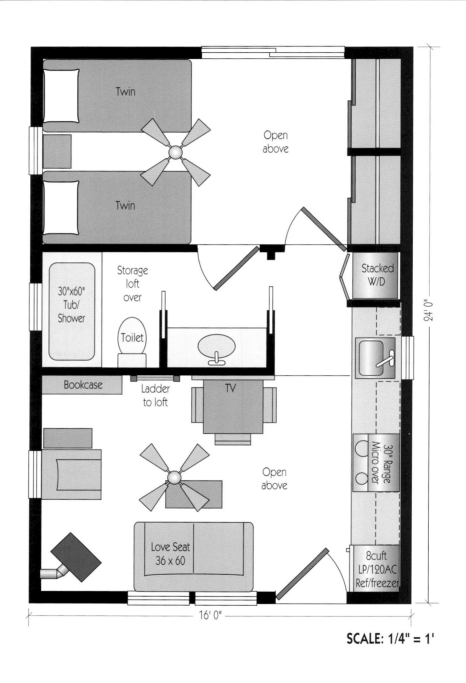

SCALE: 1/4" = 1'

Plan 20: Site-Built 20′ × 28′

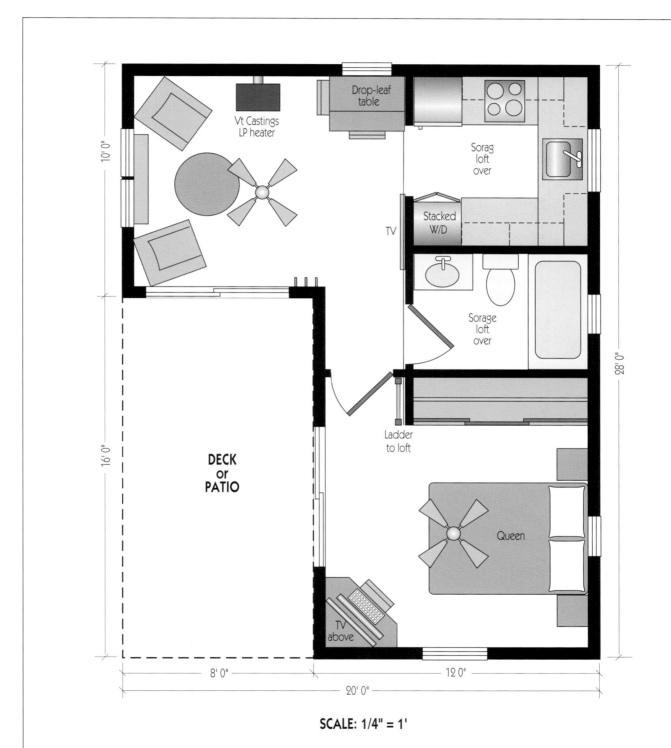

Drop-leaf table

Vt Castings LP heater

Sorag loft over

Stacked W/D

TV

Sorage loft over

Ladder to loft

DECK or PATIO

TV above

Queen

10' 0"

16' 0"

28' 0"

8' 0"

12 0"

20' 0"

SCALE: 1/4" = 1'

Plan 21: Site-Built 20′ × 20′

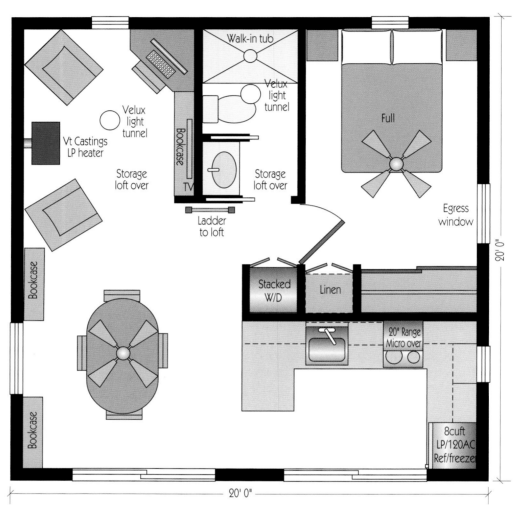

Walk-in tub

Velux light tunnel

Velux light tunnel

Vt Castings LP heater

Bookcase

Storage loft over

TV

Storage loft over

Full

Egress window

Ladder to loft

Bookcase

Stacked W/D

Linen

20″ Range Micro over

Bookcase

8cuft LP/120AC Ref/freezer

20′ 0″

20′ 0″

SCALE: 1/4″ = 1′

6 DRAWING PLANS

This chapter should provide you the basic knowledge to generate on paper a simple, but accurate and sufficient, set of plans for your tiny house.

The value of drawing accurate plans can not be overstated. The benefits include:

- reducing waste (measure twice; cut once!)
- making sure furnishings and appliances actually fit
- assuring code officials your design meets code
- generating more accurate cost estimates
- convincing loan officers you know what you are doing
- providing clear guidance to your workers.

Learning to draw house plans accurately can be as much fun as developing the conceptual design. You don't need an artistic gene, just the desire and discipline to utilize the proper tools to produce clean and precise lines. We show how to draw with pencil and paper, but the same principles apply to computer-aided drafting and drawing.

In a real sense *drawing* each physical element of the building (studs, joists, rafters, sheathing, etc,) *is constructing* it on paper. At some point in the actual construction process you will suddenly realize, "I've done this before—just on paper!"

Happy drawing and constructing!

6 DRAWING PLANS
Drafting Tools

Creating the accurate scale drawings required both for permitting and construction requires specialized drawing tools used by architects and engineers. All of the tools shown here can be purchased at art supply stores or on Amazon for less than $200. Don't even think about it. Just do it!

The following pages will show how the tools are used.

1. Any table with a perfectly smooth flat surface plus a smooth, flat, side edge as the guide for a T-square (item 10).

2. An alternative to items 1 and 10: a portable drawing board with attached gliding parallel rule. Either item 2 or the combination of items 1 and 10 are indispensable basic requirements for drawing accurate parallel lines.

3. A pad of 11" × 17" 100% rag tracing vellum paper. Although all of your drawings might also fit on 8.5" × 11" paper (as they did in Chapter 7), codes and zoning officials may require plans on 11" × 17" at a minimum.

4. Masking tape to hold the drawing paper in place on the drafting table or board. Blue painter's tape works well.

5. A 2-mm lead holder (mechanical pencil) with 4B and HB leads for initial sketches and final drawings. A mechanical lead sharpener is convenient, but a sheet of fine sandpaper will do for a single project,

6. A white vinyl plastic eraser, perfect for erasing pencil marks without smudging or leaving eraser crumbs.

7. A metal eraser shield which isolates areas (in a variety of shapes) to be removed while protecting the rest of the drawing.

8. A thin horsehair brush (designed for drafting and other artwork) for whisking off the drawing without smudging pencil lines.

9. A 12-inch triangular architectural scale ruler. Be sure to get the version marked in inches, not centimeters.

10. A 30- or 36-inch T-square. Note: this is required only to pair with item #1. A T-square is not required if you have a drafting board with attached parallel rule (item#2).

11. Adjustable triangles are used with the T-square or parallel rule to draw lines at any angle from 0° to 90°. Available in three sizes: 8", 10", and 12"; for drawing tiny house plans, the 8" triangle will do.

12. Thin, ¼-inch scale plastic templates allow tracing rather than measuring and constructing objects. They're very inexpensive, so you can purchase either one large residential template or afford separate: furnishings, appliances, bathroom, kitchens, and wiring versions.

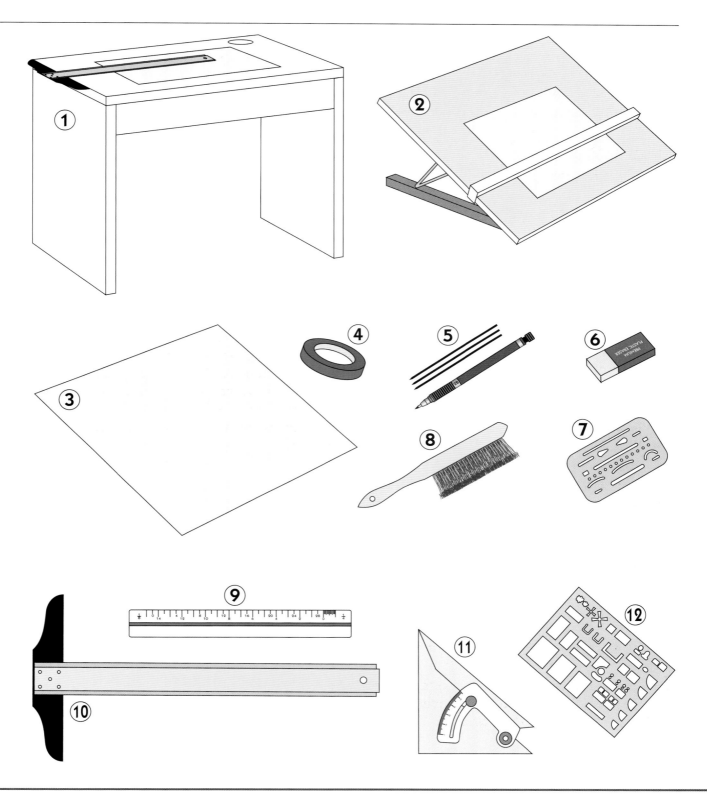

6 Drawing Lines

Horizontal Lines

Make a small tic mark at the level you wish to draw the line, then slide the T-square (or parallel rule) up to the mark. Applying firm pressure against the head of the T-square to prevent movement, draw the line through the mark from left to right.

Actually, hold the pencil parallel to the rule rather than as shown, and if the line is long, rotate the lead holder as you go to prevent wear from flattening the point of the lead.

Vertical Lines

The vertical leg of the adjustable triangle is always exactly 90° from the horizontal established by the T-square or parallel rule.

To draw a vertical line, place a tic mark at the horizontal position of the line. Holding the T-square head firmly against the table edge, slide the triangle until its vertical leg aligns with the mark. Then, pressing firmly down on the triangle, draw the line.

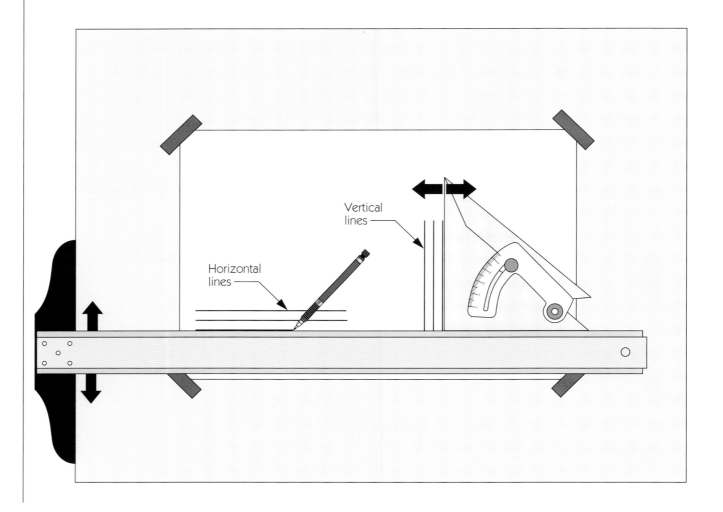

Vertical lines

Horizontal lines

Sloped Lines

Horizontal is defined as being at an angle of 0°. With its longer leg resting on the horizontal T-square or parallel rule, the adjustable triangle may be adjusted to any angle from 0° to 45°. With the triangle's shorter leg resting on the horizontal T-square or parallel rule, the adjustment range becomes 45° to 90°. Thus, after establishing horizontal (0°), we can draw straight lines at any angle as is required when drawing roof rafters.

Note that the convention in roof design is not to use degrees at all. Rather, roof slopes are usually denoted as the *pitch*: the vertical rise in inches over a horizontal run of 12 inches.

For example, the slope of rafters for a roof of pitch 4/12 may found by drawing a triangle with the vertical leg = 4″ and the horizontal leg = 12″.

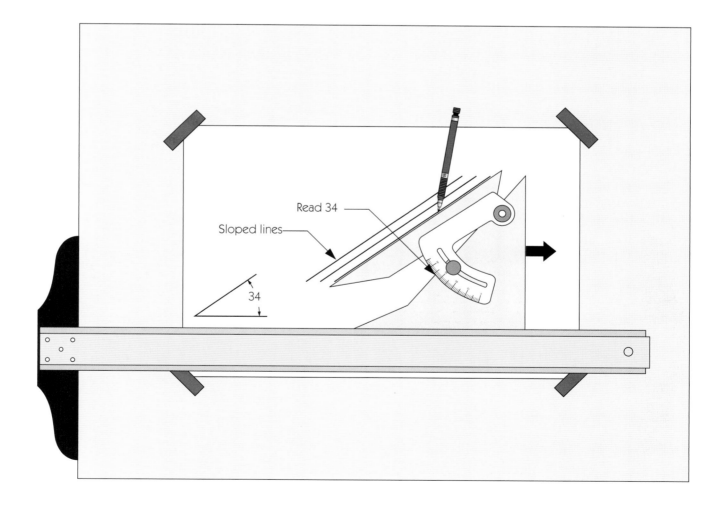

Dimensioning

Reading the Architect's Scale

The triangular architect's scale ruler is indispensable for drawing plans to scale. The ruler contains 12 scales including: 1-1/2", 1, 3/4", 3/8", 3/16", 3/32", 1/2", 1/4", 1/8". The common scale for residential drawings is 1/4" = 1'.

The illustration below shows a rule using the 1/4" scale to measure a distance of 6'–9". First place the rule so that one end mark is within the inches section at the end, Then slide the rule so the other end mark falls on a foot mark.

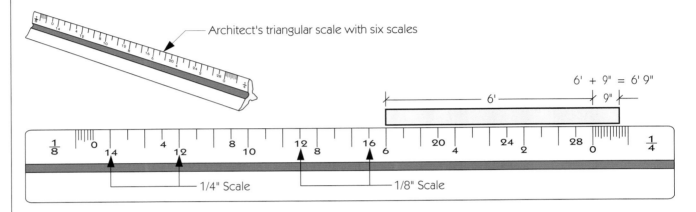

Dimension Lines

Except for elevations, all architectural drawings display dimensions in feet and inches. The idea is to provide enough dimensions that a carpenter could construct the building exactly as envisioned by the designer. Others requiring the dimensions are code officials, subcontractors, and material suppliers.

The illustration below shows how all of the critical dimensions can be shown using a minimum number of measurements. Note that calling out the *centers* of door and window locations allows changes to the unit rough openings without changing the lines of the drawing.

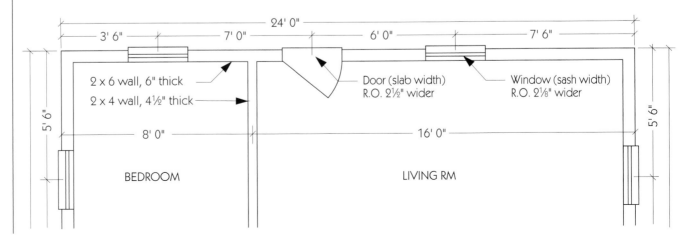

Using Templates

Using Templates

Templates are great time savers for laying out furniture and appliances, particularly in the initial stages of design. A great variety are available from either stationery stores or Amazon online, including: furniture, wiring, lighting, plumbing, bathroom fixtures, kitchen appliances, and general geometric shapes. Most can be purchased for less than $2. Be sure, however, that the ones you purchase are for 1/4-inch scale drawings.

When it comes to your final drawings, don't forget the 1/4-inch scale furniture, fixture, and appliance drawings on pages 36–37, and the catalog of furnishing for tiny spaces on pages 38–39. When dealing with tiny spaces, even fractions of inches count!

A Simple Residential Template

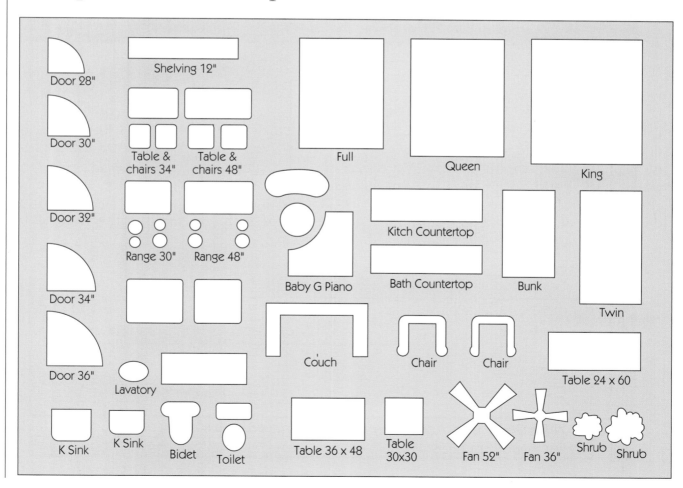

Formatting the Page

As exhibited in this book, ¼-inch scale drawings for most tiny houses (≤400 sq.ft. floor area) easily fit on 8½" × 11" pages. However, before investing hours and hours in creating finish drawings, check with your local code official for their submission requirements. Some jurisdictions require drawings on 11" x 17" sheets minimum.

Regardless of size, each drawing should be enclosed by a heavy border line indented at least ¼" (the more the better) on all edges to assure complete duplication and allow for stapling.

At the bottom of each sheet create a box containing at least:

- the title of the sheet
- the address of the proposed property
- the name of the draftsperson
- the sequential page number
- the scale of the drawing
- the date of the drawing (in case there have been changes).

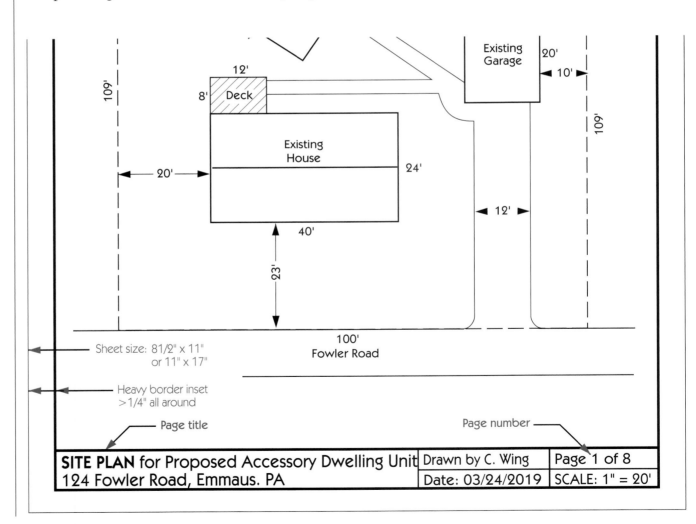

Sheet size: 8½" x 11" or 11" x 17"

Heavy border inset > 1/4" all around

Page title

Page number

SITE PLAN for Proposed Accessory Dwelling Unit 124 Fowler Road, Emmaus. PA	Drawn by C. Wing	Page 1 of 8
	Date: 03/24/2019	SCALE: 1" = 20'

7 A SET OF PLANS

If you have been reading from the beginning you may recall the evolution of the example 12' x 24' tiny house in Chapter 4. The same floor plan appears in color as Plan #11 in Chapter 5. Here we present a complete set of detailed plans for its construction. The single sheet we have omitted due to page constraints is for *Details* (larger scale drawings of items such as the built-in, wall-hung, drop-down door/desk over the living room couch). That design does appear, however, under *Furnishings for Tiny Spaces* on page 40.

Note that this set of plans is for illustrative purposes only and has not been certified by a registered architect or engineer. The plans also assume a northern, heating-climate location. If you plan to build from them, you would be advised to have them reviewed by a local professional.

And feel free to change the plans in any way to better fit your own location and lifestyle!

The following eleven pages contain a set of architectural drawings for a tiny, 12' × 24' (288 square feet) single-bedroom accessory dwelling. Omitted is a sheet of details usually included in a set for a larger and more complex structure. Being such a tiny house, it could be fabricated offsite in your driveway or by shed builders and dropped onto a prepared foundation as well as built onsite. For this reason we have included two foundations, and two floor framing options.

Site Plan (Page 80)

The site plan, drawn to scale, shows the property boundaries, building footprints (both existing and proposed), driveways and sidewalks, and the setback distances of all elements from the boundaries. The purpose is to demonstrate compliance with the applicable zoning requirements. Our example shows a lot on Fowler Street, Emmaus, PA, with frontage of 100 feet and depth of 109 feet. Existing structures include a 24' × 40' dwelling and a 16' × 20' garage. Proposed is a 12' × 24' accessory dwelling. Not included in the permit application but shown on the site plan are a possible future deck and sunspace.

Floor Plan (Page 81)

The floor plan shows building dimensions based on the outside of the frame, thickness of walls (framing plus interior finish), rough dimensions of each occupied area, and all fixed cabinets and appliances.

Though there is but a single occupied level, the second drawing shows a storage loft of 144 square feet over the bedroom.

The exterior wall thickness is shown as 6 inches (2 × 6 construction). If not required by energy code, substituting 2 × 4 construction would increase the habitable area by 11 square feet.

Foundation (Page 82)

A foundation plan shows the locations and dimensions of all footings, walls, and columns or piers. Unless otherwise stated, the bottoms of footings are below the local depth of frost penetration. Masonry foundation plans should show the locations of all embedded anchor bolts. If drainage is required the plan should show the locations of drainage pipes, both perforated and solid, as well as any sump pits. The example shows two options: 1) concrete piers and 2) masonry perimeter walls, for either a crawl space or a full basement.

Floor Framing (Page 83)

The floor framing plan shows all of the wood members: sill, joists, beams, and any supporting posts. Locations, dimensions, spacing, and minimum acceptable lumber grades are identified. The supporting foundation is shown in dashed lines.

N/S Wall Framing (Page 84)

Wall framing may be shown in any order. Here we have paired the N and S walls and E and W walls due to their similarities in sizes and shapes.

The wisdom in the carpentry rule, "Measure twice, cut once," is in the unfortunate fact that a board cut too short can never be lengthened. To coin an analogous framing rule, "Draw a dozen times, construct once."

When designing a wall frame, remember:

- Sheathing measures 48" × 96", so to minimize waste, space studs either 16" or 24" on center.

- The tops of door and window rough openings should be aligned if possible.

- Rafter loads must fall over studs or headers.

E/W Wall Framing (Page 85)

Walls are generally laid out and assembled on the subfloor then raised. However, gable- and shed-roof walls are framed in two stages. First, the rectangular lower section is framed, raised, and joined to the already-raised adjoining walls. After the rafters have been placed, the top wall section is constructed in place.

Roof Framing (Page 86)

The roof framing includes all structural members supporting roof sheathing, roofing materials, and live loads. In the case of dormers the framing includes the supporting wall sections and framing around any openings.

Conventional construction requires either roof trusses or ceiling joists to prevent the rafters from spreading and pushing the walls outward under loads. We have chosen an alternative post-and-beam style cathedral ceiling where the rafters are supported by two exposed 12-foot sections of 6 × 8 ridge beam.

To complete the aesthetic we are using exposed 4 × 6 rafters 24-inches on center.

Elevations (Page 87)

Elevations are views of the finished building from its four sides. The purpose is to project the aesthetics of the architecture. The locations of windows and doors are as shown in the floor plan and in the rough openings in the framing plans.

At this point a give-and-take often arises between interior and exterior. Which is more important: the functionality of the windows (providing light, ventilation, and view) or the exterior appearance? Nearly always the floor plan, framing, and elevations will need to be adjusted several times.

Typical Section (Page 88)

The Section drawing(s) might better be called "Slices." Their purposes are two-fold:

- Show the principle structural elements—foundation, joists, studs, and rafters—and how they connect.

- Show the remaining principle materials after framing: insulation, vapor and air barriers, sheathing, interior and exterior finishes, flooring, roofing, exterior trim, and gutters.

Think of a section drawing as what one would see under magnification if one were to pass a detailed model of the building through a saw parallel to the joists and rafters.

Electrical (Page 89)

The purpose of the electrical plan is not to show the detailed routing of wiring circuits through the building. Rather, it is a visual work order to the electrician showing all of the receptacles, switches, lighting fixtures, and fixed appliances to be installed. How the electrician chooses to route the individual cables is up to him or her to decide based on experience and the electrical code.

Plumbing (Page 90)

Unlike wiring, plumbing drain, waste, and vent pipes are subject to strict rules as to diameters, maximum lengths, slopes, and cleanouts. (Supply pipe rules allow unlimited flexibility in routing.) Thus, the plumbing plan shows all of the appliances and fixtures receiving and/or discharging water and the sizes and routing of the pipes servicing them. Unless one has much experience in plumbing they would be wise to consult with a working plumber before finalizing the plumbing plan.

7

Site Plan

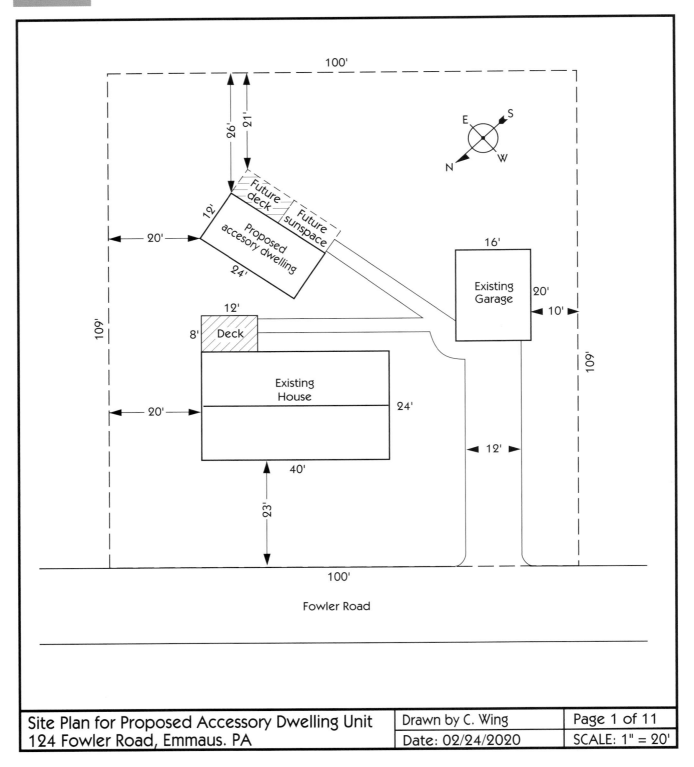

Site Plan for Proposed Accessory Dwelling Unit 124 Fowler Road, Emmaus. PA	Drawn by C. Wing	Page 1 of 11
	Date: 02/24/2020	SCALE: 1" = 20'

Floor Plan

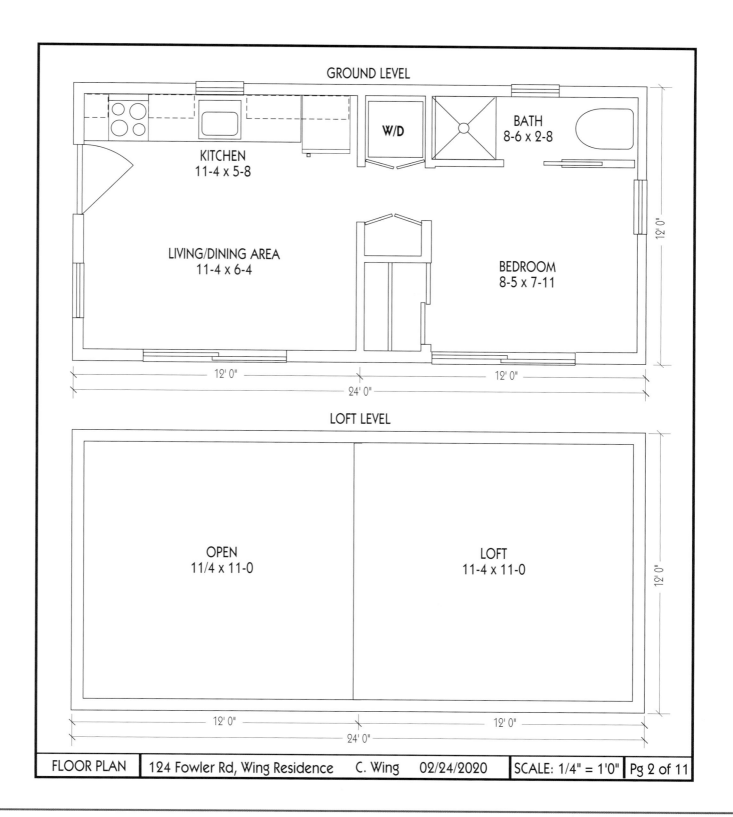

GROUND LEVEL

W/D

BATH
8-6 x 2-8

KITCHEN
11-4 x 5-8

LIVING/DINING AREA
11-4 x 6-4

BEDROOM
8-5 x 7-11

12' 0"

12' 0"

12' 0"

24' 0"

LOFT LEVEL

OPEN
11/4 x 11-0

LOFT
11-4 x 11-0

12' 0"

12' 0"

12' 0"

24' 0"

| FLOOR PLAN | 124 Fowler Rd, Wing Residence | C. Wing | 02/24/2020 | SCALE: 1/4" = 1'0" | Pg 2 of 11 |

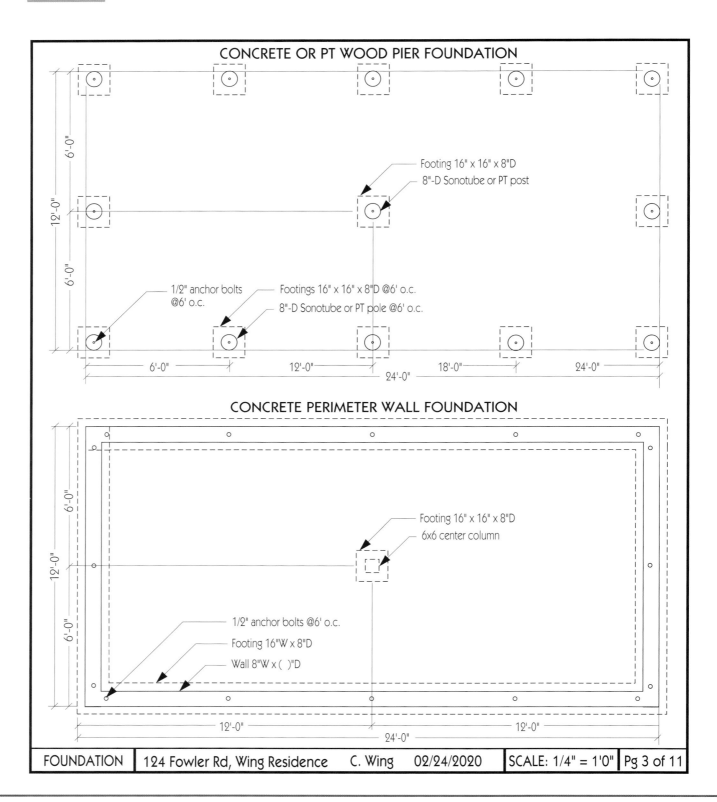

CONCRETE OR PT WOOD PIER FOUNDATION

6'-0"
12'-0"
6'-0"

Footing 16" x 16" x 8"D
8"-D Sonotube or PT post

1/2" anchor bolts @6' o.c.
Footings 16" x 16" x 8"D @6' o.c.
8"-D Sonotube or PT pole @6' o.c.

6'-0"   12'-0"   18'-0"   24'-0"
24'-0"

CONCRETE PERIMETER WALL FOUNDATION

6'-0"
12'-0"
6'-0"

Footing 16" x 16" x 8"D
6x6 center column

1/2" anchor bolts @6' o.c.
Footing 16"W x 8"D
Wall 8"W x ( )"D

12'-0"   12'-0"
24'-0"

| FOUNDATION | 124 Fowler Rd, Wing Residence | C. Wing | 02/24/2020 | SCALE: 1/4" = 1'0" | Pg 3 of 11 |

Two Floor Framing Options

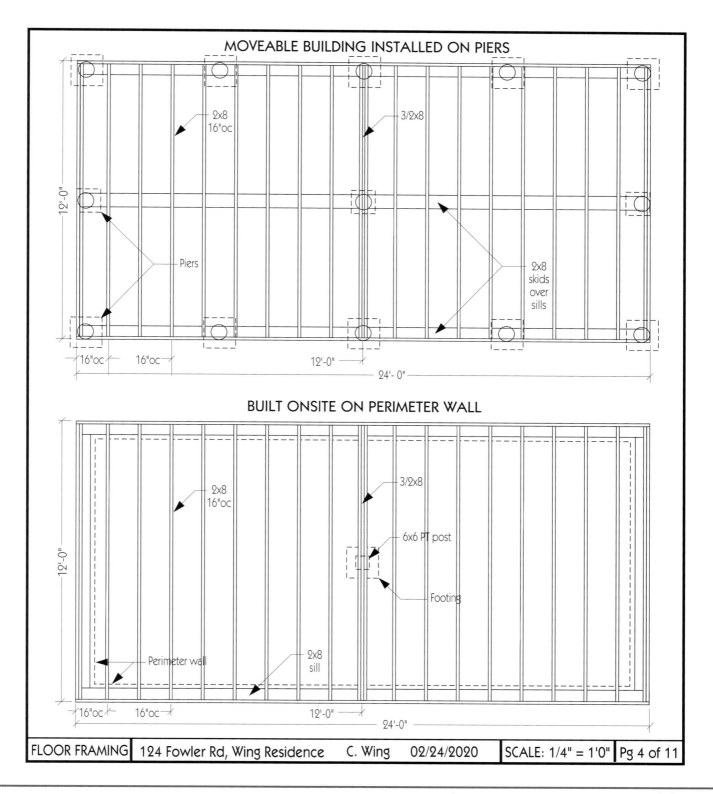

MOVEABLE BUILDING INSTALLED ON PIERS

2x8
16"oc

3/2x8

Piers

2x8
skids
over
sills

12'-0"

16"oc 16"oc 12'-0"

24'-0"

BUILT ONSITE ON PERIMETER WALL

2x8
16"oc

3/2x8

6x6 PT post

Footing

12'-0"

Perimeter wall

2x8
sill

16"oc 16"oc 12'-0"

24'-0"

| FLOOR FRAMING | 124 Fowler Rd, Wing Residence | C. Wing | 02/24/2020 | SCALE: 1/4" = 1'0" | Pg 4 of 11 |

N/S Wall Framing

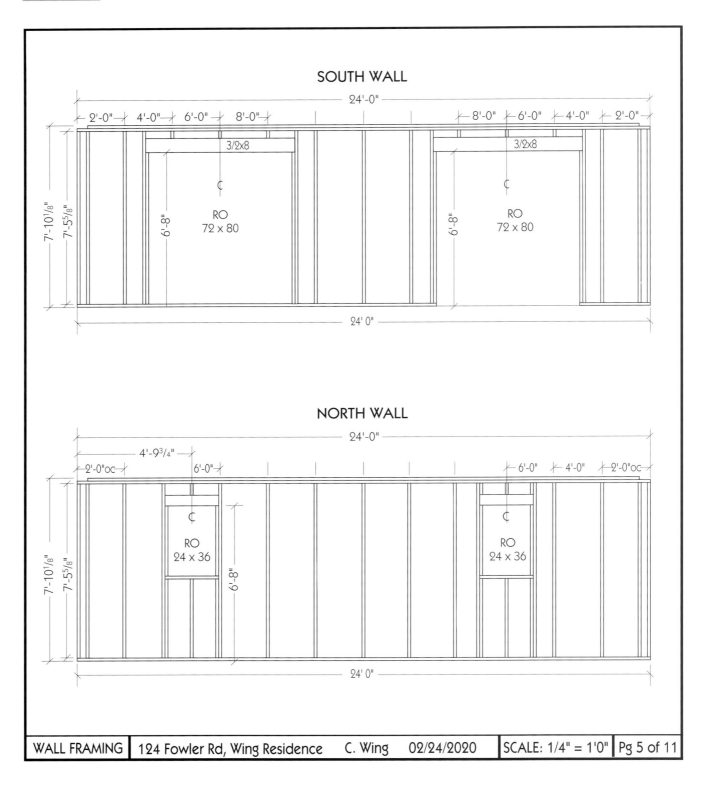

SOUTH WALL

24'-0"

2'-0" | 4'-0" | 6'-0" | 8'-0" | 8'-0" | 6'-0" | 4'-0" | 2'-0"

3/2x8

3/2x8

7'-10 1/8"
7'-5 5/8"

6'-8"

RO
72 x 80

6'-8"

RO
72 x 80

24' 0"

NORTH WALL

24'-0"

4'-9 3/4"

2'-0"oc | 6'-0" | 6'-0" | 4'-0" | 2'-0"oc

7'-10 1/8"
7'-5 5/8"

RO
24 x 36

6'-8"

RO
24 x 36

24' 0"

| WALL FRAMING | 124 Fowler Rd, Wing Residence | C. Wing | 02/24/2020 | SCALE: 1/4" = 1'0" | Pg 5 of 11 |

E/W Wall Framing

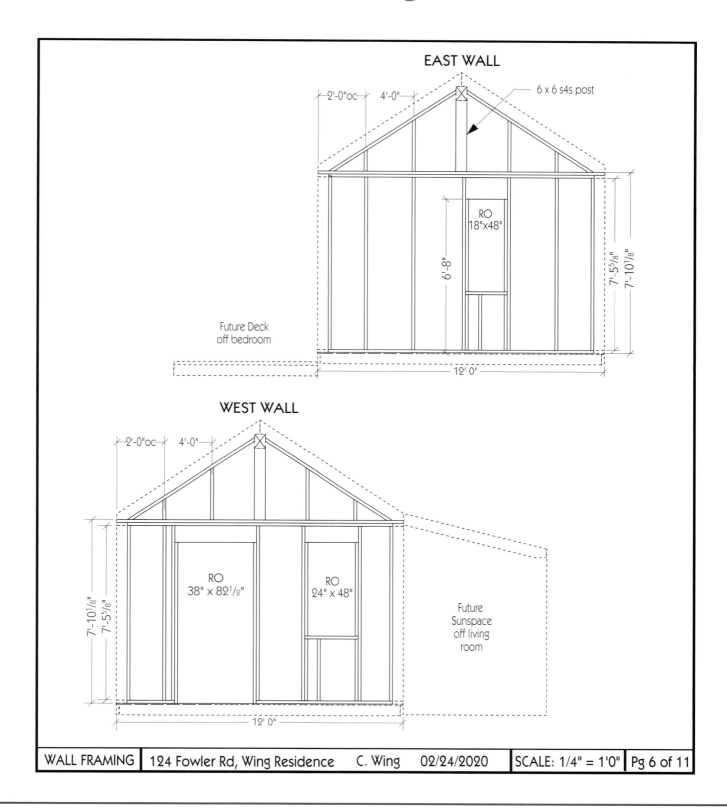

EAST WALL

6 x 6 s4s post

2'-0"oc   4'-0"

RO
18"x48"

6'-8"

7'-5⅝"
7'-10⅛"

Future Deck
off bedroom

12' 0"

WEST WALL

2'-0"oc   4'-0"

RO
38" x 82½"

RO
24" x 48"

7'-10⅛"
7'-5⅝"

Future
Sunspace
off living
room

12' 0"

| WALL FRAMING | 124 Fowler Rd, Wing Residence | C. Wing | 02/24/2020 | SCALE: 1/4" = 1'0" | Pg 6 of 11 |

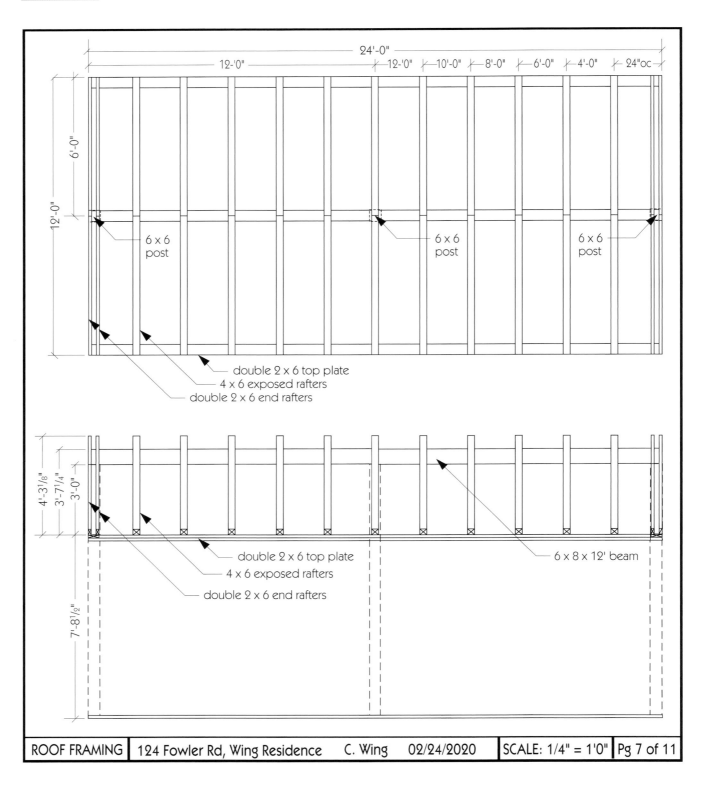

ROOF FRAMING | 124 Fowler Rd, Wing Residence | C. Wing | 02/24/2020 | SCALE: 1/4" = 1'0" | Pg 7 of 11

Elevations

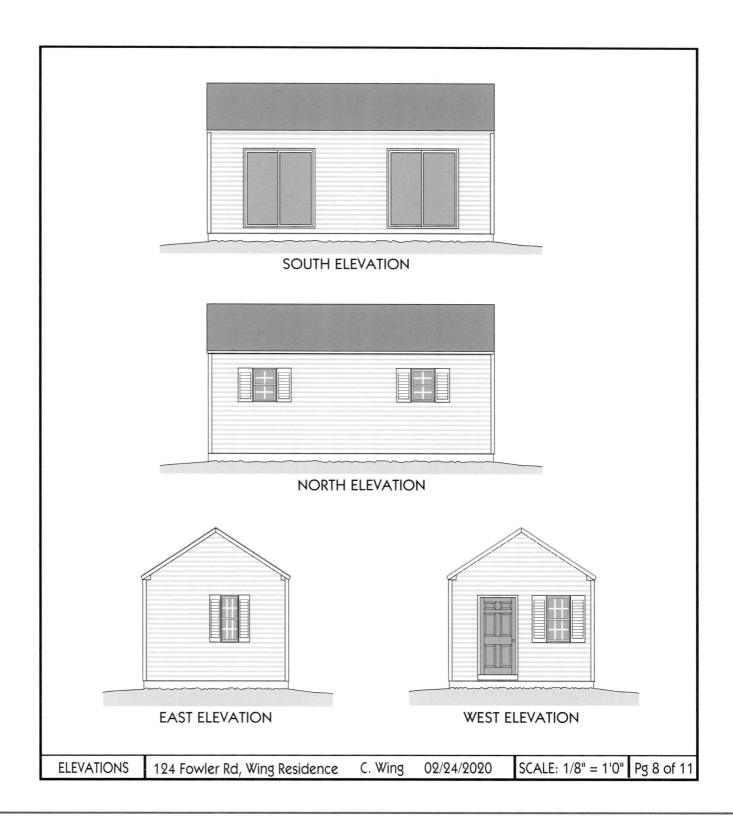

SOUTH ELEVATION

NORTH ELEVATION

EAST ELEVATION

WEST ELEVATION

| ELEVATIONS | 124 Fowler Rd, Wing Residence | C. Wing | 02/24/2020 | SCALE: 1/8" = 1'0" | Pg 8 of 11 |

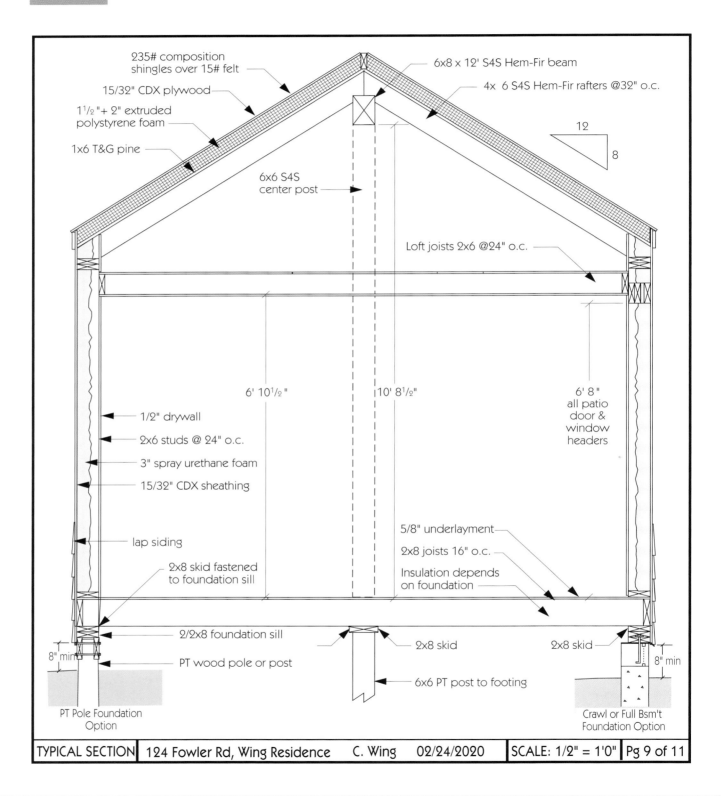

235# composition shingles over 15# felt

15/32" CDX plywood

1½"+ 2" extruded polystyrene foam

1x6 T&G pine

6x6 S4S center post

6x8 x 12' S4S Hem-Fir beam

4x 6 S4S Hem-Fir rafters @32" o.c.

12
8

Loft joists 2x6 @24" o.c.

6' 10½"

10' 8½"

6' 8" all patio door & window headers

1/2" drywall

2x6 studs @ 24" o.c.

3" spray urethane foam

15/32" CDX sheathing

lap siding

2x8 skid fastened to foundation sill

5/8" underlayment

2x8 joists 16" o.c.

Insulation depends on foundation

2/2x8 foundation sill

PT wood pole or post

8" min

2x8 skid

2x8 skid

8" min

6x6 PT post to footing

PT Pole Foundation Option

Crawl or Full Bsm't Foundation Option

| TYPICAL SECTION | 124 Fowler Rd, Wing Residence | C. Wing | 02/24/2020 | SCALE: 1/2" = 1'0" | Pg 9 of 11 |

Electrical Plan

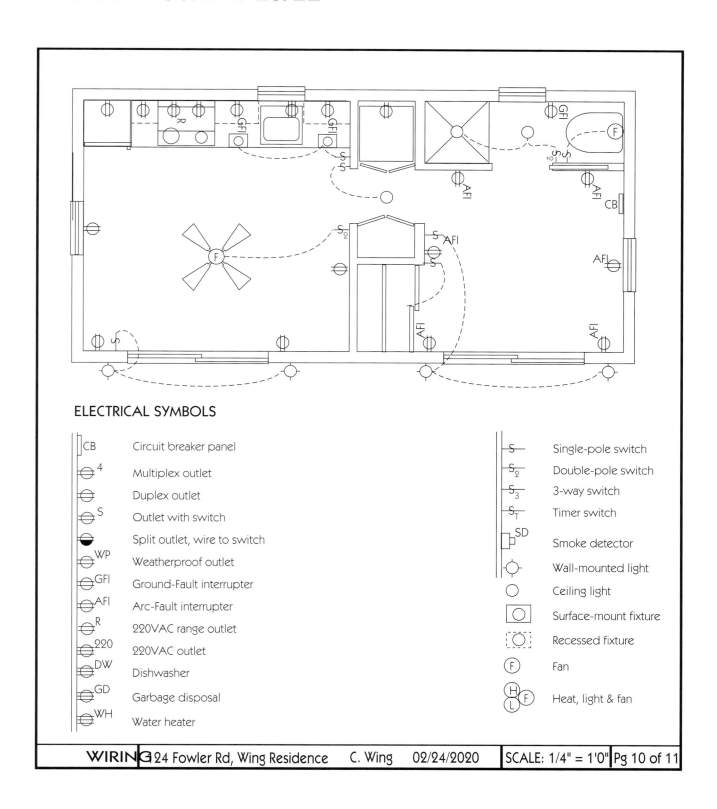

ELECTRICAL SYMBOLS

CB	Circuit breaker panel
4	Multiplex outlet
	Duplex outlet
S	Outlet with switch
	Split outlet, wire to switch
WP	Weatherproof outlet
GFI	Ground-Fault interrupter
AFI	Arc-Fault interrupter
R	220VAC range outlet
220	220VAC outlet
DW	Dishwasher
GD	Garbage disposal
WH	Water heater

S	Single-pole switch
S_2	Double-pole switch
S_3	3-way switch
S_T	Timer switch
SD	Smoke detector
	Wall-mounted light
	Ceiling light
	Surface-mount fixture
	Recessed fixture
F	Fan
H F L	Heat, light & fan

WIRING 24 Fowler Rd, Wing Residence   C. Wing   02/24/2020   SCALE: 1/4" = 1'0"   Pg 10 of 11

Plumbing Plan

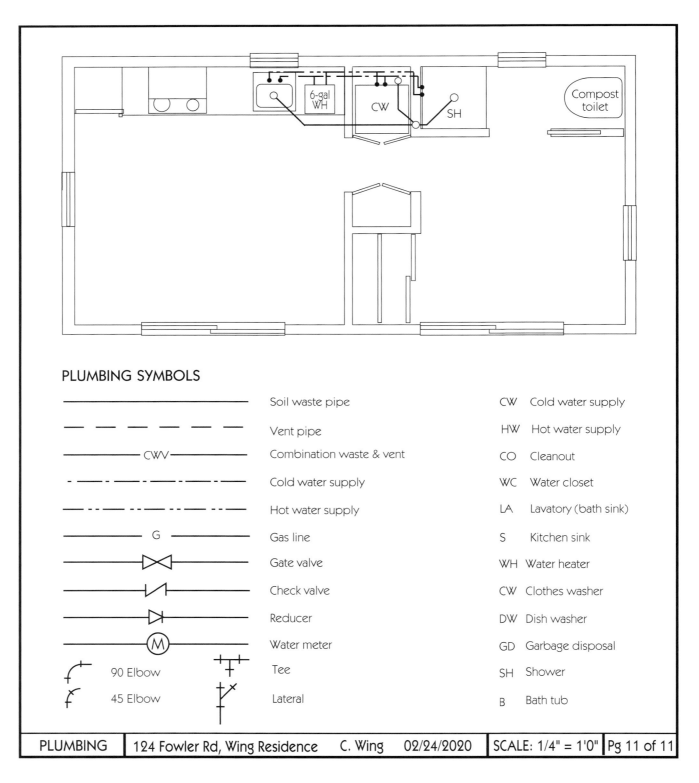

PLUMBING SYMBOLS

————————————	Soil waste pipe	CW	Cold water supply
— — — — — —	Vent pipe	HW	Hot water supply
——— CWV ———	Combination waste & vent	CO	Cleanout
– · — · — · —	Cold water supply	WC	Water closet
– · · — · · —	Hot water supply	LA	Lavatory (bath sink)
——— G ———	Gas line	S	Kitchen sink
—▷◁—	Gate valve	WH	Water heater
—▷|—	Check valve	CW	Clothes washer
—▷—	Reducer	DW	Dish washer
—Ⓜ—	Water meter	GD	Garbage disposal
90 Elbow Tee		SH	Shower
45 Elbow Lateral		B	Bath tub

PLUMBING	124 Fowler Rd, Wing Residence C. Wing 02/24/2020	SCALE: 1/4" = 1'0"	Pg 11 of 11

8 FOUNDATIONS

Tiny houses, if carefully constructed with structural sheathing, are like small boats in not requiring a stable, continuous perimeter foundation on which to rest. That is what enables them to galivant around the country on wheels or be delivered fully finished to a site.

Whether you will need an in-the-ground foundation at all (as opposed to simple leveling and blocking), and the type of permanent foundation you may require, depends both on the zoning of your site and its exposure to extreme winds.

To cover all situations this chapter details a full range of options from wind anchoring systems to pressure-treated wood posts to full basements.

Forces Due to Wind

The primary function of a foundation, providing a stable base for the building sitting on it, is obvious. Not so obvious are numerous additional functions:

- isolating the building from frost heaves
- isolating the building from expansive soil
- isolating the building from ground moisture
- anchoring the building against earthquakes
- anchoring the building against wind.

Foundation options for site-built houses are well established, but tiny houses built on trailers or delivered on skids present a special challenge: that of lightweight buildings resisting the forces of extreme winds. The best guide for dealing with such buildings is the "HUD Code"

(*National Mobile Home Construction and Safety Standards Act*), which requires manufactured homes to comply with safety standards including ground anchoring to resist wind forces in the zones indicated on the map below:

- HUD Zone III. Areas of wind speed over 110 mph including the Gulf coasts of Texas, Louisiana, Mississippi, Alabama and Florida, plus the entire eastern seaboard.
- HUD Zone II. Areas of wind over 100 mph.
- HUD Zone I. Areas of wind over 70 mph (the rest of the country).

For site-built tiny houses we include detailed illustrations for four conventional foundations: piers or poles, slab on grade, crawl space, and full basement.

HUD Wind Zones

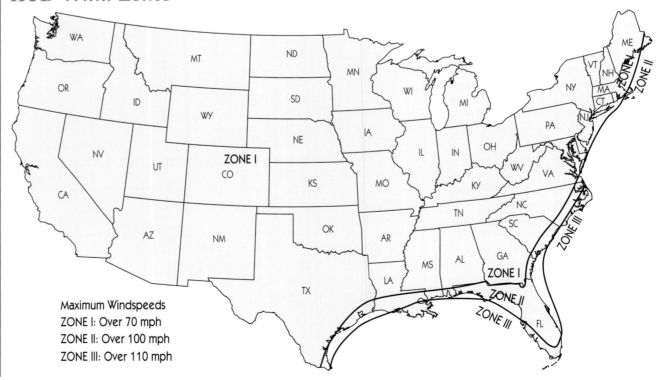

Maximum Windspeeds
ZONE I: Over 70 mph
ZONE II: Over 100 mph
ZONE III: Over 110 mph

The Forces Exerted by Wind

If you have never done so, stick your hand out a car window while traveling at 65 mph. Surprised at the force? Now try to hold a 4' × 8' sheet of plywood into a 20 mph wind. Wow! Air has mass, and stopping its moving mass requires force. A simple formula relates the total force exerted on a surface facing the wind to the area of the surface and the windspeed:

$$F = 0.00256AV^2$$

where:

A = area of surface in square feet
V = wind speed in miles per hour

The illustration at right shows the calculated forces against a typical tiny house wall measuring 8' high and 24' long in the three HUD zones. In Zone 3 at 110 mph, the force against the wall is 5,952 lb. Imagine!

Effects of Wind on a Building

Wind creates additional forces on a building including suction on the leeward (downwind) wall and uplift on the roof, but we will concentrate here on the two effects related to the building's foundation: translation and rotation.

Translation is simply sliding across the ground or off the foundation when the force of the wind exceeds the weight of the building times the coefficient of friction between the building and its support.

Rotation can occur when the building sits on sloping ground, especially when the foundation is closed except on the side facing the wind. The combination of horizontal pressure and pressure from beneath the building results in a lever action rotating the building.

HUD Wind Zone Forces

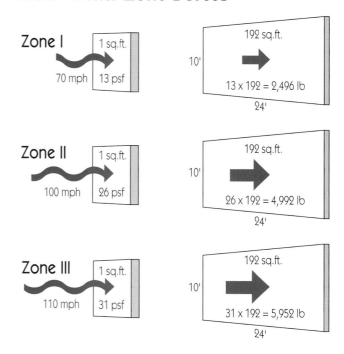

Effects of Wind

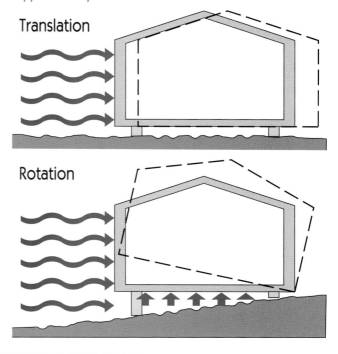

Anchoring Homes on Wheels

Tiny homes on wheels are designed to be mobile, and local zoning ordinances generally prohibit their occupation in one site for more than three to six months at a time, so building a foundation under them is impractical. However, occupied or not, hurricanes and microbursts pose a constant danger.

The illustration below shows an anchoring system of auger anchors and cabling commonly used on mobile homes. With the tiny home in place, 3- or 4-foot auger anchors are driven as close as possible under and outside

D-rings welded to the main beams close to the four corners of the trailer. Turnbuckles then connect the anchor eyes to the D-rings. Each auger is then connected horizontally to the D-ring on the opposite side of the trailer. Non-stretch marine halyard rope or cargo straps may substitute for aircraft cable. Note the thrust plates driven into the soil inside the auger eyes to resist the horizontal force.

With all turnbuckles tightened, the tiny house will move neither vertically nor horizontally.

Securing a Tiny Home on Wheels with Auger Anchors

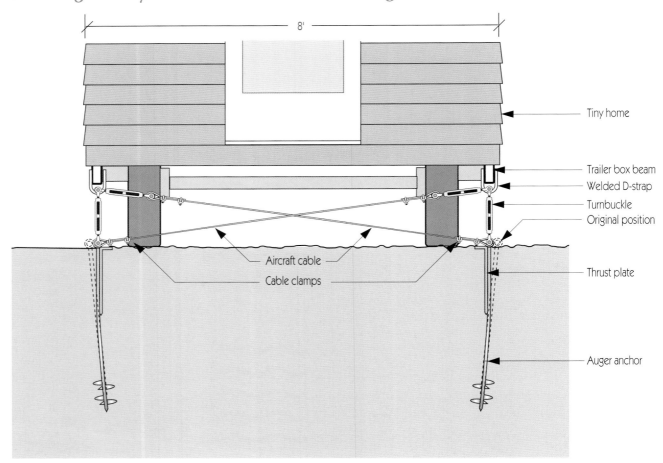

8'

Tiny home

Trailer box beam
Welded D-strap
Turnbuckle
Original position

Thrust plate

Aircraft cable
Cable clamps

Auger anchor

Anchoring Homes on Skids

Having no wheels, tiny homes on skids aren't exactly mobile, but they are designed to be easily transported, even moved several times. Unless one intends to make the building's first site its final site, any foundation should be removable.

As the illustration below shows, the same mobile home auger anchor system may be used to secure a building on skids against high winds.

Instead of D-rings welded to trailer beams, simple galvanized tie straps (available at big box home stores) can be bolted or lag-screwed through the wall sheathing to the outside faces of the building's rim joists. The attachment point could also be the bottom skids except for the difficulty of driving anchor augers vertically from beneath the building.

Note that the horizontal cables or straps need not extend all the way to the opposite rim joists but may be fastened to floor joists provided their angles from vertical exceed 40 degrees.

If the site is intended to be permanent the building may be jacked and then lowered onto any of the following site-built foundations.

Securing a Tiny Home on Skids with Auger Anchors

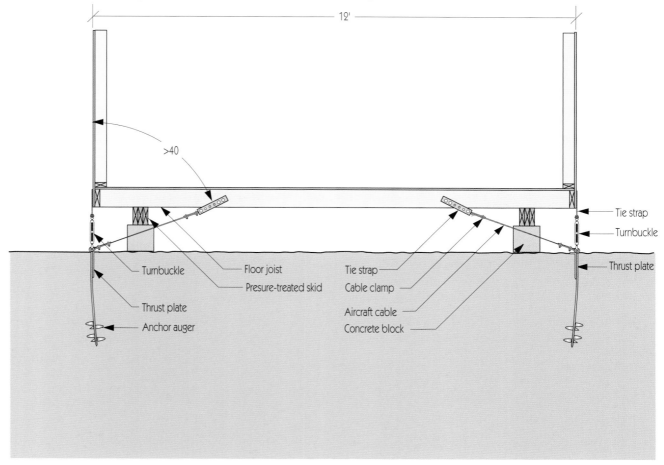

8 Pole Foundation

Farmers know the simplest and lowest-cost building foundation uses pressure-treated telephone poles. Though new poles are expensive and hard to procure, the butts of poles damaged from vehicular impact are often available for free from the electric utility. With no exposure to UV, the below-ground portion is as good as new.

How can you place poles accurately? You don't need to! The poles are set inside the building perimeter with the floor joists cantilevered over the sill beams by up to 2 feet.

Two solutions are shown. At left the building is constructed onsite. At right a tiny house on skids is dropped onto the sills and the building fastened down with lag bolts into the joists.

The Simple But Practical Telephone Pole Foundation

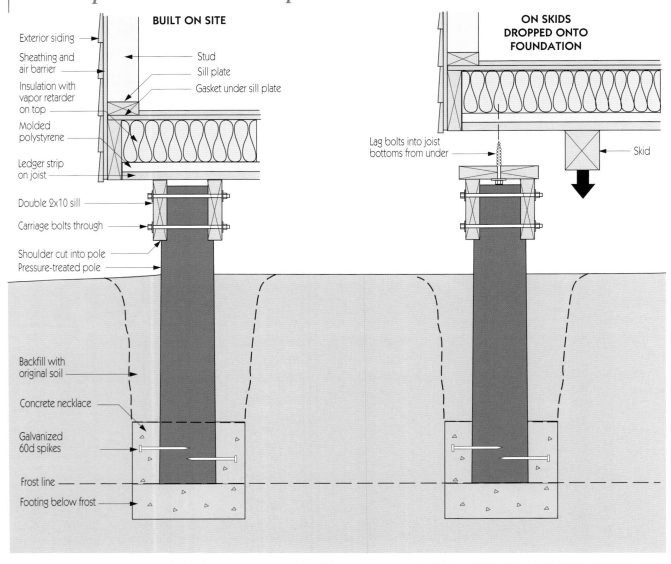

BUILT ON SITE

Exterior siding

Sheathing and air barrier

Insulation with vapor retarder on top

Molded polystyrene

Ledger strip on joist

Stud

Sill plate

Gasket under sill plate

Double 2x10 sill

Carriage bolts through

Shoulder cut into pole

Pressure-treated pole

Backfill with original soil

Concrete necklace

Galvanized 60d spikes

Frost line

Footing below frost

ON SKIDS DROPPED ONTO FOUNDATION

Lag bolts into joist bottoms from under

Skid

Slab on Grade

Slabs on grade are the simplest and least expensive contracted foundations. Again, two solutions are shown. At left the building is constructed onsite. At right a tiny house on skids is dropped onto a built-up sill and the building fastened down with a plywood splice plate.

Without perimeter insulation, the slab edges experience heat loss and condensation. The bottom illustration adds perimeter insulation. The protective coating protects the foam from UV degradation, and the termite shield blocks termites from tunneling up behind the foam.

Slab in a Cooling Climate

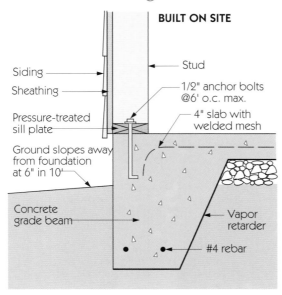

BUILT ON SITE

Siding

Sheathing

Pressure-treated sill plate

Ground slopes away from foundation at 6" in 10'

Concrete grade beam

Stud

1/2" anchor bolts @6' o.c. max.

4" slab with welded mesh

Vapor retarder

#4 rebar

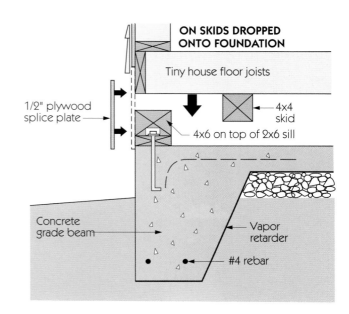

ON SKIDS DROPPED ONTO FOUNDATION

Tiny house floor joists

1/2" plywood splice plate

4x4 skid

4x6 on top of 2x6 sill

Concrete grade beam

Vapor retarder

#4 rebar

Slab in a Heating Climate

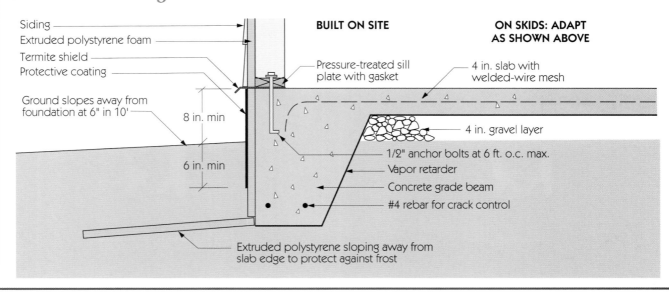

Siding

Extruded polystyrene foam

Termite shield

Protective coating

Ground slopes away from foundation at 6" in 10'

8 in. min

6 in. min

BUILT ON SITE

Pressure-treated sill plate with gasket

ON SKIDS: ADAPT AS SHOWN ABOVE

4 in. slab with welded-wire mesh

4 in. gravel layer

1/2" anchor bolts at 6 ft. o.c. max.

Vapor retarder

Concrete grade beam

#4 rebar for crack control

Extruded polystyrene sloping away from slab edge to protect against frost

Masonry Crawl Space

A crawl space foundation provides enclosed space beneath a building for plumbing, wiring, space and water heating equipment, and, depending on moisture conditions, storage. Important shoulds and musts include:

- footings placed below the maximum frost depth for the area

- pressure-treated sill
- termite shield between masonry and sill
- 6-mil polyethylene vapor barrier covering the ground
- crawl space cleared of untreated wood.

A tiny house on skids could be dropped onto the 2×6 + 4×6 sill shown on page 97.

For Cooling Climates

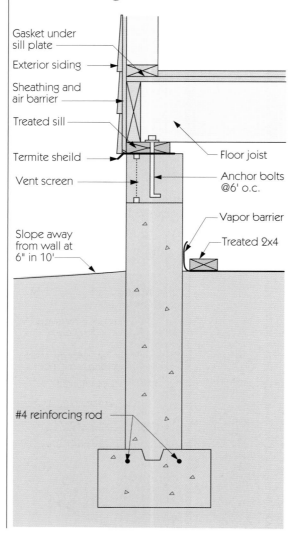

Gasket under sill plate
Exterior siding
Sheathing and air barrier
Treated sill
Termite sheild
Vent screen
Slope away from wall at 6" in 10'
#4 reinforcing rod
Floor joist
Anchor bolts @6' o.c.
Vapor barrier
Treated 2x4

For Heating Climates

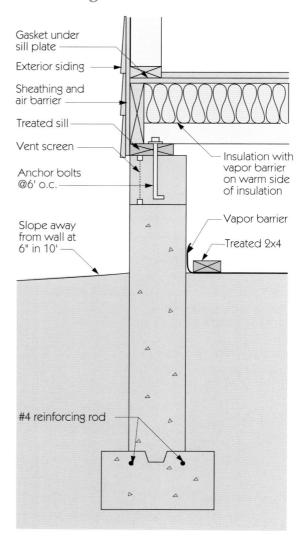

Gasket under sill plate
Exterior siding
Sheathing and air barrier
Treated sill
Vent screen
Anchor bolts @6' o.c.
Slope away from wall at 6" in 10'
#4 reinforcing rod
Insulation with vapor barrier on warm side of insulation
Vapor barrier
Treated 2x4

Full Basement (South)

A full-height basement foundation can provide storage or even habitable space at a far lower cost per square foot than the structure it supports. However, to be successful certain rules must be observed:

- the soil be well drained sand or gravel and the water table below basement level, or the site be sloped so drainage water flows to grade by gravity, or a utility drainage pipe be available as a sink

- the basement wall be coated with exterior waterproofing and/or provided with a drainage mat
- the roof be provided with gutters
- the slab be poured over a 6-mil polyethylene vapor barrier
- the area around the basement be sloped away at least 6 inches per 10 feet.

A tiny house on skids could be dropped onto the 2×6 + 4×6 sill shown on page 97.

For Cooling Climates

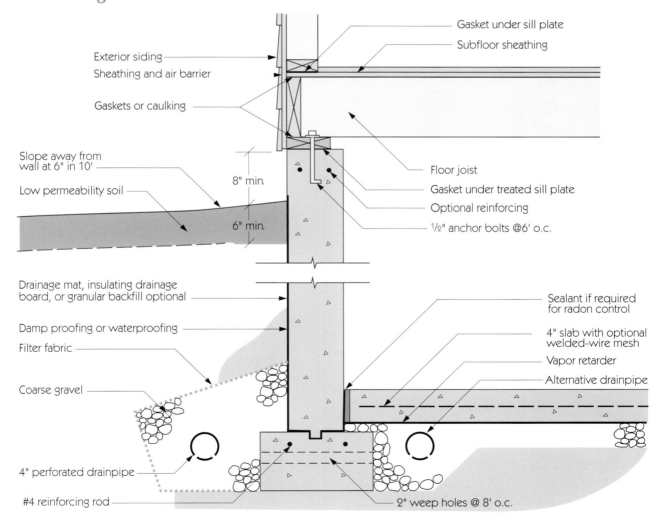

Exterior siding
Sheathing and air barrier
Gaskets or caulking

Gasket under sill plate
Subfloor sheathing

Slope away from wall at 6" in 10'
Low permeability soil

8" min.
6" min.

Floor joist
Gasket under treated sill plate
Optional reinforcing
1/2" anchor bolts @6' o.c.

Drainage mat, insulating drainage board, or granular backfill optional
Damp proofing or waterproofing
Filter fabric
Coarse gravel

Sealant if required for radon control
4" slab with optional welded-wire mesh
Vapor retarder
Alternative drainpipe

4" perforated drainpipe
#4 reinforcing rod

2" weep holes @ 8' o.c.

8 Full Basement (North)

Most homes in heating climates have basements. Part of the reason is historical. Before the advent of central heating systems and refrigeration, a deep hole beneath the house provided the perfect conditions for storing fruits, vegetables, and hams through the winter. Now the basement houses appliances and pool tables, but heat loss through uninsulated concrete walls accounts for about 25% of the home's heating bill. The illustration below shows the concrete wall insulated with 2-inch (R-value 10) extruded polystyrene. A latex-modified, fiberglass-reinforced stucco coating protects the plastic foam above grade from the sun.

For Heating Climates

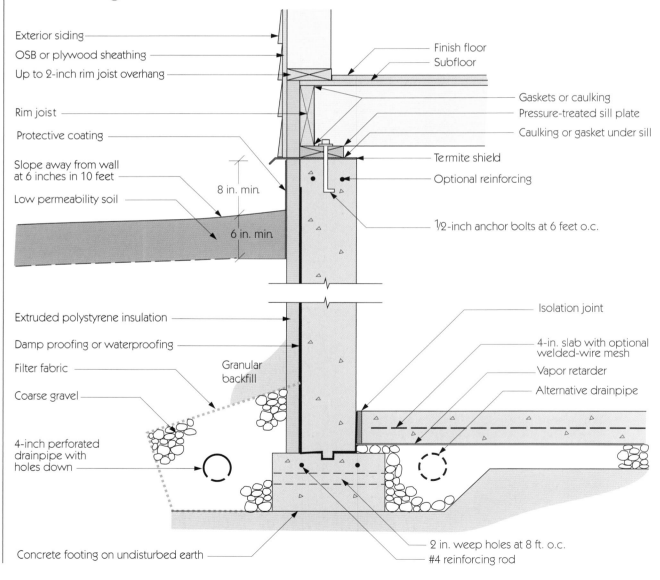

Exterior siding
OSB or plywood sheathing
Up to 2-inch rim joist overhang

Rim joist

Protective coating

Slope away from wall at 6 inches in 10 feet

Low permeability soil

8 in. min.

6 in. min.

Extruded polystyrene insulation

Damp proofing or waterproofing

Filter fabric

Coarse gravel

4-inch perforated drainpipe with holes down

Granular backfill

Concrete footing on undisturbed earth

Finish floor
Subfloor

Gaskets or caulking
Pressure-treated sill plate
Caulking or gasket under sill

Termite shield
Optional reinforcing

1/2-inch anchor bolts at 6 feet o.c.

Isolation joint

4-in. slab with optional welded-wire mesh
Vapor retarder
Alternative drainpipe

2 in. weep holes at 8 ft. o.c.
#4 reinforcing rod

9 FRAMING

In the sequential phases of construction, framing is both the most gratifying and the most demanding. The gratification comes when, after grovelling on the ground with foundation and floor, the wall frames go up. For the first time you find yourself inside your tiny house. At this point it resembles a big wooden cage, but the interior spaces are clearly defined, allowing you to picture yourself standing at the kitchen sink, sitting by the sunny south window, and waking to the eastern sunrise.

But framing is demanding because, unless you purchase a professionally drawn set of plans, you need to understand structure. You need to understand the loads, how they act on each member of the frame, and the sizes of those members required to resist each load.

To that end we begin with a "tiny" course on structural analysis. Don't skip! The knowledge this preliminary section imparts makes the following sections on floor, wall, and roof framing seem obvious, almost intuitive

When it comes time to actually assemble and raise the various parts of the frame, hire an experienced builder as your temporary foreman (or forewoman). The tricks and shortcuts they know will more than pay their one- or two-day's wages.

Forces on a House Frame

Dead Loads

Dead loads are the weights, in pounds per square foot (psf), of the building itself. In standard wood frame construction, they are assumed to be:

- *Roof:* light 10 psf, medium 15 psf, heavy 20 psf
- *Ceiling:* no storage 10 psf
- *Floor:* wood framed 10 psf
- *Exterior wall:* 10 psf
- *Interior wall* wood framed 10 psf

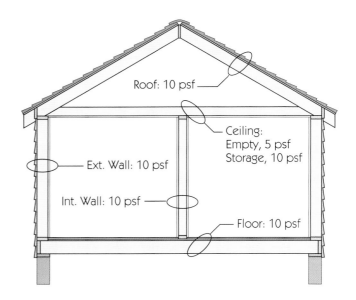

Roof: 10 psf

Ceiling:
Empty, 5 psf
Storage, 10 psf

Ext. Wall: 10 psf

Int. Wall: 10 psf

Floor: 10 psf

Live Loads

Live loads, in psf, are the weights added to the building by occupancy (furnishings plus people). The International Residential Code prescribes:

- *Attic:* no storage 10 psf, with storage 20 psf
- *Deck:* 40 psf
- *Balcony:* 60 psf
- *Bedrooms:* 30 psf
- *Living spaces other than bedrooms:* 40 psf
- *Roof:* light 10 psf, medium 15 psf, heavy 20
- *Stairs:* 40 psf
- *Roof:* pitch less than 4/12, 20 psf
- *Roof:* pitch 4–12/12, 16 psf
- *Roof:* pitch greater than 12/12, 12 psf

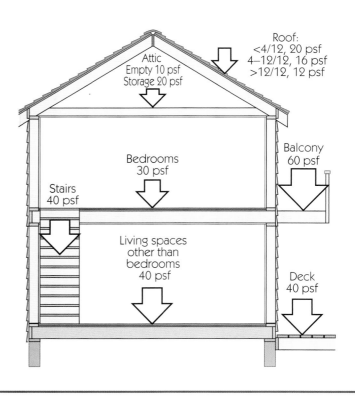

Attic
Empty 10 psf
Storage 20 psf

Roof:
<4/12, 20 psf
4–12/12, 16 psf
>12/12, 12 psf

Balcony
60 psf

Bedrooms
30 psf

Stairs
40 psf

Living spaces
other than
bedrooms
40 psf

Deck
40 psf

Wind Loads

Wind loads are defined as the pressure against an upwind wall and uplift on a down-wind roof due to the maximum sustained wind. These winds and resulting pressures are described in more detail in Chapter 8, pages 92–93.

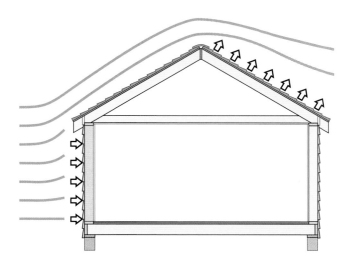

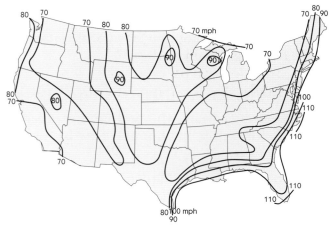

Snow Loads

Snow load is the maximum weight of snow, in psf, expected on a horizontal surface once in 50 years. The snow load for your area may be found on the map at right, but local snow accumulations can vary considerably, so it is wise to consult your local building code official or an architect with experience in residential construction.

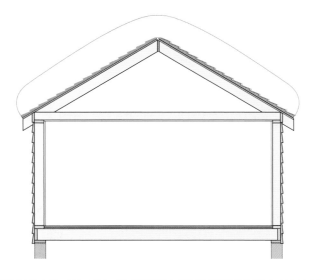

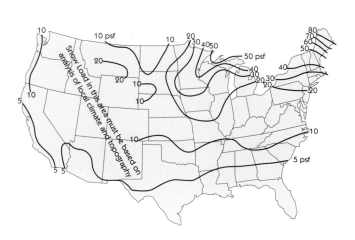

How Beams Support Loads

Bending and Deflection

If a load is placed on a beam, the beam bends or deflects. The amount of deflection under full load, D, is not as important as the deflection ratio, D/L, where L is the unsupported span.

Building codes specify maximum deflection ratios of 1/360 for floor joists, 1/240 for ceiling joists, and 1/180 for rafters without ceilings.

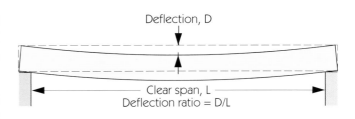

Deflection, D

Clear span, L
Deflection ratio = D/L

Long Beam Failure in Bending

In a bending beam, the bottommost fibers are in tension, while the top fibers are in compression.

The most common failure in a long beam is due to the bottom fibers pulling apart and the beam breaking, as shown. This explains why many joist and rafter tables show maximum allowed span as a function of extreme fiber stress in bending, f_b.

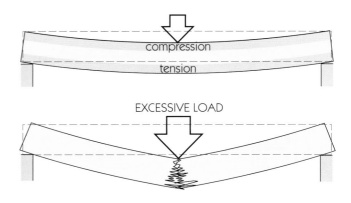

compression
tension

EXCESSIVE LOAD

Short Beam Failure in Shear

Individual wood fibers are long and extremely strong. This gives a beam great strength in both tension and compression in the direction of the fibers (lengthwise). The "glue" (lignin) that holds the fibers together is not very strong, however.

As a beam bends, the top layers compress, while the bottom layers stretch. The combined forces thus conspire to separate or shear the beam into several thinner beams. Because the pair of thinner beams is not as strong in bending as the original beam, the end result is most often failure in bending.

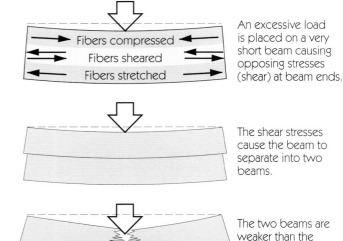

Fibers compressed
Fibers sheared
Fibers stretched

An excessive load is placed on a very short beam causing opposing stresses (shear) at beam ends.

The shear stresses cause the beam to separate into two beams.

The two beams are weaker than the original beam and break by bending.

Beams: Natural & Manufactured

Natural Wood Beams

Natural solid beams are sawn green, full-size from logs (i.e. a "2 × 4" measures a full 2 inches by 4 inches). Because it shrinks during drying, commercial structural lumber is first dried, then planed (Surfaced 4 Sides, or "S4S") to the finished sizes shown in the illustration.

Because planing removes wood fibers, a rough-sawn timber is stronger than its S4S equivalent. However, S4S lumber offers several advantages:

- It's graded so you can count on its strength.
- Its sizes are exact.
- It's available or can be special ordered in lengths to 20 feet at nearly all lumberyards.

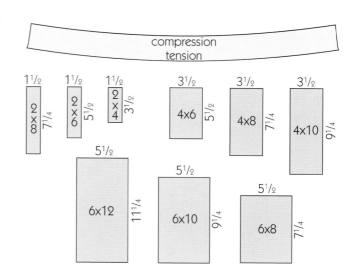

I-Joists

I-joists are wood versions of steel I-beams. Capitalizing on wood's natural strength in tension and compression and a structural panel's (such as plywood) strength in shear, the I-joist achieves greater strength than a solid beam of the same weight by gluing a structural panel between two 2 × 4s.

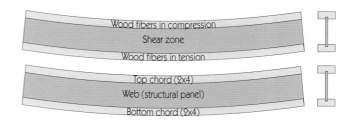

Laminated Beams

Since most of the tension in a beam is concentrated in its bottom-most layers, sawing a solid beam into thin layers, rearranging the layers with the strongest on the top and bottom, then gluing the whole pile together results in a much stronger beam. Glue-laminated beams are known collectively as "engineered beams."

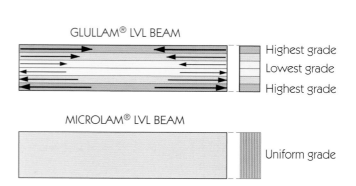

Building on Skids

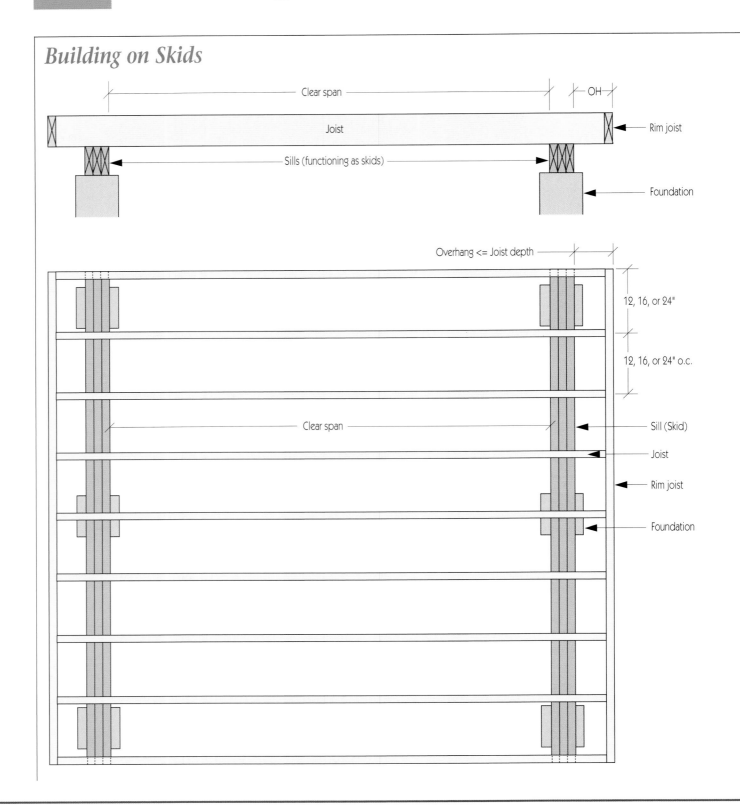

Clear span | OH

Joist

Rim joist

Sills (functioning as skids)

Foundation

Overhang <= Joist depth

12, 16, or 24"

12, 16, or 24" o.c.

Clear span

Sill (Skid)

Joist

Rim joist

Foundation

Building on Poles

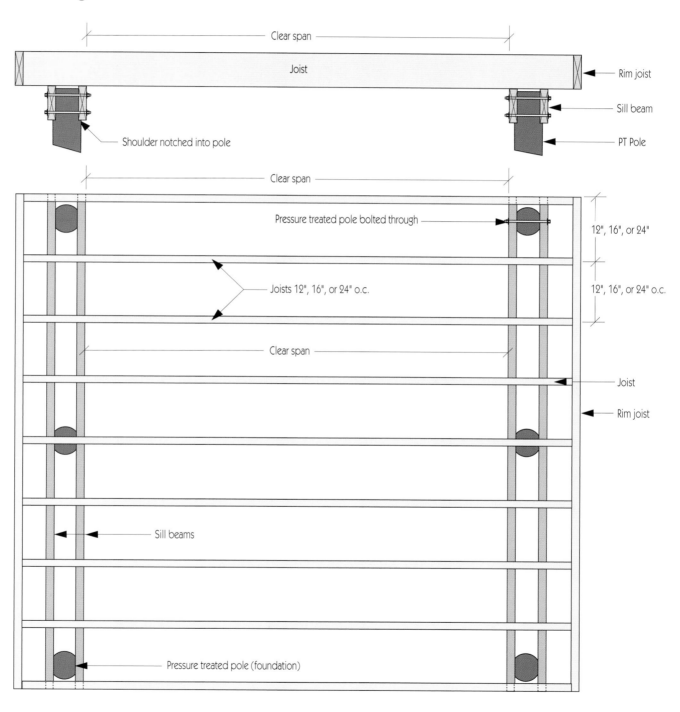

Clear span

Joist ← Rim joist

Shoulder notched into pole

Sill beam

PT Pole

Clear span

Pressure treated pole bolted through

12", 16", or 24"

Joists 12", 16", or 24" o.c.

12", 16", or 24" o.c.

Clear span

Joist

Rim joist

Sill beams

Pressure treated pole (foundation)

Narrow Building (12' Maximum Width) on Masonry

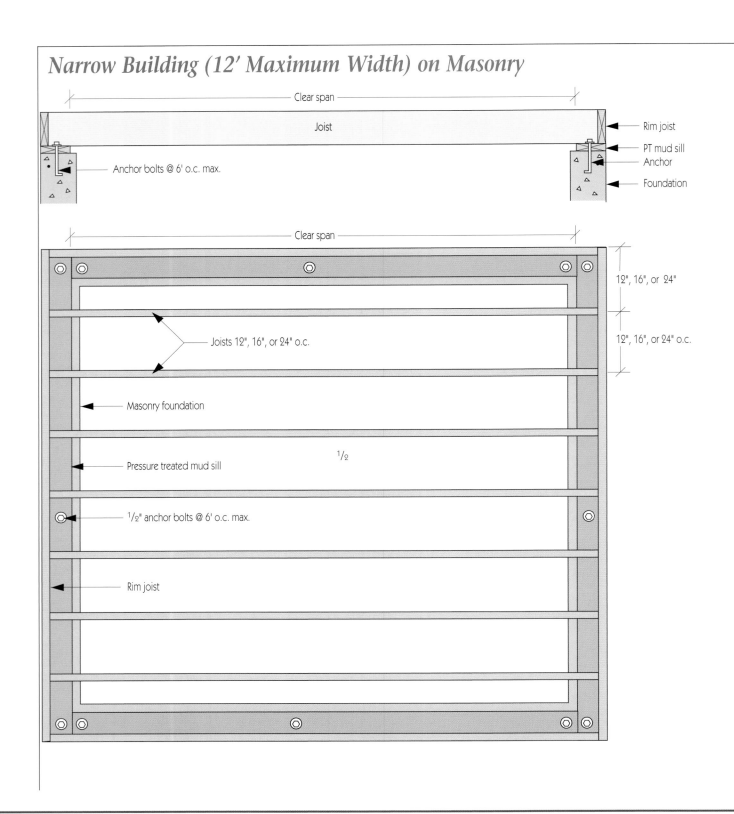

Clear span

Joist

Rim joist

PT mud sill

Anchor

Foundation

Anchor bolts @ 6' o.c. max.

Clear span

12", 16", or 24"

12", 16", or 24" o.c.

Joists 12", 16", or 24" o.c.

Masonry foundation

Pressure treated mud sill

$^1/_2$

$^1/_2$" anchor bolts @ 6' o.c. max.

Rim joist

Wide Building (Over 12') with Framed Openings on Masonry

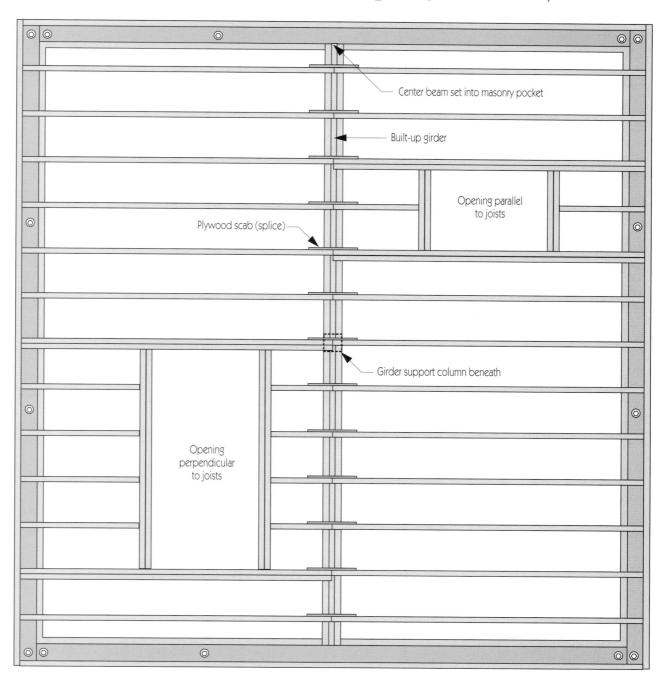

Center beam set into masonry pocket

Built-up girder

Opening parallel to joists

Plywood scab (splice)

Girder support column beneath

Opening perpendicular to joists

Span Tables for Floor Joists

All Rooms Except Sleeping Rooms and Attics: 40 PSF Live, 10 PSF Dead

Species Group	Spacing inches oc	2 × 6 Sel Str	No.1	No.2	No.3	2 × 8 Sel Str	No.1	No.2	No.3	2 × 10 Sel Str	No.1	No.2	No.3	2 × 12 Sel Str	No.1	No.2	No.3
Douglas fir-larch	12	11-4	10-11	10-9	8-11	15-0	14-5	14-2	11-3	19-1	18-5	18-0	13-9	23-3	22-0	20-11	16-0
	16	10-4	9-11	9-9	7-8	13-7	13-1	12-9	9-9	17-4	16-5	15-7	11-11	21-1	19-1	18-1	13-10
	24	9-0	8-8	8-3	6-3	11-11	11-0	10-5	8-0	15-2	13-5	12-9	9-9	18-5	15-7	14-9	11-3
Hem-fir	12	10-9	10-6	10-0	8-8	14-2	13-10	13-2	11-0	18-0	17-8	16-10	13-5	21-11	21-6	20-4	15-7
	16	9-9	9-6	9-1	7-6	12-10	12-7	12-0	9-6	16-5	16-0	15-2	11-8	19-11	18-10	17-7	13-6
	24	8-6	8-4	7-11	6-2	11-3	10-10	10-2	7-9	14-4	13-3	12-5	9-6	17-5	15-5	14-4	11-0
Southern pine	12	11-2	10-11	10-9	9-4	14-8	14-5	14-2	11-11	18-9	18-5	18-0	14-0	22-10	22-5	21-9	16-8
	16	10-2	9-11	9-9	8-1	13-4	13-1	12-10	10-3	17-0	16-9	16-1	12-2	20-9	20-4	18-10	14-6
	24	8-10	8-8	8-6	6-7	11-8	11-5	11-0	8-5	14-11	14-7	13-1	9-11	18-1	17-5	15-5	11-10

Sleeping Rooms and Attics: 30 PSF Live, 10 PSF Dead

Species Group	Spacing inches oc	2 × 6 Sel Str	No.1	No.2	No.3	2 × 8 Sel Str	No.1	No.2	No.3	2 × 10 Sel Str	No.1	No.2	No.3	2 × 12 Sel Str	No.1	No.2	No.3
Douglas fir-larch	12	12-6	12-0	11-10	9-11	16-6	15-10	15-7	12-7	21-0	20-3	19-10	15-5	25-7	24-8	23-4	17-10
	16	11-4	10-11	10-9	8-7	15-0	14-5	14-2	10-11	19-1	18-5	17-5	13-4	23-3	21-4	20-3	15-5
	24	9-11	9-7	9-3	7-0	13-1	12-4	11-8	8-11	16-8	15-0	14-3	10-11	20-3	17-5	16-6	12-7
Hem-fir	12	11-10	11-7	11-0	9-8	15-7	15-3	14-6	12-4	19-10	19-5	18-6	15-0	24-2	23-7	22-6	17-5
	16	10-9	10-6	10-0	8-5	14-2	13-10	13-2	10-8	18-0	17-8	16-10	13-0	21-11	21-1	19-8	15-1
	24	9-4	9-2	8-9	6-10	12-4	12-1	11-4	8-8	15-9	14-10	13-10	10-7	19-2	17-2	16-1	12-4
Southern pine	12	12-3	12-0	11-10	10-5	16-2	15-10	15-7	13-3	20-8	20-3	19-10	15-8	25-1	24-8	24-2	18-8
	16	11-2	10-11	10-9	9-0	14-8	14-5	14-2	11-6	18-9	18-5	18-0	13-7	22-10	22-5	21-1	16-2
	24	9-9	9-7	9-4	7-4	12-10	12-7	12-4	9-5	16-5	16-1	14-8	11-1	19-11	19-6	17-2	13-2

Attic—No Rooms and Limited Storage: 20 PSF Live, 10 PSF Dead

Species Group	Spacing inches oc	2 × 6				2 × 8				2 × 10				2 × 12			
		Sel Str	No.1	No.2	No.3	Sel Str	No.1	No.2	No.3	Sel Str	No.1	No.2	No.3	Sel Str	No.1	No.2	No.3
Douglas fir-larch	12	10-5	10-0	9-10	7-10	16-4	15-9	15-0	11-6	21-7	20-1	19-1	14-7	27-6	24-6	23-3	17-9
	16	9-6	9-1	8-11	6-10	14-11	13-9	13-0	9-11	19-7	17-5	16-6	12-7	25-0	21-3	20-2	15-5
	24	8-3	7-8	7-3	5-7	13-0	11-2	10-8	8-1	17-2	14-2	13-6	10-3	21-3	17-4	16-5	12-7
Hem-fir	12	9-10	9-8	9-2	7-8	15-6	15-2	14-5	11-2	20-5	19-10	18-6	14-2	26-0	24-3	22-7	17-4
	16	8-11	8-9	8-4	6-8	14-1	13-7	12-8	9-8	18-6	17-2	16-0	12-4	23-8	21-0	19-7	15-0
	24	7-10	7-7	7-1	5-5	12-3	11-1	10-4	7-11	16-2	14-0	13-1	10-0	20-6	17-1	16-0	12-3
Southern pine	12	10-3	10-0	9-10	8-2	16-1	15-9	15-6	12-0	21-2	20-10	20-1	15-4	27-1	26-6	23-11	18-1
	16	9-4	9-1	8-11	7-1	14-7	14-4	13-6	10-5	19-3	18-11	17-5	13-3	24-7	23-1	20-9	15-8
	24	8-1	8-0	7-8	5-9	12-9	12-6	11-0	8-6	16-10	15-10	14-2	10-10	21-6	18-10	16-11	12-10

Attic—No Rooms and No Storage: 10 PSF Live, 5 PSF Dead

Species Group	Spacing inches oc	2 × 6				2 × 8				2 × 10				2 × 12			
		Sel Str	No.1	No.2	No.3	Sel Str	No.1	No.2	No.3	Sel Str	No.1	No.2	No.3	Sel Str	No.1	No.2	No.3
Douglas fir-larch	12	13-2	12-8	12-5	11-1	20-8	19-11	19-6	16-3	27-2	26-2	25-8	20-7	34-8	33-5	32-9	25-2
	16	11-11	11-6	11-3	9-7	18-9	18-1	17-8	14-1	24-8	23-10	23-4	17-10	31-6	30-0	28-6	21-9
	24	10-5	10-0	9-10	7-10	16-4	15-9	15-0	11-6	21-7	20-1	19-1	14-7	27-6	24-6	23-3	17-9
Hem-fir	12	12-5	12-2	11-7	10-10	19-6	19-1	18-2	15-10	25-8	25-2	24-0	20-1	32-9	32-1	30-7	24-6
	16	11-3	11-0	10-6	9-5	17-8	17-4	16-6	13-9	23-4	22-10	21-9	17-5	29-9	29-2	27-8	21-3
	24	9-10	9-8	9-2	7-8	15-6	15-2	14-5	11-2	20-5	19-10	18-6	14-2	26-0	24-3	22-7	17-4
Southern pine	12	12-11	12-8	12-5	11-6	20-3	19-11	19-6	17-0	26-9	26-2	25-8	21-8	34-1	33-5	32-9	25-7
	16	11-9	11-6	11-3	10-0	18-5	18-1	17-8	14-9	24-3	23-10	23-4	18-9	31-0	30-5	29-4	22-2
	24	10-3	10-0	9-10	8-2	16-1	15-9	15-6	12-0	21-2	20-10	20-1	15-4	27-1	26-6	23-11	18-1

Parts of a Wall Frame

Wall framing has evolved for efficiency in the use of materials. In the US sheathing, drywall, and rigid insulation all come in standard 48-inch by 96-inch sheets. So that sheathing joints fall on studs, they are spaced 12, 16, or 24 inches on-center from the ends of the wall. To eliminate cutting, blanket and batt insulations come in widths that fit snugly between the studs. Other studs with special names are used to frame windows and doors and to form corners with intersecting walls. The illustration below identifies the elements in a typical exterior wall. Starting at the bottom:

- *Bottom plate:* single bottommost continuous horizontal member.

- *Stud:* vertical full-height repetitive member.

- *Top plate:* horizontal member connecting the tops of studs

- *Double plate:* second plate serving to splice the top plates in a long wall

- *King stud:* outer full-height stud on either side of a window or door opening

- *Trimmers:* short studs supporting header ends

- *Top/bottom cripples:* filler studs over headers and under windows to maintain spacing

- *Corner studs:* extra studs providing interior nailing surfaces at intersecting wall corners

- *Headers:* beams above door/window openings.

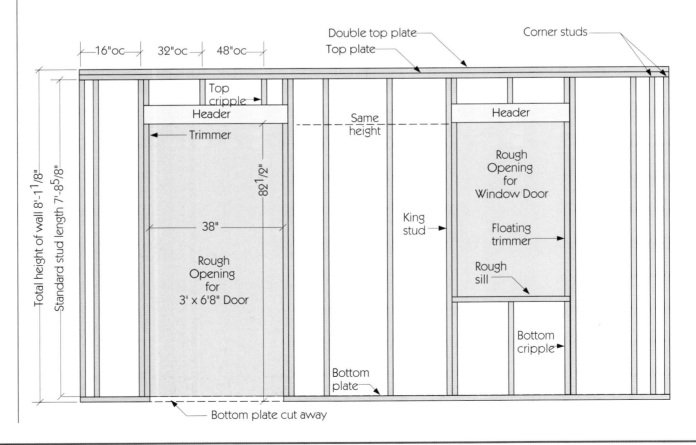

Dealing with Non-Standard Doors

Due to the height limitations for both mobile and moveable tiny houses, the International Residential Code allows shorter than standard ceiling heights. Since standard door heights are 6'8" (80 inches), their door frames won't fit under the lower ceilings.

Custom doors can be ordered, but they are very expensive. The most cost effective solution is to trim both top and bottom from standard solid wood doors. Unfortunately, this will not work on fiberglas and steel doors!

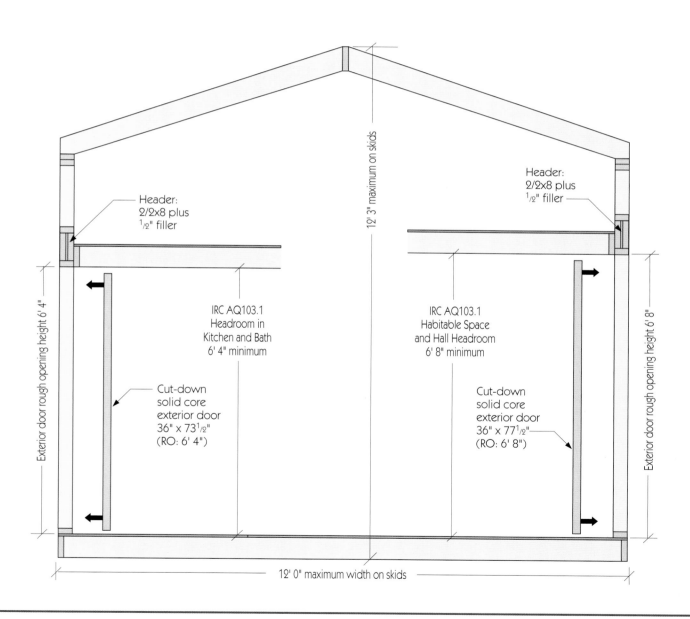

Header:
2/2x8 plus
1/2" filler

Header:
2/2x8 plus
1/2" filler

12' 3" maximum on skids

Exterior door rough opening height 6' 4"

IRC AQ103.1
Headroom in
Kitchen and Bath
6' 4" minimum

IRC AQ103.1
Habitable Space
and Hall Headroom
6' 8" minimum

Exterior door rough opening height 6' 8"

Cut-down
solid core
exterior door
36" x 73 1/2"
(RO: 6' 4")

Cut-down
solid core
exterior door
36" x 77 1/2"
(RO: 6' 8")

12' 0" maximum width on skids

Door and Window Headers in Exterior Walls

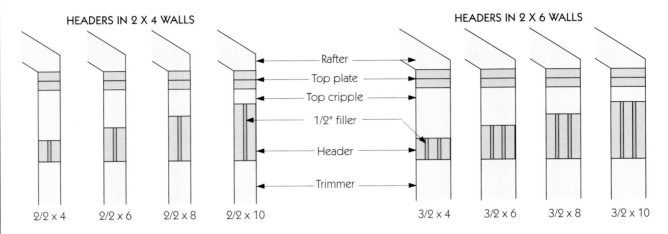

HEADERS IN 2 X 4 WALLS — 2/2 x 4, 2/2 x 6, 2/2 x 8, 2/2 x 10

HEADERS IN 2 X 6 WALLS — 3/2 x 4, 3/2 x 6, 3/2 x 8, 3/2 x 10

Labels: Rafter, Top plate, Top cripple, 1/2" filler, Header, Trimmer

Maximum Allowed Header Span (feet-inches)

Roof Snow Load	20 psf				30 psf				40 psf				50 psf			
	Building Width, ft				Building Width, ft				Building Width, ft				Building Width, ft			
Header	8	12	16	20	8	12	16	20	8	12	16	20	8	12	16	20
2-2x4	5-10	4-9	4-1	3-8	5-0	4-1	3-7	3-2	4-6	3-8	3-2	2-10	4-1	3-4	2-11	2-7
2-2x6	9-2	7-6	6-6	5-10	7-11	6-6	5-7	5-0	7-1	5-10	5-0	4-6	6-6	5-3	4-7	4-1
2-2x8	12-1	9-10	8-6	7-8	10-5	8-6	7-5	6-7	9-4	7-8	6-7	5-11	8-6	7-0	6-0	5-4
2-2x10	15-5	12-7	10-11	9-9	13-4	10-11	9-5	8-5	11-11	9-9	8-5	7-7	10-11	8-11	7-8	6-11
3-2x4	7-2	5-10	5-1	4-6	6-2	5-1	4-4	3-11	5-6	4-6	3-11	3-6	5-0	4-1	3-7	3-2
3-2x6	11-3	9-2	7-11	7-1	9-9	7-11	6-11	6-2	8-8	7-1	6-2	5-6	7-11	6-6	5-7	5-0
3-2x8	14-9	12-1	10-5	9-4	12-10	10-5	9-1	8-1	11-5	9-4	8-1	7-3	10-5	8-6	7-5	6-7
3-2x10	18-11	15-5	13-4	11-11	16-4	13-4	11-7	10-4	14-8	11-11	10-4	9-3	13-4	10-10	9-5	8-5
2-2x4	4-0	3-3	2-10	2-6	3-8	3-0	2-7	2-4	3-6	2-10	2-5	2-2	3-3	2-8	2-4	2-1
2-2x6	6-3	5-1	4-5	3-11	5-10	4-9	4-1	3-8	5-5	4-5	3-10	3-5	5-2	4-2	3-8	3-3
2-2x8	8-2	6-8	5-10	5-2	7-8	6-3	5-5	4-10	7-2	5-10	5-1	4-6	6-9	5-6	4-10	4-3
2-2x10	10-6	8-7	7-5	6-8	9-9	8-0	6-11	6-2	9-2	7-6	6-6	5-10	8-8	7-1	6-2	5-6
3-2x4	4-10	4-0	3-5	3-1	4-6	3-8	3-2	2-10	4-3	3-6	3-0	2-8	4-0	3-3	2-10	2-6
3-2x6	7-8	6-3	5-5	4-10	7-1	5-10	5-0	4-6	6-8	5-5	4-9	4-3	6-4	5-2	4-6	4-0
3-2x8	10-0	8-2	7-1	6-4	9-4	7-8	6-7	5-11	8-9	7-2	6-2	5-7	8-4	6-9	5-10	5-3
3-2x10	12-10	10-6	9-1	8-1	11-11	9-9	8-5	7-7	11-3	9-2	7-11	7-1	10-7	8-8	7-6	6-9

Assembling and Raising Walls

① Assemble frame on floor deck

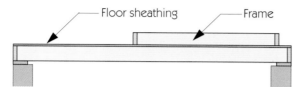

Floor sheathing   Frame

② Sheath frame

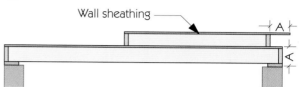

Wall sheathing

A

A

③ Raise wall with one helper per 4' of wall.

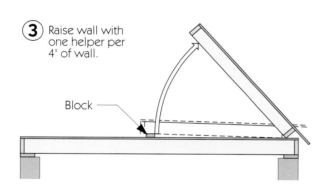

Block

④ Adjust base with sledge, fasten sheathing to rim joist, bring to vertical with level, fasten braces at each end.

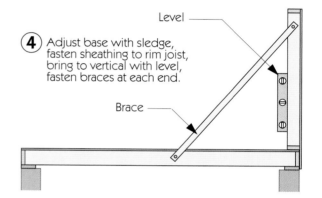

Level

Brace

Connecting Intersecting Walls

OUTSIDE CORNERS — 2 X 4 WALLS

Blocking   ½" filler

OUTSIDE CORNERS — 2 X 6 WALLS

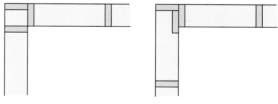

INSIDE CORNERS — 2 X 4 WALLS

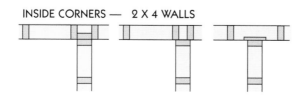

INSIDE CORNERS — 2 X 6 WALLS

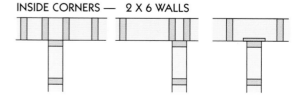

9 FRAMING
Framing Roofs

Rafters and Ceiling Joists

The weight on a roof includes dead and snow loads. Like floor joists, rafters are sized to prevent failure in bending, but that is not the whole story. The joint at the ridge acts as a hinge, so vertical loads act to open the joint and thrust the rafter/wall joint outward. The three common solutions are:

- *Trusses,* not considered here because they render valuable underroof spaces unuseable.

- *Ceiling or loft joists,* shown at right, prevent the rafter/wall joints from spreading.

- A *ridge beam,* below, counteracts the downward force at the ridge to eliminate the outward thrust on the walls.

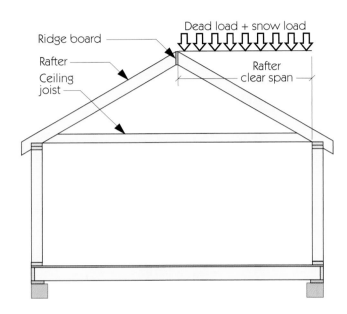

Rafters and Ridge Beams

In the ridge beam solution the rafters are loaded, as usual, by combined dead and snow loads across their clear spans. The ridge beam supports the load on a rectangular area defined by half the building width less two wall thicknesses and

the beam's clear span. Span tables for rafters and ridge beams are found on pages 118–120.

The facing page illustrates the possible solutions for four common building styles.

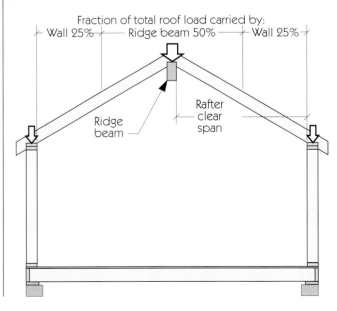

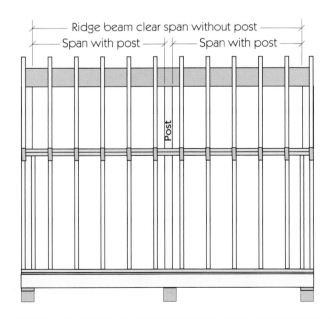

Roof Support Solutions

GABLE

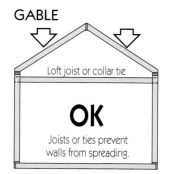

OK

Joists or ties prevent walls from spreading.

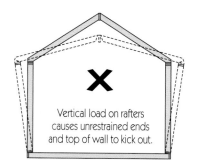

Ridge beam

Posts both ends

OK

Ridge beam supported by posts creates two sheds.

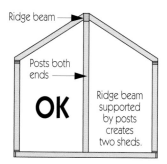

X

Vertical load on rafters causes unrestrained ends and top of wall to kick out.

SHED

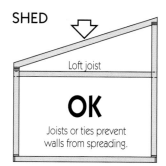

Loft joist

OK

Joists or ties prevent walls from spreading.

OK

No horizontal forces, so no horizontal ties required.

OK

No horizontal forces, so no horizontal ties required.

SALTBOX

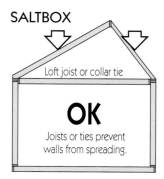

Loft joist or collar tie

OK

Joists or ties prevent walls from spreading.

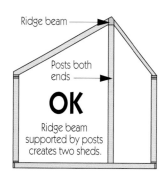

Ridge beam

Posts both ends

OK

Ridge beam supported by posts creates two sheds.

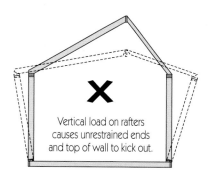

X

Vertical load on rafters causes unrestrained ends and top of wall to kick out.

DORMER

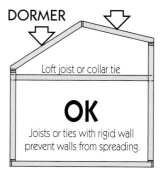

Loft joist or collar tie

OK

Joists or ties with rigid wall prevent walls from spreading.

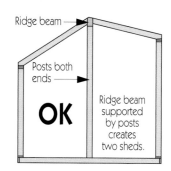

Ridge beam

Posts both ends

OK

Ridge beam supported by posts creates two sheds.

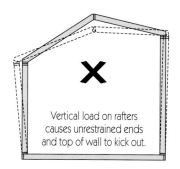

X

Vertical load on rafters causes unrestrained ends and top of wall to kick out.

9 FRAMING
Span Tables for Rafters

Snow Region, No Attic: 20 PSF Live, 10 PSF Dead

Species Group	Spacing inches oc	2 × 6 Sel Str	No.1	No.2	No.3	2 × 8 Sel Str	No.1	No.2	No.3	2 × 10 Sel Str	No.1	No.2	No.3	2 × 12 Sel Str	No.1	No.2	No.3
Douglas fir-larch	12	16-4	15-9	15-6	12-4	21-7	20-10	20-5	15-7	27-6	26-4	24-11	19-1	33-6	30-6	28-11	22-1
	16	14-11	14-4	14-0	10-8	19-7	18-8	17-8	13-6	25-0	22-9	21-7	16-6	30-5	26-5	25-1	19-2
	24	13-0	12-0	11-5	8-9	17-2	15-3	14-5	11-0	21-10	18-7	17-8	13-6	26-5	21-7	20-5	15-7
Hem-fir	12	15-6	15-2	14-5	12-0	20-5	19-11	19-0	15-3	26-0	25-5	24-3	18-7	31-8	30-1	28-1	21-7
	16	14-1	13-9	13-1	10-5	18-6	18-2	17-2	13-2	23-8	22-6	21-0	16-1	28-9	26-1	24-4	18-8
	24	12-3	11-10	11-1	8-6	16-2	15-0	14-0	10-9	20-8	18-4	17-2	13-2	25-1	21-3	19-11	15-3
Southern pine	12	16-1	15-9	15-6	12-11	21-2	20-10	20-5	16-5	27-1	26-6	25-8	19-5	32-11	32-3	30-1	23-1
	16	14-7	14-4	14-1	11-2	19-3	18-11	18-6	14-3	24-7	24-1	22-3	19-10	29-11	29-4	26-1	20-0
	24	12-9	12-6	11-9	9-2	16-10	16-6	15-3	11-8	21-6	20-3	18-2	13-9	26-1	24-1	21-3	16-4

Snow Region, No Attic: 30 PSF Live, 10 PSF Dead

Species Group	Spacing inches oc	2 × 6 Sel Str	No.1	No.2	No.3	2 × 8 Sel Str	No.1	No.2	No.3	2 × 10 Sel Str	No.1	No.2	No.3	2 × 12 Sel Str	No.1	No.2	No.3
Douglas fir-larch	12	14-4	13-9	13-6	10-8	18-10	18-2	17-8	13-6	24-1	22-9	21-7	16-6	29-3	26-5	25-1	19-2
	16	13-0	12-6	12-1	9-3	17-2	16-2	15-4	11-8	21-10	19-9	18-9	14-3	26-7	22-10	21-8	16-7
	24	11-4	10-5	9-10	7-7	15-0	13-2	12-6	9-7	19-1	16-1	15-3	11-8	22-10	18-8	17-9	13-6
Hem-fir	12	13-6	13-3	12-7	10-5	17-10	17-5	16-7	13-2	22-9	22-3	21-0	16-1	27-8	26-1	24-4	18-8
	16	12-3	12-0	11-5	9-0	16-2	15-10	14-11	11-5	20-8	19-6	18-2	13-11	25-1	22-7	21-1	16-2
	24	10-3	10-3	9-7	7-4	14-2	13-0	12-2	9-4	18-0	15-11	14-10	11-5	21-11	18-5	17-3	13-2
Southern pine	12	14-1	13-9	13-6	11-2	18-6	18-2	17-10	14-3	23-8	23-2	22-3	16-10	28-9	28-2	26-1	20-0
	16	12-9	12-6	12-3	9-8	16-10	16-6	16-2	12-4	21-6	21-1	19-3	14-7	26-1	25-7	22-7	17-4
	24	11-2	10-11	10-2	7-11	14-8	14-5	13-2	10-1	18-9	17-6	15-9	11-11	22-10	20-11	18-5	14-2

Snow Region, No Attic: 40 PSF Live, 10 PSF Dead

Species Group	Spacing inches oc	2 × 6 Sel Str	No.1	No.2	No.3	2 × 8 Sel Str	No.1	No.2	No.3	2 × 10 Sel Str	No.1	No.2	No.3	2 × 12 Sel Str	No.1	No.2	No.3
Douglas fir-larch	12	13-2	12-6	12-3	9-6	17-2	16-6	15-10	12-1	21-10	20-4	19-4	14-9	26-7	23-7	22-5	17-1
	16	11-10	11-5	10-10	8-3	15-7	14-5	13-8	10-6	19-10	17-8	16-9	12-9	24-2	20-5	19-5	14-10
	24	10-4	9-4	8-10	6-9	13-7	11-9	11-2	8-7	17-4	14-5	13-8	10-5	20-5	16-8	15-10	12-1
Hem-fir	12	12-3	12-0	11-5	9-4	16-2	15-10	15-1	11-9	20-8	20-1	18-9	14-5	25-1	23-4	21-9	16-8
	16	11-2	10-11	10-5	8-1	14-8	14-3	13-4	10-3	18-9	17-5	16-3	12-6	22-10	20-2	18-10	14-6
	24	9-9	9-2	8-7	6-7	12-10	11-8	10-10	8-4	16-5	14-3	13-3	10-2	19-9	16-6	15-5	11-10
Southern pine	12	12-9	12-6	12-3	10-0	16-10	16-6	16-2	12-9	21-6	21-1	19-11	15-1	26-1	25-7	23-4	17-11
	16	11-7	11-5	11-2	8-8	15-3	15-0	14-5	11-0	19-6	19-2	17-3	13-0	23-9	22-10	20-2	15-6
	24	10-2	9-11	9-2	7-1	13-4	13-1	11-9	9-0	17-0	15-8	14-1	10-8	20-9	18-8	16-6	12-8

Snow Region, No Attic: 50 PSF Live, 10 PSF Dead

Species Group	Spacing inches oc	2 × 6 Sel Str	No.1	No.2	No.3	2 × 8 Sel Str	No.1	No.2	No.3	2 × 10 Sel Str	No.1	No.2	No.3	2 × 12 Sel Str	No.1	No.2	No.3
Douglas fir-larch	12	12-1	11-8	11-5	8-9	15-11	15-3	14-5	11-0	20-3	18-7	17-8	13-6	24-8	21-7	20-5	15-7
	16	11-0	10-5	9-10	7-7	14-5	13-2	12-6	9-7	18-5	16-1	15-3	11-8	22-5	18-8	17-9	13-6
	24	9-7	8-6	8-1	6-2	12-7	10-9	10-3	7-10	16-1	13-2	12-6	9-6	18-8	15-3	14-6	11-1
Hem-fir	12	11-5	11-2	10-8	8-6	15-0	14-8	14-0	10-9	19-2	18-4	17-2	13-2	23-4	21-3	19-11	15-3
	16	10-4	10-2	9-7	7-4	13-8	13-0	12-2	9-4	17-5	15-11	14-10	11-5	21-2	18-5	17-3	13-2
	24	9-1	8-5	7-10	6-0	11-11	10-8	9-11	7-7	15-2	13-0	12-1	9-4	18-0	15-1	14-1	10-9
Southern pine	12	11-10	11-8	11-5	9-2	15-7	15-4	15-0	11-8	19-11	19-7	18-2	13-9	24-3	23-9	21-3	16-4
	16	10-9	10-7	10-2	7-11	14-2	13-11	13-2	10-1	18-1	17-6	15-9	11-11	22-0	20-11	18-5	14-2
	24	9-5	9-3	8-4	6-5	12-5	12-0	10-9	8-3	15-10	14-4	12-10	9-9	19-3	17-1	15-1	11-7

Understanding the Ridge Beam Span Table

The spans in the table below are the maximum allowed clear spans between end supports. Spans in excess of 20'–0" are not shown because of the impracticality of obtaining longer lengths. Remember, the table is for *tiny* houses!

Snow loads of 20 to 50 pounds per square foot (psf) are listed, but the table assumes an addition dead load of 10 psf. The snow load for your area may be found on the map on page 103, but local snow loads may vary considerably, so it is wise to consult your local building code official. (It is politic to consult him or her anyway since you may need their approval for what many consider out of bounds!)

The four building widths (in the direction of the rafters) correspond to the maximum widths of mobile tiny homes, movable tiny homes on skids and delivered over the highway without special permit, and two common widths up to the likely maximum for a home of area 400 square feet.

As an example we'll select the minimally acceptable ridge beam with a clear span of 11'5" in a 12-foot wide building in an area having a snow load of 40 psf. We shade the column under both *40 psf snow load* and *12-foot building width*. Running down the column we find the smallest beam with a maximum allowed clear span in excess of 11'5", a 4 × 10.

Note the alternate solution of a 6 × 8 beam. Sometimes your choice may be determined by aesthetics.

Maximum Allowed Ridge Beam Spans (feet-inches)

Snow Load	20 psf				30 psf				40 psf				50 psf			
	Building Width, ft				Building Width, ft				Building Width, ft				Building Width, ft			
Ridge Beam	8	12	16	20	8	12	16	20	8	12	16	20	8	12	16	20
2×4	4-11	4-0	3-5	3-1	4-3	3-5	3-0	2-8	3-9	3-1	—	—	3-5	—	—	—
2×6	7-10	6-3	5-5	4-10	6-8	5-10	4-8	4-2	5-11	4-10	4-2	3-9	5-5	4-5	3-10	3-5
2×8	10-1	8-3	7-2	6-6	8-9	7-2	6-2	5-6	7-10	6-5	5-6	4-11	7-2	5-10	5-1	4-6
4×6	11-8	9-7	8-3	7-5	10-2	8-3	7-2	6-5	9-1	7-5	6-5	5-9	8-3	6-9	5-10	5-3
4×8	15-5	12-7	10-11	9-9	13-5	10-11	9-6	8-6	12-0	9-9	8-6	7-7	10-11	8-11	7-9	6-11
4×10	19-8	16-1	13-11	12-6	17-1	13-11	12-1	10-9	15-3	12-6	10-9	9-8	13-11	11-4	9-10	8-10
6×8	20-0	16-4	14-2	12-8	17-4	14-2	12-3	11-0	15-6	12-8	11-0	9-10	14-2	11-7	10-0	9-0
6×10	—	—	17-11	16-0	—	17-11	15-6	13-11	19-8	16-0	13-11	12-5	17-11	14-8	12-8	11-4
6×12	—	—	—	19-5	—	—	18-9	16-10	—	19-5	16-10	15-0	—	17-8	15-4	13-9

Maximum spans assume S4S solid wood beams, grade #2 or better, with 1-month fiber stress in bending of 1,400 psi.

10 SHEATHING

If the frame is the skeleton of a house, the sheathing is its skin. The frame provides the compressive and bending strengths to resist and support the loads (forces of wind and weight). The sheathing holds it all together.

The sheathing also:

- prevents the frame from distorting (shearing)
- makes the building air tight
- provides a substrate for the attachment of flooring, siding, and roofing.

If the house you are building is on wheels or intended to be trucked to its site, don't skimp on its sheathing. The sheathing provides the rigidity to keep drywall from cracking, windows from popping, and doors from jamming. Even though both may be labeled "structural," plywood is stronger than oriented strand board (OSB), and 5/8-inch thickness is stronger than 1/2-inch.

Except for the possible upgrading of panels, sheath your floor, walls, and roof exactly as shown in the illustrations on the following pages adapted from the *APA Engineered Wood Construction Guide, Form E30*.

Sheathing Materials

APA Engineered Wood Panels

Engineered panels are manufactured in several ways, primarily plywood (cross-laminated wood veneer) and oriented strand board (OSB).

Some plywood is manufactured under Voluntary Product Standard PS 1-09 for Construction and Industrial Plywood. Other plywood panels, as well as composite and OSB panels, are manufactured under APA Performance Standard PRP-108, or Voluntary Product Standard PS 2-04.

APA performance-rated panels are easy to use because recommended end uses and maximum support spacings are printed in the APA grade stamp (see illustration at right).

The list at right describes the face (outside) veneer grading system. The opposite panel sides are often of different grade so that less expensive veneers can be used on the side of the panel that will not show.

Bond Classification

Bond classification specifies the moisture resistance of the panel's glue.

Exterior panels are rated for repeated wetting and redrying or constant exposure.

Exposure 1 panels are intended to resist the effects of moisture during construction and for exterior use where not directly exposed to water. Exposure 1 panels are made with the same adhesives used in Exterior panels. However, due to other factors affecting bond performance, only Exterior panels should be used for long-term exposure to weather.

Interior panels are manufactured with interior glue and are intended for interior uses only.

Typical APA Grade Stamp

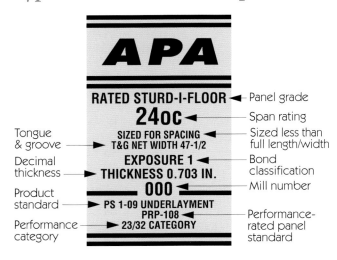

Plywood Face Grades

A – Smooth and paintable. Not more than 18 neatly made repairs parallel to grain permitted. Wood or synthetic repairs permitted.

B – Solid surface permits shims, sled or router repairs, tight knots to 1 inch across the grain, and minor splits. Wood or synthetic repairs permitted.

C-Plugged – has splits limited to $1/8$ -inch width and knotholes and other open defects limited to $1/4 \times 1/2$ inch. Admits some broken grain. Wood or synthetic repairs permitted.

C – Tight knots to 1½ inches. Knotholes to 1 inch across grain with some to $1^1/2$ inches if total width is within specified limits. Repairs are synthetic or wood. Limited splits and stitching allowed.

D – Knots and knotholes to $2^1/2$-inch across grain and $1/2$ inch larger within specified limits. Limited splits and stitching permitted. This face grade is limited to Exposure I or Interior panels.

APA Rated Sheathing

Bond Classifications: Exterior, Exposure 1

Specially designed for subflooring and wall and roof sheathing.

Also good for a broad range of other construction and industrial applications.

Can be manufactured as OSB, plywood, or other wood-based panel.

THICKNESSES
$3/8"$
$7/16"$
$15/32"$
$1/2"$
$19/32"$
$5/8"$
$23/32"$
$3/4"$

APA Structural I Rated Sheathing

Bond Classifications: Exterior, Exposure 1

Unsanded grade for use where shear and cross-panel strength properties are of maximum importance, such as panelized roofs and diaphragms.

Can be manufactured as OSB, plywood, or other wood-based panel.

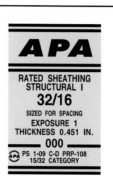
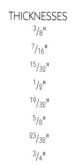

THICKNESSES
$3/8"$
$7/16"$
$15/32"$
$1/2"$
$19/32"$
$5/8"$
$23/32"$
$3/4"$

APA Rated Sturd-I-Floor

Bond Classifications: Exterior, Exposure 1

Designed as combination subfloor/underlayment. Provides smooth surface for application of carpet and pad and possesses high concentrated and impact load resistance.

Can be manufactured as OSB, plywood, or other wood-based panel. Available square edge or tongue-and-groove.

THICKNESSES
$19/32"$
$5/8"$
$23/32"$
$3/4"$
$7/8"$
$1-1/8"$

APA Underlayment

Bond Classifications: Exposure 1

For application over structural subfloor. Provides smooth surface for application of carpet and pad and possesses high concentrated and impact load resistance.

For areas to be covered with resilient flooring, specify panels with "sanded face."

THICKNESSES
$1/4"$
$11/32"$
$3/8"$
$15/32"$
$1/2"$
$19/32"$
$5/8"$
$23/32"$
$3/4"$

10 Floor Sheathing

APA Panel Subflooring

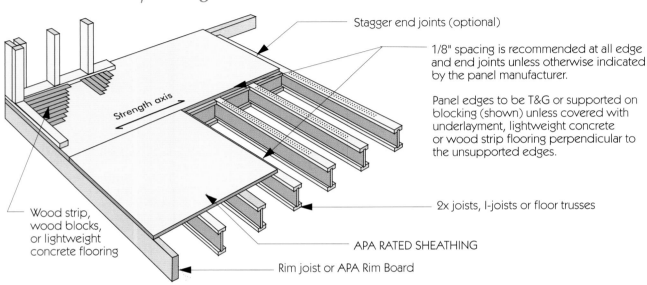

Stagger end joints (optional)

1/8" spacing is recommended at all edge and end joints unless otherwise indicated by the panel manufacturer.

Panel edges to be T&G or supported on blocking (shown) unless covered with underlayment, lightweight concrete or wood strip flooring perpendicular to the unsupported edges.

Strength axis

2x joists, I-joists or floor trusses

Wood strip, wood blocks, or lightweight concrete flooring

APA RATED SHEATHING

Rim joist or APA Rim Board

Note:
Provide adequate moisture control and use ground cover vapor retarder in a crawl space. Subfloor must be dry before applying subsequent layers.

APA Plywood Underlayment

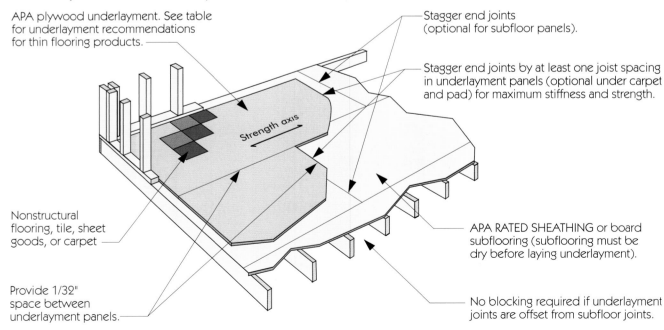

APA plywood underlayment. See table for underlayment recommendations for thin flooring products.

Stagger end joints (optional for subfloor panels).

Stagger end joints by at least one joist spacing in underlayment panels (optional under carpet and pad) for maximum stiffness and strength.

Strength axis

Nonstructural flooring, tile, sheet goods, or carpet

Provide 1/32" space between underlayment panels.

APA RATED SHEATHING or board subflooring (subflooring must be dry before laying underlayment).

No blocking required if underlayment joints are offset from subfloor joints.

APA Sturd-I-Floor

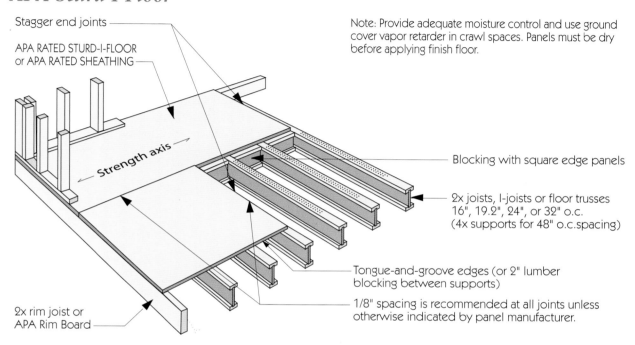

Stagger end joints

APA RATED STURD-I-FLOOR or APA RATED SHEATHING

Strength axis

Note: Provide adequate moisture control and use ground cover vapor retarder in crawl spaces. Panels must be dry before applying finish floor.

Blocking with square edge panels

2x joists, I-joists or floor trusses 16", 19.2", 24", or 32" o.c. (4x supports for 48" o.c.spacing)

Tongue-and-groove edges (or 2" lumber blocking between supports)

1/8" spacing is recommended at all joints unless otherwise indicated by panel manufacturer.

2x rim joist or APA Rim Board

APA Glued Floor

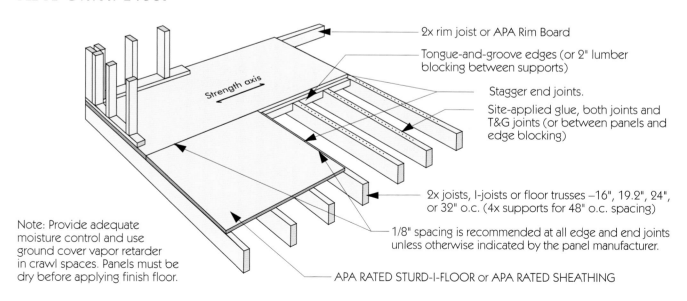

Strength axis

2x rim joist or APA Rim Board

Tongue-and-groove edges (or 2" lumber blocking between supports)

Stagger end joints.

Site-applied glue, both joints and T&G joints (or between panels and edge blocking)

2x joists, I-joists or floor trusses −16", 19.2", 24", or 32" o.c. (4x supports for 48" o.c. spacing)

1/8" spacing is recommended at all edge and end joints unless otherwise indicated by the panel manufacturer.

Note: Provide adequate moisture control and use ground cover vapor retarder in crawl spaces. Panels must be dry before applying finish floor.

APA RATED STURD-I-FLOOR or APA RATED SHEATHING

Wall Sheathing

APA Panel Wall Sheathing

APA engineered 4' × 8' panels are ideal for sheathing the walls of tiny houses because they:

- form a nearly airtight membrane with a minimum of waste,

- provide a continuous nail base for siding,

- brace the walls against shear (racking), making the tiny house rigid enough to be easily transported without damage to the structure.

Make sure the panels, either plywood or OSB, are labeled APA RATED SHEATHING. For maximum racking resistance panels should be installed horizontally across the wall studs as shown in the illustration below.

Nails should be spaced 6 inches on center along the panel edges and 12 inches on center into interior studs with a minimum nail length of 1½ inches.

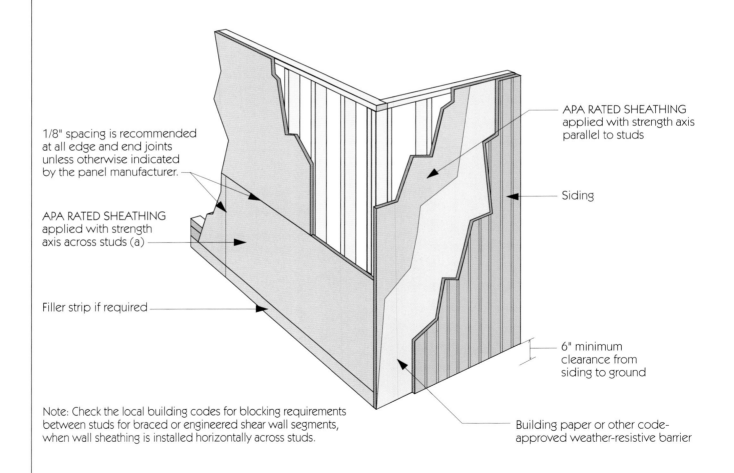

1/8" spacing is recommended at all edge and end joints unless otherwise indicated by the panel manufacturer.

APA RATED SHEATHING applied with strength axis across studs (a)

Filler strip if required

APA RATED SHEATHING applied with strength axis parallel to studs

Siding

6" minimum clearance from siding to ground

Building paper or other code-approved weather-resistive barrier

Note: Check the local building codes for blocking requirements between studs for braced or engineered shear wall segments, when wall sheathing is installed horizontally across studs.

Roof Sheathing

APA Panel Roof Sheathing

Roofs may be sheathed with either APA RATED SHEATHING or with APA RATED STURD-I-FLOOR panels.

For rafters spaced 16 inches on center panel span ratings may be 20/0, 24/0, 24/16 or greater. For rafters spaced 24 inches on center panel span ratings may be 24/16, 32/16, or greater. For rafters spaced 32 inches on center panel span ratings may be 32/16, 40/20, or greater.

Panels should be fastened with 8d nails spaced

6 inches on center along panel edges and 12 inches on center into interior rafters with minimum nail lengths of 1½ inches.

Closer nail spacings may be required in high wind zones. Check with your local building code official.

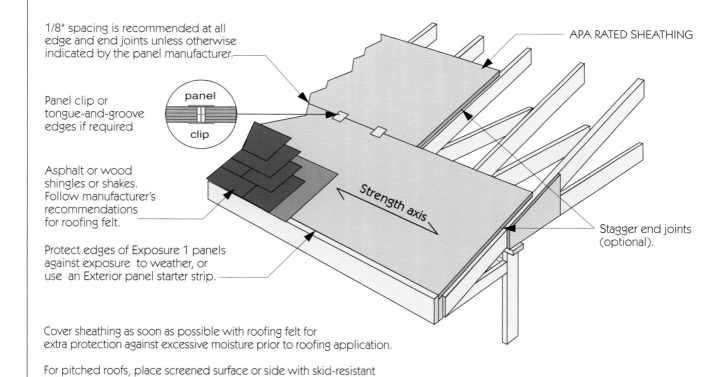

1/8" spacing is recommended at all edge and end joints unless otherwise indicated by the panel manufacturer.

Panel clip or tongue-and-groove edges if required

panel
clip

Asphalt or wood shingles or shakes. Follow manufacturer's recommendations for roofing felt.

Protect edges of Exposure 1 panels against exposure to weather, or use an Exterior panel starter strip.

APA RATED SHEATHING

Strength axis

Stagger end joints (optional).

Cover sheathing as soon as possible with roofing felt for extra protection against excessive moisture prior to roofing application.

For pitched roofs, place screened surface or side with skid-resistant coating up if OSB panels are used. Keep the roof surface free of dirt, sawdust, and debris, and wear skid-resistant shoes when installing roof sheathing.

SHEATHING
T&G Roof Sheathing

APA Panel and T&G Board Roofs

In a tiny house every cubic foot of interior space is both valuable and visually important. The roof illustrated below features a cathedral ceiling with exposed timbers. The high ceiling relieves the oppression of the otherwise low ceilings, while the stout timbers promise to protect from Mother Nature.

The sheathing immediately over the rafters consists of T&G pine boards, aesthetically more pleasing than plywood and thick enough (¾-inch) to span 32 inches. On top of the boards are a continuous polyethylene vapor barrier and sheets of rigid, closed-cell foam, the thickness of the foam being determined by

the desired R-factor. Nailing strips fastened to the rafters below and of the same thickness as the foam provide a solid base for fastening the plywood or OSB panel sheathing on top.

The roof construction described is known as a "hot roof" because it lacks the normal ventilation channel below the sheathing designed to prevent ice dams. Since the entire surface of the roof is at a uniform temperature, there is no melting and refreezing at the eaves.

This roof will be further described in the chapter on insulation.

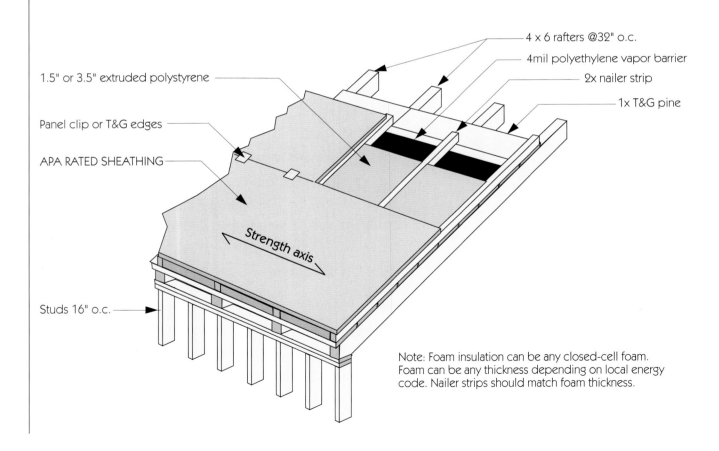

4 x 6 rafters @32" o.c.

4mil polyethylene vapor barrier

2x nailer strip

1x T&G pine

1.5" or 3.5" extruded polystyrene

Panel clip or T&G edges

APA RATED SHEATHING

Strength axis

Studs 16" o.c.

Note: Foam insulation can be any closed-cell foam. Foam can be any thickness depending on local energy code. Nailer strips should match foam thickness.

11 SIDING

Siding has two primary functions:

- taking the brunt of abuse assaulting the building from sun (ultraviolet radiation), wind, and rain
- enhancing the building's appearance, particularly in blending with the architecture of its neighborhood.

This chapter contains detailed application instructions for four of the most appropriate sidings for tiny houses:

- cedar shingles
- horizontal lap siding (such as clapboards)
- panel siding (such as T-111 textured sheathing/siding)
- vinyl siding.

SIDING
Cedar Shingle Siding

Cedar Shingle Grades and Specifications

Grade	Length, inches	Butt, inches	Bundles/ Square	Maximum Exposure, in., and Nails			
				Single Course		Double Course	
RED CEDAR							
No. 1 blue label	16	0.40	4	7½	3d	12	5d
(premium grade, 100% heartwood,	18	0.45	4	8½	3d	14	5d
100% clear, 100% edge grain	24	0.50	4	11½	4d	16	6d
No. 2 red label	16	0.40	4	7½	3d	12	5d
(good grade, 10" clear on 16" shingle,	18	0.45	4	8½	3d	14	5d
16" clear on 24" shingle)	24	0.50	4	11½	4d	16	6d
WHITE CEDAR							
Extra (perfectly clear)	16	0.40	4	7½	3d	12	5d
1st clear (7" clear, no sapwood	16	0.40	4	7½	3d	12	5d
2nd clear (sound knots, no sapwood)	16	0.40	4	7½	3d	12	5d

Application

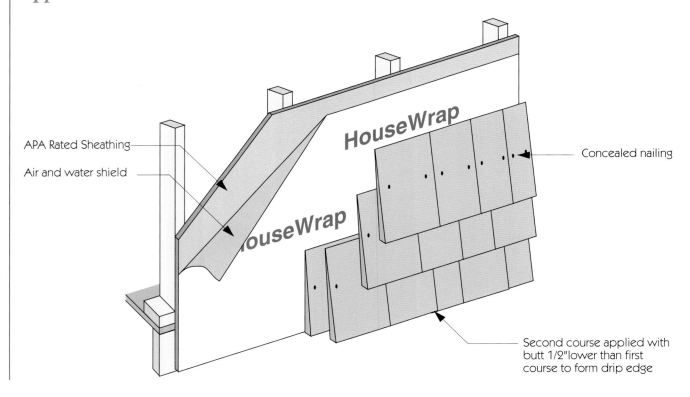

APA Rated Sheathing

Air and water shield

Concealed nailing

Second course applied with butt 1/2"lower than first course to form drip edge

Cedar Shingle Application Details

WITH ZIP SYSTEM SHEATHING

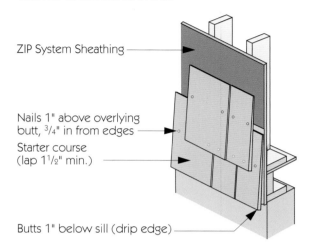

ZIP System Sheathing

Nails 1" above overlying butt, 3/4" in from edges

Starter course (lap 1 1/2" min.)

Butts 1" below sill (drip edge)

WITH RAIN SCREEN

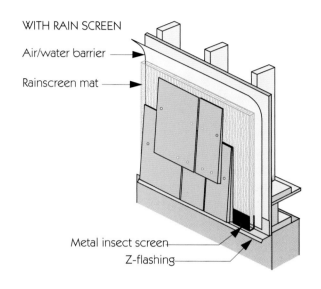

Air/water barrier

Rainscreen mat

Metal insect screen

Z-flashing

OUTSIDE CORNER

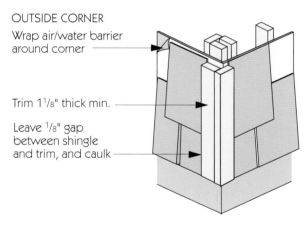

Wrap air/water barrier around corner

Trim 1 1/8" thick min.

Leave 1/8" gap between shingle and trim, and caulk

INSIDE CORNER

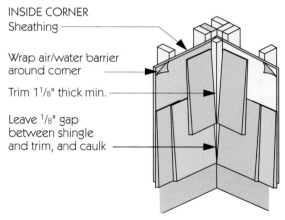

Sheathing

Wrap air/water barrier around corner

Trim 1 1/8" thick min.

Leave 1/8" gap between shingle and trim, and caulk

CLEARANCE

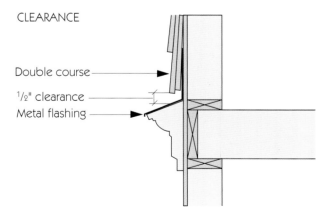

Double course

1/2" clearance

Metal flashing

CLEARANCE

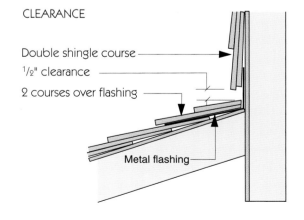

Double shingle course

1/2" clearance

2 courses over flashing

Metal flashing

11 Horizontal Lap Siding

Horizontal Lap Siding Profiles

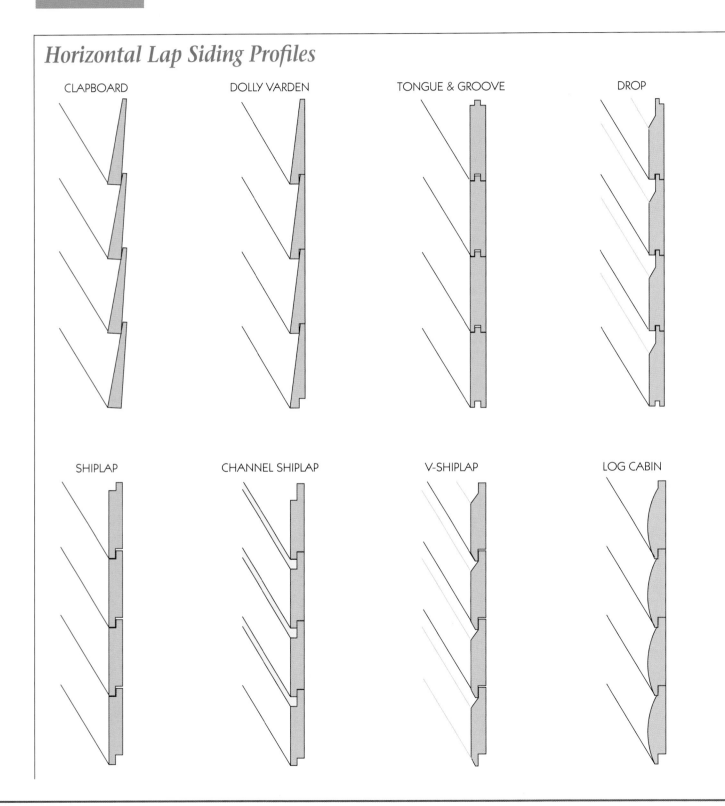

CLAPBOARD

DOLLY VARDEN

TONGUE & GROOVE

DROP

SHIPLAP

CHANNEL SHIPLAP

V-SHIPLAP

LOG CABIN

Horizontal Lap Siding Application Details

CLAPBOARD

Stud

Sheathing

1" min. overlap

Air/water barrier

Nail tip clears tip
of undercourse

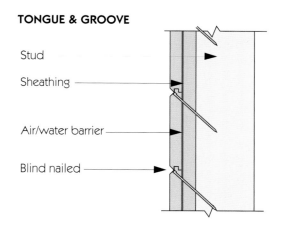

DOLLY VARDEN

Stud

Sheathing

Air/water barrier

Nail must penetrate
solid wood by $1\frac{1}{2}$"

$\frac{1}{8}$" expansion clearance

All nails must be aluminum,
stainless steel, or galvanized

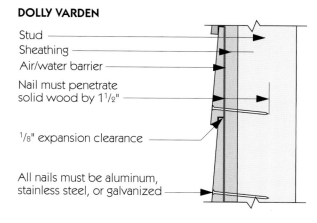

TONGUE & GROOVE

Stud

Sheathing

Air/water barrier

Blind nailed

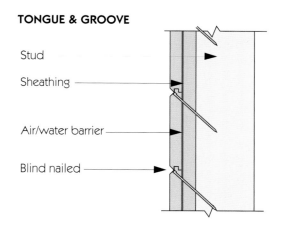

V - SHIPLAP

Stud

Sheathing

Nail must penetrate
solid wood by $1\frac{1}{2}$"

Nails for all patterns
must be aluminum,
stainless steel, or hot-
dipped galvanized

Air/water barrier

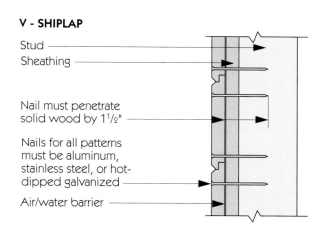

OUTSIDE CORNER

Caulk

Siding

Air/water barrier

Sheathing

Stud

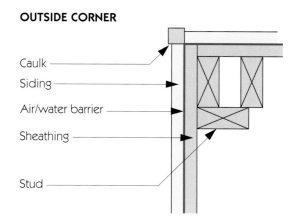

INSIDE CORNER

Stud

Sheathing

Air/water barrier

Siding

Caulk joints

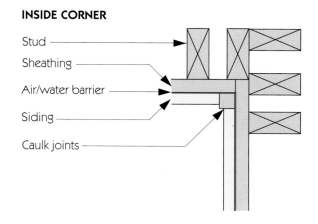

Plywood Panel Siding

APA Performance-Rated Siding

APA Rated Siding may be applied directly to studs or over nonstructural fiberboard, gypsum, or rigid foam insulation. Panel siding eliminates the cost of additional structural sheathing.

The panels are usually installed vertically but may also be placed horizontally if the horizontal joints are blocked.

Nails will be visible at panel edges, so non-staining box, siding, or casing nails should be used. Stainless nails are preferred. Nail sizes should be 6d for thickness ≤ ½"; 8d for thicker.

Panels should be treated according to manufacturer's directions within six weeks of installation.

Panel Styles

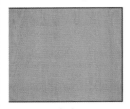 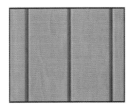 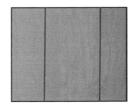  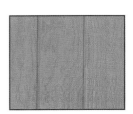

| Rough Sawn | Texture 1-11 | Kerfed Rough Sawn | Reverse Board & Batten | Channel Groove |

Source: American Plywood Association

Vertical Panel Application

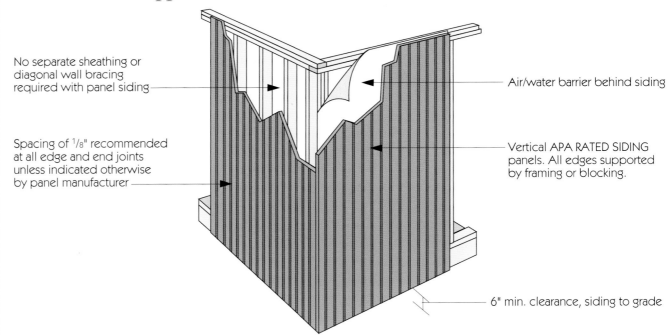

No separate sheathing or diagonal wall bracing required with panel siding

Spacing of ⅛" recommended at all edge and end joints unless indicated otherwise by panel manufacturer

Air/water barrier behind siding

Vertical APA RATED SIDING panels. All edges supported by framing or blocking.

6" min. clearance, siding to grade

APA Siding Joint Details

HORIZONTAL WALL JOINTS

Butt & Flash
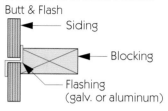
Siding — Blocking — Flashing (galv. or aluminum)

Lap
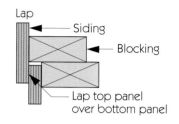
Siding — Blocking — Lap top panel over bottom panel

Shiplap
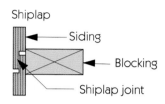
Siding — Blocking — Shiplap joint

HORIZONTAL BELTLINE JOINTS

Jog Exterior Stud Line
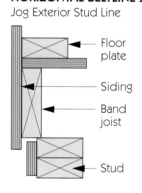
Floor plate — Siding — Band joist — Stud

Band Board Over Panel Filler

Band Board In Relief
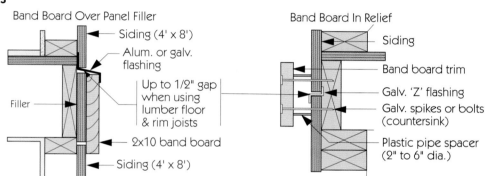
Siding (4' x 8') — Alum. or galv. flashing — Up to 1/2" gap when using lumber floor & rim joists — 2x10 band board — Siding (4' x 8') — Filler

Siding — Band board trim — Galv. 'Z' flashing — Galv. spikes or bolts (countersink) — Plastic pipe spacer (2" to 6" dia.)

VERTICAL WALL JOINTS

Butt

Treat panel edges with water repellent

Shiplap
Reverse Board and Batten
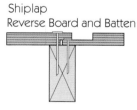

Shiplap
T1-11 & Channel Groove

Use ring-shank nails for the battens, applied near edges in two staggered rows

Vertical Batten
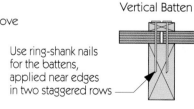

VERTICAL INSIDE & OUTSIDE CORNER JOINTS

Butt & Caulk
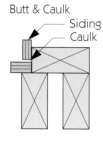
Siding — Caulk

Corner Board Lap Joints
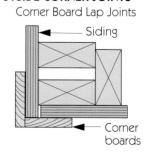
Siding — Corner boards

Lap Siding (APA Sturd-I-Wall)
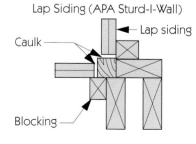
Caulk — Lap siding — Blocking

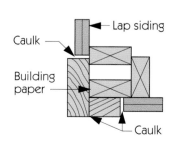
Caulk — Lap siding — Building paper — Caulk

Vinyl Siding

Vinyl Siding Fastening

NAIL DRIVING

Too tight

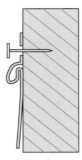

Too loose

1/16"

Correct

HORIZONTAL LENGTHS

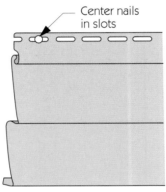

Center nails in slots

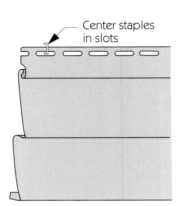

Center staples in slots

VERTICAL LENGTHS

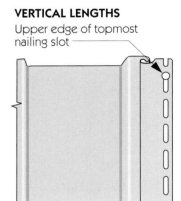

Upper edge of topmost nailing slot

ENDS OF HORIZONTALS

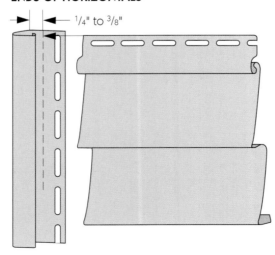

1/4" to 3/8"

ENDS OF VERTICALS

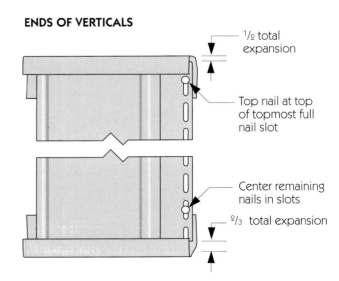

1/2 total expansion

Top nail at top of topmost full nail slot

Center remaining nails in slots

2/3 total expansion

Starting Vinyl Siding

STARTING AT AN OUTSIDE CORNER

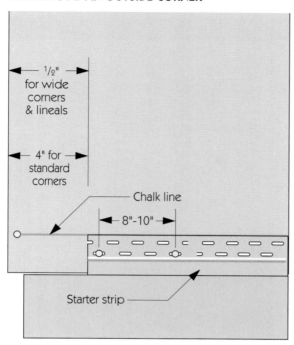

1/2" for wide corners & lineals

4" for standard corners

Chalk line

8"-10"

Starter strip

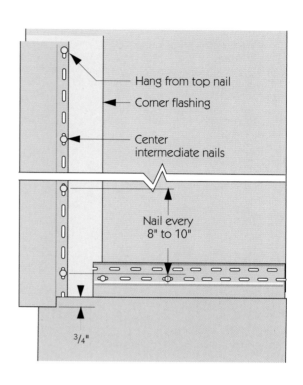

Hang from top nail

Corner flashing

Center intermediate nails

Nail every 8" to 10"

3/4"

STANDARD 3/4" INSIDE CORNER POST

INSIDE CORNER SPLICE

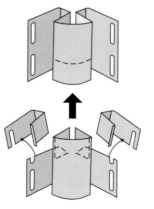

OUTSIDE CORNER SPLICE

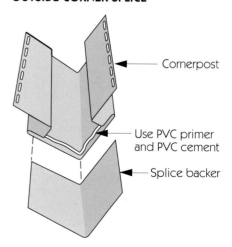

Cornerpost

Use PVC primer and PVC cement

Splice backer

Vinyl Siding (Continued)

Eaves and Intersections

ROOF/WALL INTERSECTION

To prevent water infiltration along the intersection of roof and wall, install step flashing before installing J-channel. At points where vinyl siding and accessories will meet at a roof line—such as areas where a gable dormer or a second-story side wall intersect with the roof—it is best to position the J-channel so it is $3/4$" to 1" away from the roof line. Placing the J-channel directly on the roof line would subject it to a buildup of heat, which could result in excessive expansion.

NOTE: If you use more than one length of J-channel to span a wall surface, be sure to overlap J-channels $3/4$". Do not butt J-channel pieces end-to-end.

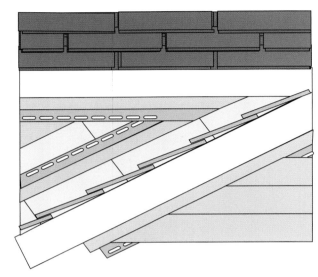

FITTING AT GABLE ENDS

Make a pattern duplicating the slope of the gable. Use this pattern as a cutting guide to panels to fit into the gable ends.

To make the pattern, lock a short piece of siding into the panel gable starter course as, shown in illustration. Hold a second piece of siding against the J-channel at the slope. Run a pencil along the edge of this piece, transferring the slope angle to the horizontal piece. Cut along the pencil line using a power saw or tin snips. Use the resulting pattern to mark the siding panels before cutting.

NOTE: Double-check the angle of the pattern at every course. If necessary, cut a new pattern.

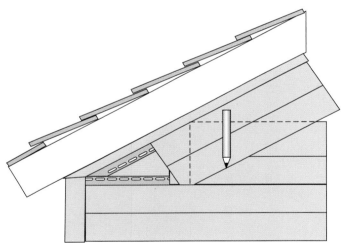

INSTALLING CUT PANELS

Slip the angled end of the panel into the J-channel along the gable edge, leaving space for expansion. Interlock with the siding panel below.

If necessary to securely fasten the last panel at the peak of the gable, face nail as shown in the illustration. This is the only place you will face nail. Use a $1^1/4$" to $1^1/2$" aluminum nail with painted head that matches the siding.

NOTE: Do not cover ventilation louvers in gables.

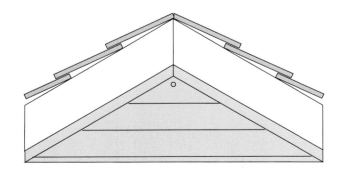

Soffit Treatments

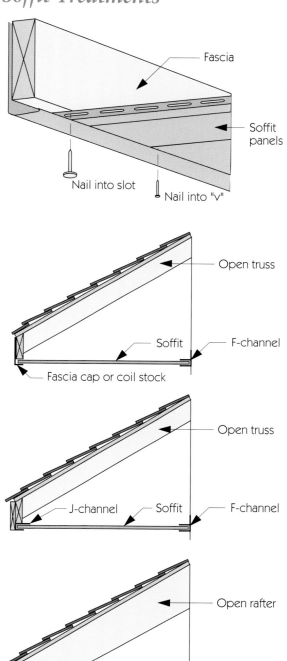

Fascia

Soffit panels

Nail into slot

Nail into "v"

Open truss

Soffit

F-channel

Fascia cap or coil stock

Open truss

J-channel

Soffit

F-channel

Open rafter

Soffit

F-channel

Fascia cap or coil stock

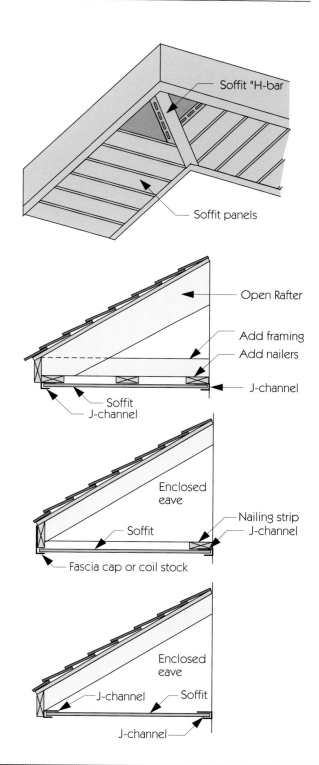

Soffit "H-bar

Soffit panels

Open Rafter

Add framing

Add nailers

J-channel

Soffit

J-channel

Enclosed eave

Soffit

Nailing strip

J-channel

Fascia cap or coil stock

Enclosed eave

J-channel

Soffit

J-channel

NOTES

12 ROOFING

Writing about building, particularly DIY or owner building, I am sometimes asked whether I think the questioner should attempt a roofing job themselves. Unless the person is young, obviously in good physical condition, and has previous carpentry experience, I tend to discourage the idea.

Roofing is dangerous. Nearly every roofer I know has fallen off a roof at some time, and the injuries sustained from falling 10 to 20 feet onto the ground can live with you the rest of your life.

On the other hand, the roof of a tiny house **is** tiny compared to that of the average house, and its eave is rarely more than 10 feet above ground. If you do decide to play roofer, make sure you have help, the proper equipment (sturdy ladders, staging, and safety harnesses), and a safety-minded attitude.

Whether you choose to do it yourself or hire a roofer, this chapter shows in detail how to apply:

- roll roofing
- double-coverage roll roofing
- asphalt shingles
- cedar shingles
- metal panels
- rubber (EPDM) roofing

ROOFING
Roofing Materials

12

Roofing Choices Compared

Roll Roofing is a single layer of material with only three inches lapped and sealed. The cost is lowest of all, minimum recommended roof slope 2/12, and estimated life 10 years.

Double Coverage is a double layer of roofing with no cutouts. Half of the surface is lapped and sealed, the remainer mineral surfaced. Cost is low, minimum recommended roof slope only 1/12, and estimated life 15 years.

Asphalt Shingles, with and without cutouts, are popular due to shingle-like appearance and longevity. Cost is medium, minimum recommended roof slope 4/12, and estimated life 20–25 years.

Cedar Shingles are popular due to their rustic appearance. Installed cost is moderately high, minimum recommended roof slope 3/12, and estimated life if installed properly 25–30 years.

Metal Panels are popular in snow country due to their ability to shed snow. Panels are available in colorful baked enamel finishes. Cost is medium, minimum recommended roof slope 3/12, and estimated life 30–50 years.

Ethylene Propylene Diene Terpolymer Membrane, EPDM, is an extremely durable synthetic rubber roofing membrane. Installed cost is moderately high, minimum roof slope zero, and estimated life 20–30 years.

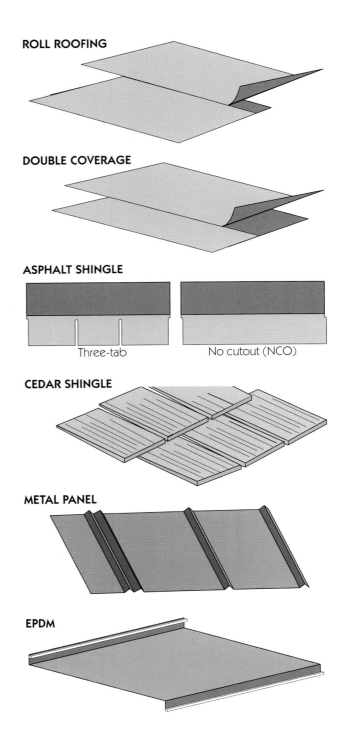

ROLL ROOFING

DOUBLE COVERAGE

ASPHALT SHINGLE

Three-tab

No cutout (NCO)

CEDAR SHINGLE

METAL PANEL

EPDM

Roof Edge Details

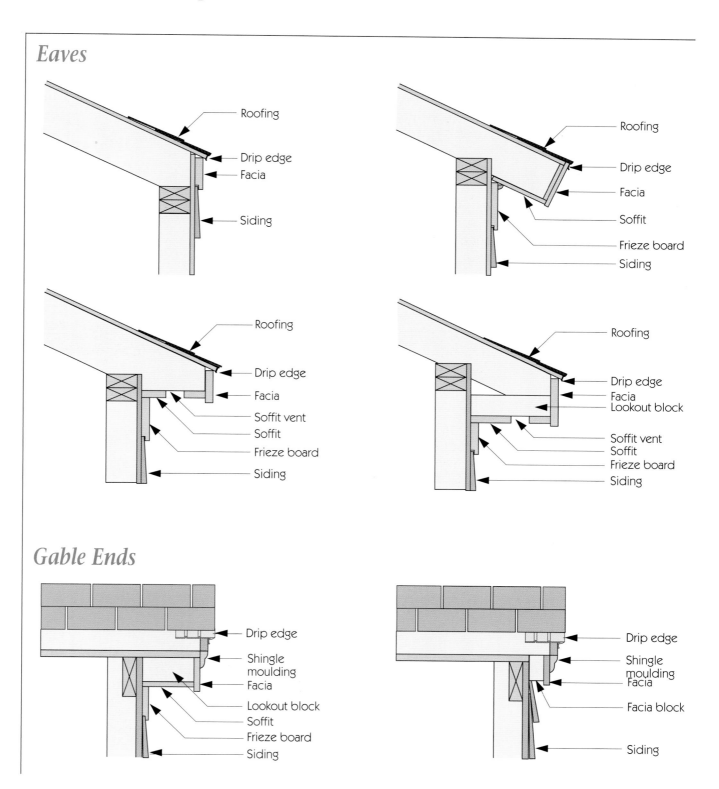

Eaves

Roofing — **Drip edge** — **Facia** — **Siding**

Roofing — **Drip edge** — **Facia** — **Soffit** — **Frieze board** — **Siding**

Roofing — **Drip edge** — **Facia** — **Soffit vent** — **Soffit** — **Frieze board** — **Siding**

Roofing — **Drip edge** — **Facia** — **Lookout block** — **Soffit vent** — **Soffit** — **Frieze board** — **Siding**

Gable Ends

Drip edge — **Shingle moulding** — **Facia** — **Lookout block** — **Soffit** — **Frieze board** — **Siding**

Drip edge — **Shingle moulding** — **Facia** — **Facia block** — **Siding**

Application

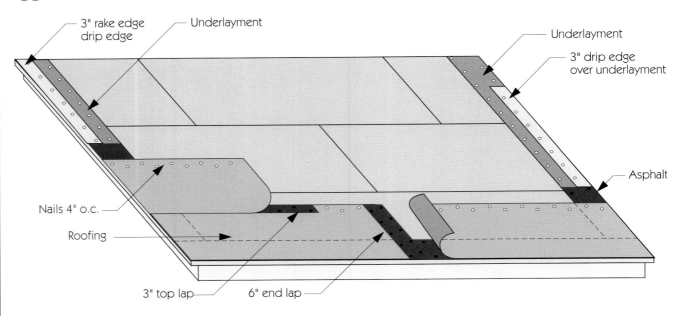

3" rake edge drip edge

Underlayment

Underlayment

3" drip edge over underlayment

Nails 4" o.c.

Roofing

Asphalt

3" top lap

6" end lap

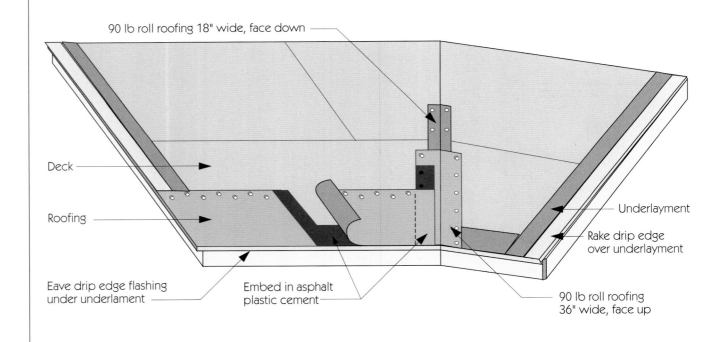

90 lb roll roofing 18" wide, face down

Deck

Roofing

Underlayment

Rake drip edge over underlayment

Eave drip edge flashing under underlament

Embed in asphalt plastic cement

90 lb roll roofing 36" wide, face up

Double Coverage Roofing

Application

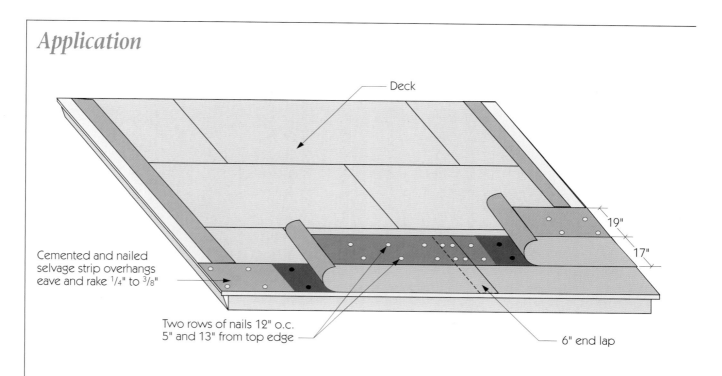

Deck

19"

17"

Cemented and nailed
selvage strip overhangs
eave and rake 1/4" to 3/8"

Two rows of nails 12" o.c.
5" and 13" from top edge

6" end lap

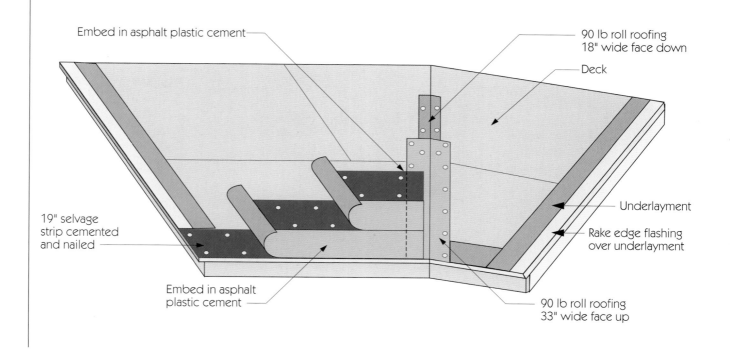

Embed in asphalt plastic cement

90 lb roll roofing
18" wide face down

Deck

Underlayment

Rake edge flashing
over underlayment

19" selvage
strip cemented
and nailed

Embed in asphalt
plastic cement

90 lb roll roofing
33" wide face up

Application

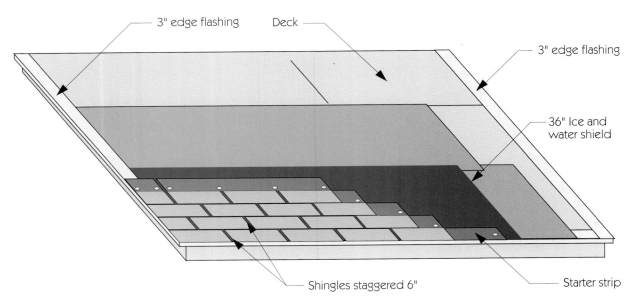

3" edge flashing

Deck

3" edge flashing

36" Ice and water shield

Shingles staggered 6"

Starter strip

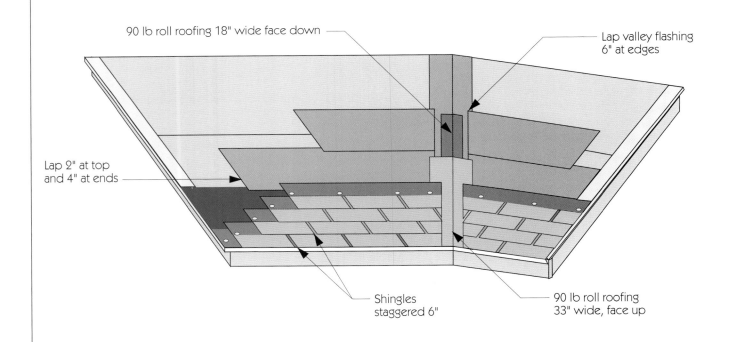

90 lb roll roofing 18" wide face down

Lap valley flashing 6" at edges

Lap 2" at top and 4" at ends

Shingles staggered 6"

90 lb roll roofing 33" wide, face up

Application Details

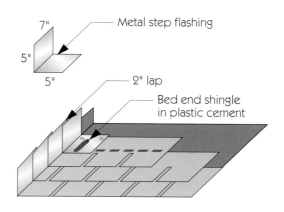

Metal step flashing

7"
5"
5"

2" lap

Bed end shingle
in plastic cement

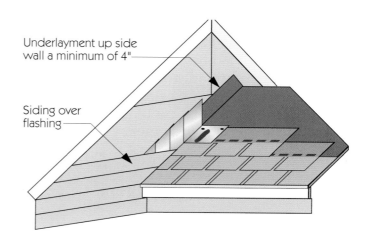

Underlayment up side
wall a minimum of 4"

Siding over
flashing

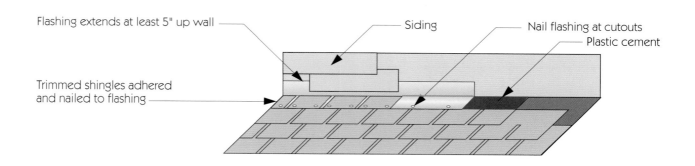

Flashing extends at least 5" up wall

Siding

Nail flashing at cutouts

Plastic cement

Trimmed shingles adhered
and nailed to flashing

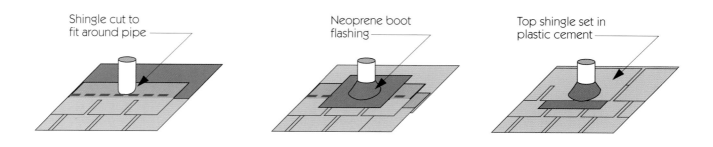

Shingle cut to
fit around pipe

Neoprene boot
flashing

Top shingle set in
plastic cement

12 Cedar Shingles

Application

Alone among roofing materials, cedar shingles can become saturated and expand across the grain. For this reason, wood shingles should be applied over sheathing strips having the same on-center spacing as the exposure of the shingles. To allow room for swelling, the shingles should be spaced at least ¼ inch.

In areas where ice dams occur, the eaves should be flashed with special ice-shield membrane for at least 24 inches inside the wall line.

As shown in the illustrations on the facing page, the first course should be doubled, with an eave projection (drip edge) of 1½ inches. The joints of successive courses should be spaced horizontally by 1½ inches minimum. Succeeding courses should be laid with exposure and nailing as shown in the table below.

Red Cedar Shingle Grades

Shingle Grade	Max. Exposure @ Slope Length, in.	<4 in 12	Nails for >4 in 12	New Roof	Reroof
No.1 (blue label)	16	3¾	5	3d	5d
Premium grade, 100% heartwood,	18	4¼	5½	3d	5d
100% clear. 100% edge grain	24	5½	7½	4d	6d
No.2 (red label)	16	3½	4	3d	5d
Good grade, flat grain permitted,	18	4	4½	3d	5d
10" clear on 16" shingle, 11" clear on 18" shingle, 16" clear on 24" shingle	24	5½	6½	4d	6d
No.3 (black label)	16	3	3½	3d	5d
Utility grade, flat grain permitted,	18	3½	4	3d	5d
6" clear on 16" and 18" shingle, 10" clear on 24" shingle	24	5	5½	4d	6d

Note: Exposure is given in inches

Application

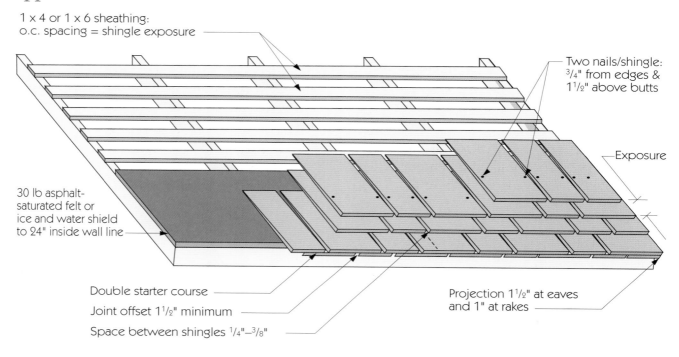

1 x 4 or 1 x 6 sheathing:
o.c. spacing = shingle exposure

Two nails/shingle:
$3/4$" from edges &
$1\frac{1}{2}$" above butts

Exposure

30 lb asphalt-
saturated felt or
ice and water shield
to 24" inside wall line

Double starter course

Joint offset $1\frac{1}{2}$" minimum

Space between shingles $1/4$"–$3/8$"

Projection $1\frac{1}{2}$" at eaves
and 1" at rakes

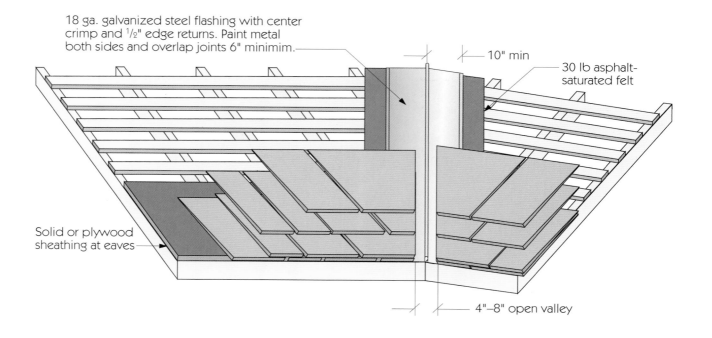

18 ga. galvanized steel flashing with center
crimp and $1/2$" edge returns. Paint metal
both sides and overlap joints 6" minimim.

10" min

30 lb asphalt-
saturated felt

Solid or plywood
sheathing at eaves

4"–8" open valley

Metal Panel Roofing

Application

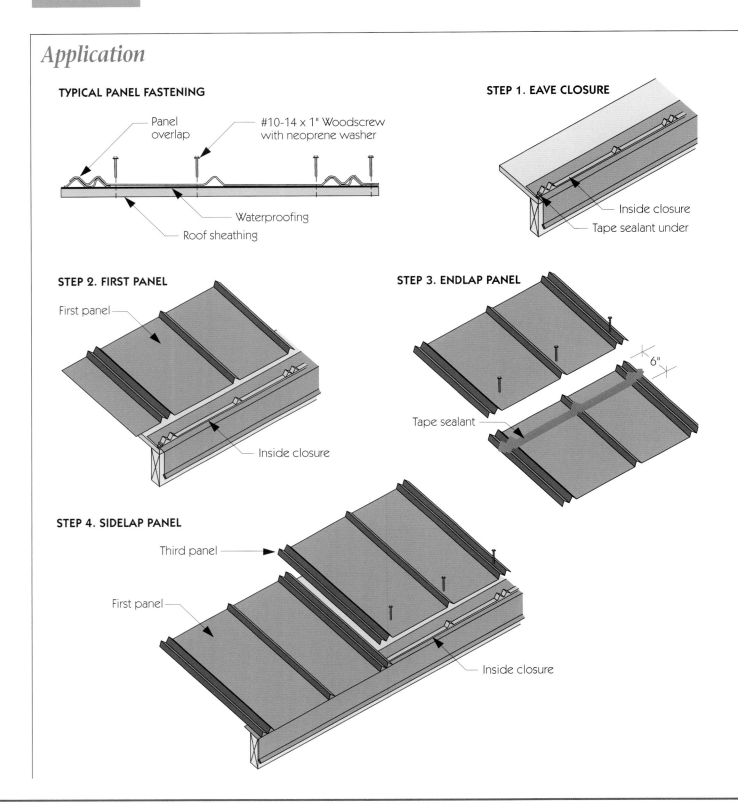

TYPICAL PANEL FASTENING

Panel overlap

#10-14 x 1" Woodscrew with neoprene washer

Waterproofing

Roof sheathing

STEP 1. EAVE CLOSURE

Inside closure

Tape sealant under

STEP 2. FIRST PANEL

First panel

Inside closure

STEP 3. ENDLAP PANEL

6"

Tape sealant

STEP 4. SIDELAP PANEL

Third panel

First panel

Inside closure

Edge Details

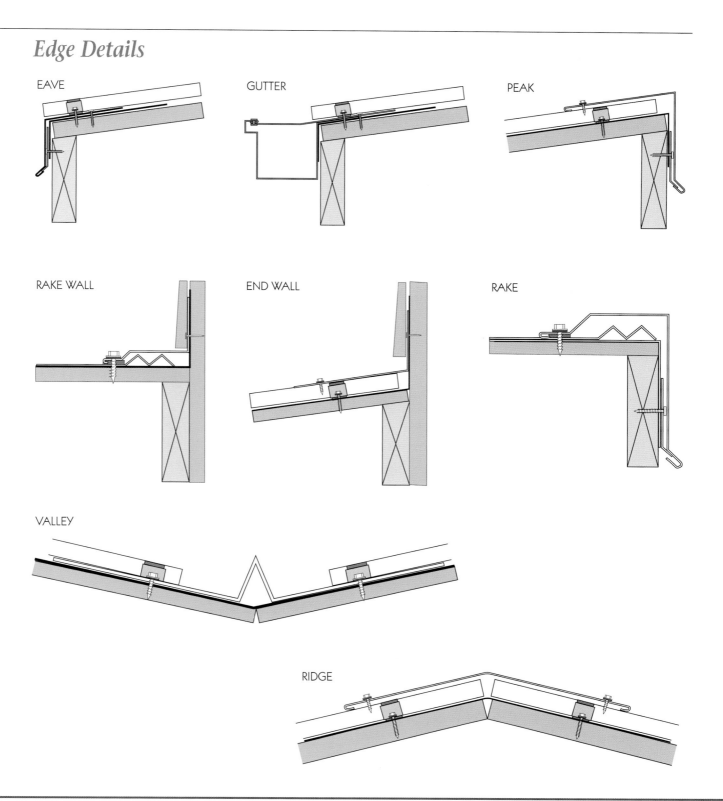

EAVE

GUTTER

PEAK

RAKE WALL

END WALL

RAKE

VALLEY

RIDGE

Application

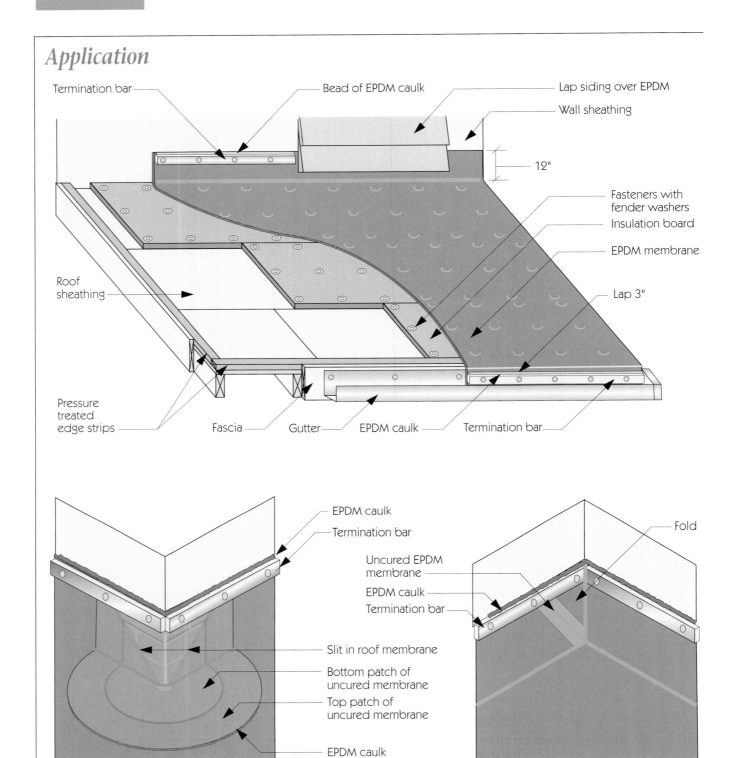

Termination bar

Bead of EPDM caulk

Lap siding over EPDM

Wall sheathing

12"

Fasteners with fender washers

Insulation board

EPDM membrane

Lap 3"

Roof sheathing

Pressure treated edge strips

Fascia

Gutter

EPDM caulk

Termination bar

EPDM caulk

Termination bar

Slit in roof membrane

Bottom patch of uncured membrane

Top patch of uncured membrane

EPDM caulk

Fold

Uncured EPDM membrane

EPDM caulk

Termination bar

13 LOFTS & STAIRS

"Why?" you might wonder, "is a whole chapter devoted to what are usually but small parts of a whole house?" The answer is *IRC Appendix Q* (pages 13–14).

A devoted group of tiny home proponents brought to the attention of the governing body of the *International Residential Code* a serious problem: as dictated by the present IRC rules, a legal stairway including top and bottom landings takes up about 50 square feet. In a 200-square-foot tiny house, this would represent 25 percent of the habitable space. Further, the tiny house on wheels or skids height limitation of 13 feet 6 inches over the ground doesn't allow sufficient headroom in lofts to make them habitable. The solution, adopted in 2018, is a group of compromises embodied in *Appendix Q*. The full wording can be found on pages 13–14.

Nowhere is it more true that, "A picture is worth 1,000 words," than in building codes. This chapter deconstructs *Appendix Q* in nine pages of clear illustrations.

Loft Headroom

Because both mobile and moveable tiny houses are limited in height to 13'6", *IRC Appendix Q* grants exceptions to normal ceiling height requirements. As the illustration shows, the allowed minima are 6'4" in kitchens and bathrooms and 6'8" in other habitable spaces and halls.

Most tiny houses incorporate lofts either as sleeping spaces or storage. Legal sleeping spaces must measure at least 35 sq.ft. in area and 5' in both directions. Areas under ceilings sloping <6/12 must have a ceiling height of 36" minimum. Under ceilings sloping at least 6/12 minimum ceiling height is 16".

Minimum Headroom and Loft Area Dimensions

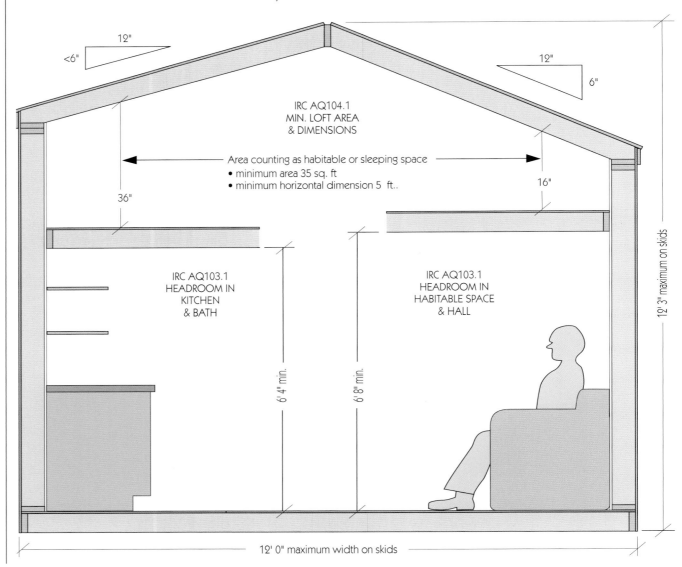

Loft Access

IRC *Appendix Q* recognizes four methods for accessing lofts: stairways, ladders, alternating tread devices, and ship's ladders. Specifications for each method are shown on the following pages.

As with decks, open loft edges are dangerous. In each case the open loft edge must be protected by a guard at least 36" high (or half the ceiling height) and not allowing the passage of a sphere 4" in diameter. Note also that all methods except ladders require handrails except where one side abuts a wall. Handrails must be continuous and either return to a wall or terminate at a Newell post.

Four Methods of Accessing a Loft

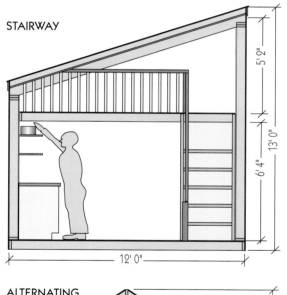

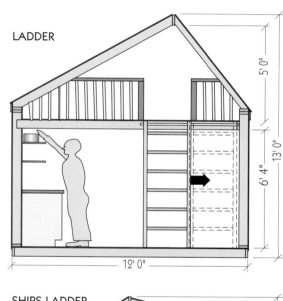

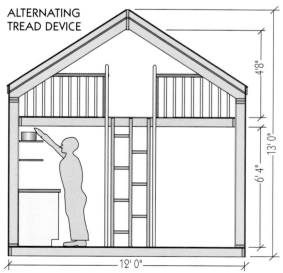

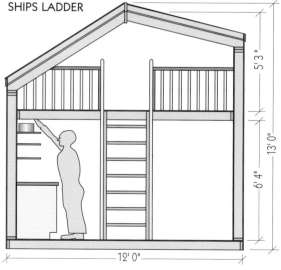

A normal residential stairway requires about 36 sq.ft. of living area, 54 sq.ft. counting top and bottom landings. This would represent between nine and fourteen percent of the total floor area of even the largest (400 sq.ft.) tiny house. For this reason *IRC Appendix Q* reduces both stairway width and slope requirements, as well as allowing alternate means for accessing lofts. As the illustration below shows, maximum allowed stairway slopes approach those of ladders.

Stairway Slopes

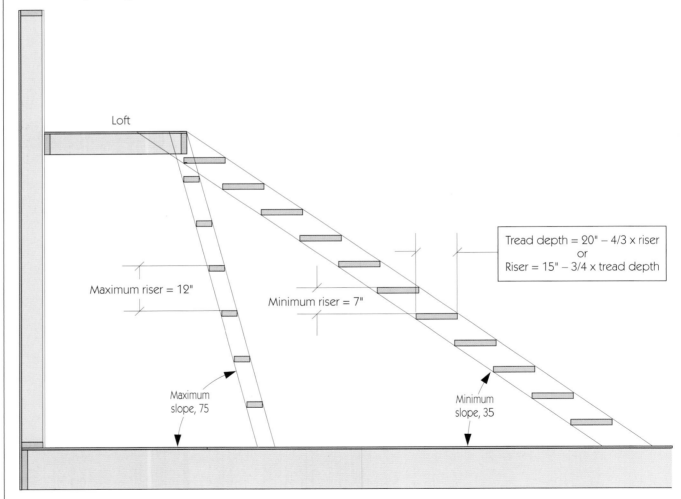

Loft

Maximum riser = 12"

Minimum riser = 7"

Tread depth = 20" − 4/3 x riser
or
Riser = 15" − 3/4 x tread depth

Maximum slope, 75

Minimum slope, 35

Due to the extreme dangers posed by unguarded stairways and lofts more than 30" above floor level, the IRC has retained the rules for railings and balusters or other means of blocking specified for normal residential buildings. That these rules are often ignored in tiny houses is unfortunate because the dangers of falling due to age, sleepwalking, or inebriation are the same regardless of the size of the house.

Stairway Guards

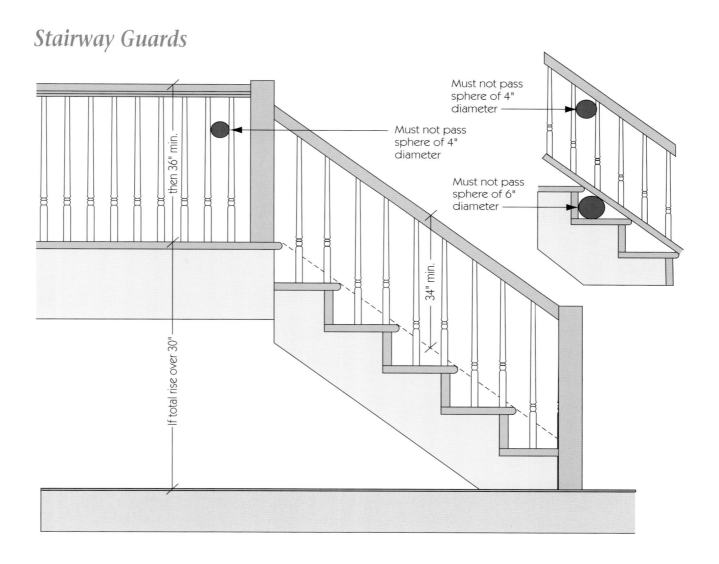

Must not pass sphere of 4" diameter

Must not pass sphere of 4" diameter

Must not pass sphere of 6" diameter

then 36" min.

If total rise over 30"

34" min.

Stairways (Continued)

IRC Appendix Q specifies a minimum headroom of 6'2" at the top of a straight run of stairs (see illustration at bottom left). For a mobile or moveable tiny house, this is impossible unless the roof is flat or the stairway ends under a shed dormer. To get around this limitation, Appendix Q allows an exemption where the top stair is actually a landing 16 to 18 inches below the loft floor. This allows one to transition from standing on the top tread to sitting on the loft.

Note that the minimum widths of tiny house stairways are reduced from the normal 36 inches to 20 inches.

In the left illustration the stair rail and loft guard are shown for clarity without balusters and Newell posts. These two required features were illustrated on the previous page.

Stairway Widths and Headroom

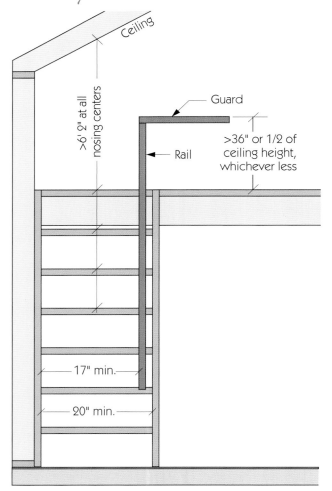

Stairway Landing Platforms

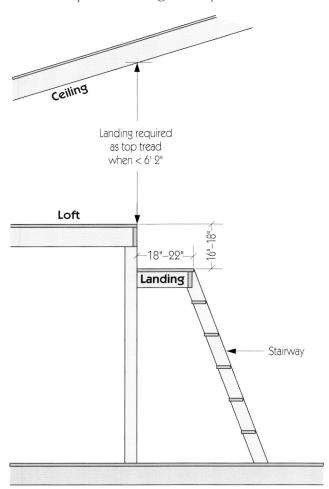

Ladders

In normal residential buildings, ladders are allowed only for occasional access to attics and storage spaces. *IRC Appendix Q* allows ladders because of their obvious minimal space requirements.

Alone of the four allowed means of accessing lofts, the ladder is not required to have separate handrails. Due to its steep (70 to 80 degree) slope, the ladder's structural rails and treads serve as hand holds.

Although it is unusual that a person weighing in excess of 200 pounds would choose a loft as a sleeping space, it is not unlikely that they would at least use the loft as a storage area. For this reason it would be wise to increase the required minimum point load from the code-specified 200 pounds.

Note that ladders in tiny houses are often hung from horizontal pipes or tracks, allowing them to be slid out of the way when not in use.

Tiny House Ladder Specifications

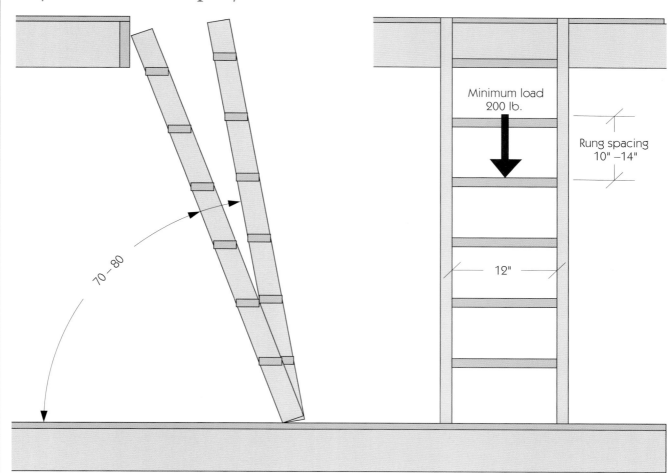

70–80

Minimum load
200 lb.

Rung spacing
10"–14"

12"

Alternating-Tread Devices

Alternating-tread ladders are commonly found in industrial applications but rarely in homes. They do, however, offer several advantages:

- Since sequential treads on either side have no overlap, one is less likely to trip over the tread nosings.

- With the added clearance it is easier to descend facing forward than with an ordinary ladder or ships ladder.

The device illustrated at lower right shows three stringers, but single, central stringers are also common. Single stringer devices are usually made of steel or aluminum, while three-stringer versions are of wood.

Note that handrails are required on both sides and that they are returned to floor level so as not to hook loose clothing or objects with straps.

Alternating Tread Devices

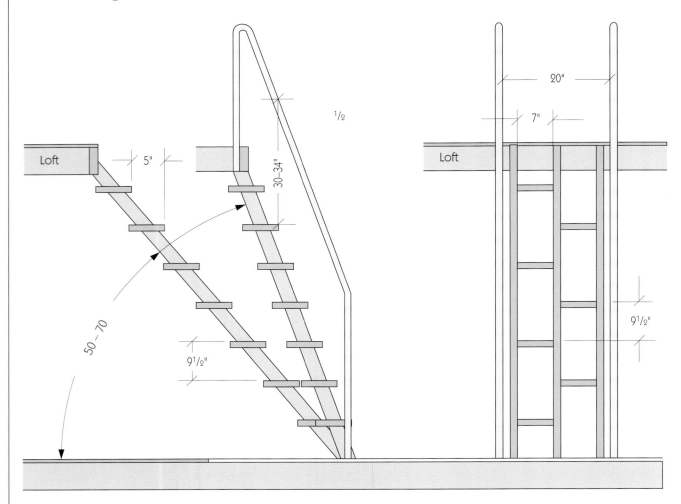

Ships Ladders

As their name implies, ships ladders are common on vessels. Any one who has been at sea in rough weather can attest to their utility. When a ship is heaving, pitching, and rolling, one needs both handrails to avoid being thrown off the ladder.

A second advantage is the small required footprint where space is at a premium (as it is in a tiny house as well as in a vessel).

Ships Ladders

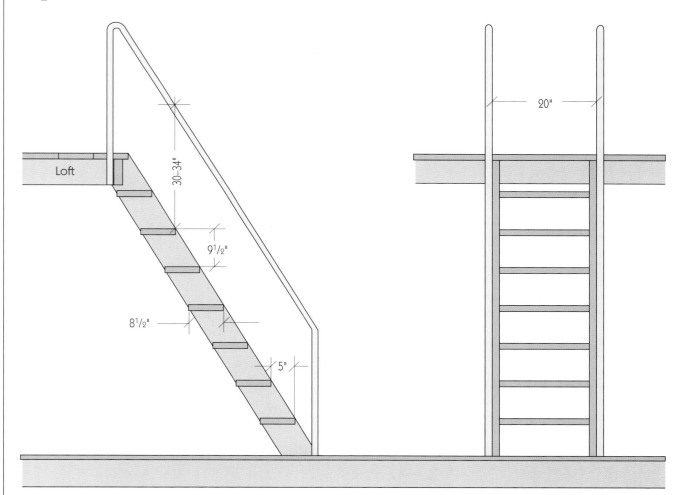

Handrails

Since the function of a stair handrail is to prevent falling, the two most important qualities are strength/rigidity and grippability.

The code requirements for tiny house handrails are the same as for all other residential structures and are listed in IRC section 311.7.8.

Handrail heights and guard spacings are illustrated on page 157. The illustrations below show permitted sizes and shapes. Note that 2 × 4s and 2 × 6s, either on edge or flat, are NOT allowed!

Allowed Handrail Sizes and Shapes

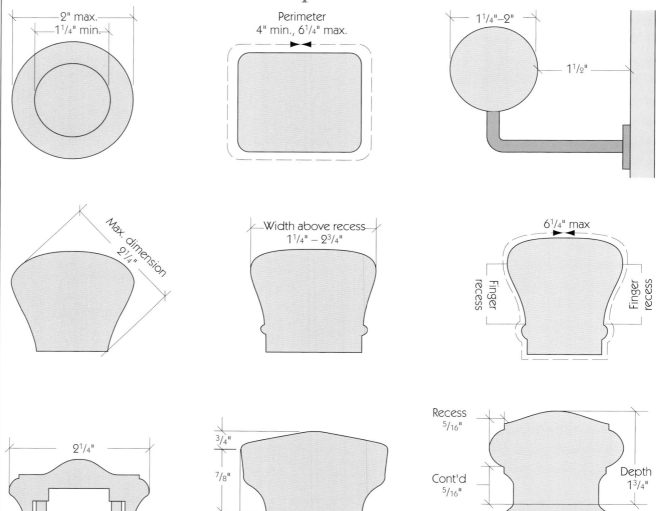

14 WINDOWS & DOORS

Liveaboard boaters and tiny house dwellers have two things in common: they both live in very small spaces, and they both spend a large percentage of time outdoors. As you might guess, the two spaces are related. Henry David Thoreau, in describing his 10' × 15' cabin on Walden Pond, wrote:

"My 'best' room, however, my withdrawing room, always ready for company, on whose carpet the sun rarely fell, was the pine wood behind my house."

In other words, a tiny home tends to, and well should, incorporate the outdoor spaces around it.

What separates the two spaces? Walls. And what connects indoors to outdoors? Windows and doors. The importance of the ways in which your tiny home's windows and doors facilitate this connection cannot be overstressed,

In addition to how to choose and install your windows and doors, this chapter discusses:

- making the most of natural daylighting
- utilizing natural ventilation for cooling
- window placement for seeing out.

Window Types

A Window for Every Purpose

All of the window types depicted at right are available through home centers as well as specialty window and door stores.

Single- and **Double-Hung** windows are the most popular. Available in both wood and vinyl, they are economical and durable. As shown on the following page, they are available in a wide range of standard sizes.

Sliding or Gliding panels are the next most popular. Smaller versions are often used in bathrooms and kitchens. Sliding-glass, or patio, doors are designed to function both as windows and as doors.

Casement windows often flank picture windows to provide ventilation. Alone of window types, they have the unique ability to "scoop" moving air into a building, similar to the old side windows in earlier automobiles.

Awning windows, available in a limited range of sizes, are hinged at the top. This feature allows for ventilation even when it is raining. While most often used as basement windows, they are perfect for tiny house lofts. Hinged at the bottom, **Hopper** windows find few uses.

Picture or **Fixed** windows, because they are often combined with double-hung and casement units, are available in all of the standard heights. A cost-saving option is installation of plain glazed units on site, a rather simple operation.

Skylights or **Roof Windows** may be fixed or openable. Several openable products qualify as egress windows, satisfying the often difficult code requirement of an egress opening for tiny house sleeping lofts.

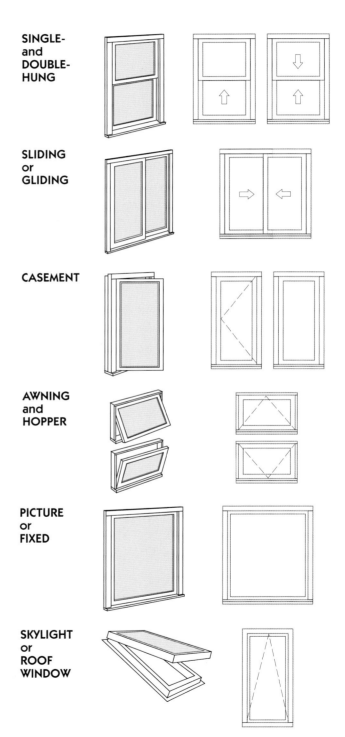

SINGLE-
and
DOUBLE-
HUNG

SLIDING
or
GLIDING

CASEMENT

AWNING
and
HOPPER

PICTURE
or
FIXED

SKYLIGHT
or
ROOF
WINDOW

Sizing Windows

Shown below is the size chart for Andersen Series 100 single-hung windows. This is not an endorsement for either Andersen or the particular windows, but an example of what one will find at any of the major home centers.

The dimensions shown are for the rough openings (R.O.) in the framing. The dimensions of the window unit (the part that fits inside the framed opening) are ½" smaller in both directions..

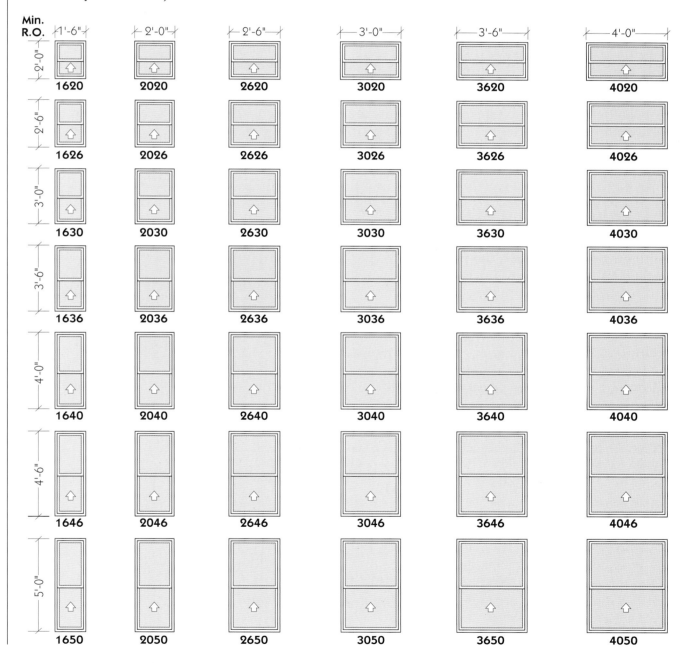

Window Energy Efficiency

The Window Performance Label

U-factor. The rate at which the window conducts heat flow, expressed in Btu/hr-ft²-°F.

Solar heat gain coefficient (SHGC). The fraction of solar radiation striking the window and passing through into the building.

Visible transmittance (VT). The fraction of visible sunlight transmitted through the window's glazing.

Air leakage. The rate of air infiltration around or through the window in cubic feet per minute per square foot of framed area at a standard test pressure (cfm/ft²).

NFRC
National Fenestration Rating Council
CERTIFIED

ACME Energy Window Co.

Millenium 2000⁺
Vinyl-Clad Wood Frame
Double Glazing • Argon Fill • Low E
Product Type: **Vertical Slider**

ENERGY PERFORMANCE RAINGS	
U-Factor (U.S./I-P)	Solar Heat Gain Coefficient
0.35	**0.32**

ADDITIONAL PERFORMANCE RATINGS	
Visible Transmittance	Air Leakage (U.S./I-P)
0.51	**0.2**

Manufacturer stipulates that these ratings conform to applicable NFRC procedures for determining whole product performance. NFRC ratings are determined for a fixed set of environmental conditions and a specific product size. Consult manufacturer's literature for other product performance information.
www.nfrc.org

Choosing Windows by Climate

Annual heat loss and/or heat gain through a window depend on both the performance characteristics listed above and the climate where the window is located.

The relative performances of eight window types (see table below) in eight climates across the US (see map) are shown in the bar graphs on the facing page. Blue represents the annual cost of cooling, red the cost of heating.

Seattle • Burlington • Chicago • DC • St Louis • Los Angeles • Phoenix • Miami

Window Types

Window #	Glazings	Tint	Coating	Ar/Kr Gas?	Frame	U-value	SHGC	VT
1	Single	Clear	None	No	Metal	>=1.00	>=.60	>=.60
2	Double	Clear	None	No	Metal	.71–.99	>=.60	>=.60
3	Single	Clear	None	No	Non-metal	.71-.99	>=.61	>=.60
4	Double	Clear	None	No	Non-metal	.41-.55	.41-.60	.51-.60
5	Double	Clear	HSG Low-E	Yes	Non-metal	.31-.40	.41-.60	.51-.60
6	Double	Clear	LSG Low-E	Yes	Non-metal	.31-.40	<=.25	.41-.50
7	Triple	Clear	MSG Low-E	Yes	Non-metal	.21-.25	.26-.40	.41-.50
8	Triple	Clear	MSG Low-E	Yes	Non-metal, TI	<=.20	.26-.40	.41-.50

KEY: HSG = High Solar Gain, MSG = Medium Solar Gain, LSG = Low Solar Gain, TI = Thermally Improved

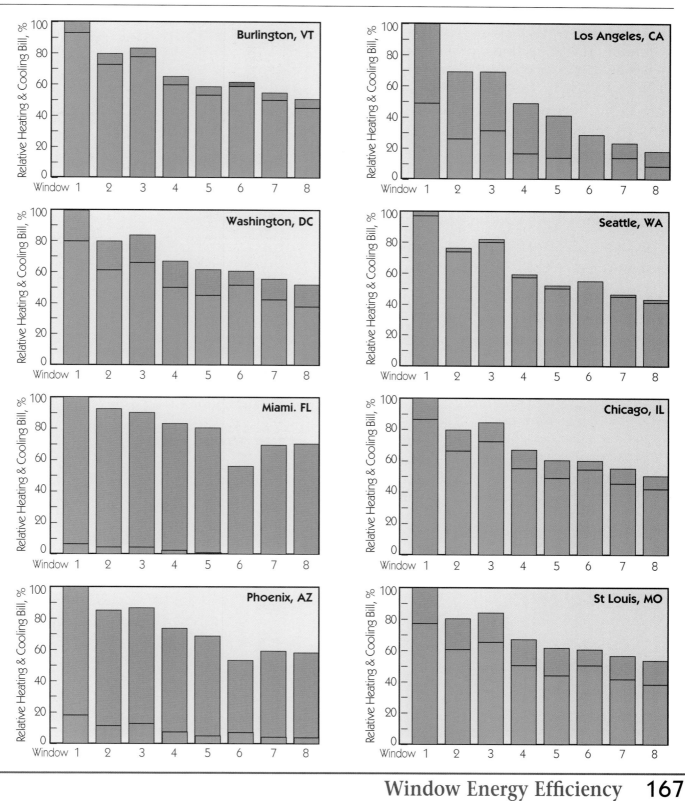

Egress Openings

The fire safety sections of building codes require egress openings from all sleeping spaces directly to the outside leading to a public way without obstruction. Why sleeping spaces only? Because a sleeping person may not awake to a fire until escape through the building interior is impossible.

In order to qualify as egress openings windows must meet the minimum dimension requirements illustrated at right:

- a window sill height of 44 inches maximum

- for windows both above and below grade level, a minimum clear opening 5.7 sq. ft.; for windows at grade, 5.0 sq. ft.

- a minimum opening height of 24 inches

- a minimum opening width of 20 inches.

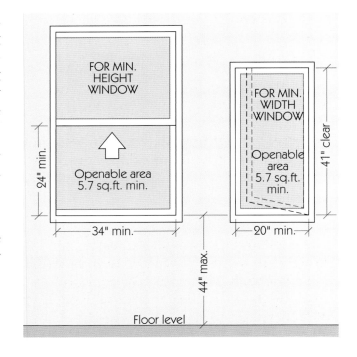

Roof Egress Windows

Because most tiny houses are restricted in height, sleeping lofts may not have wall heights sufficient to contain legal egress windows. For this reason *Appendix Q* of the *International Residential Code* allows egress skylights and roof windows. Such units must also conform to the dimensional requirements of the wall mounted windows above.

Most skylight manufacturers now offer egress versions. Two models from Velux are shown at right.

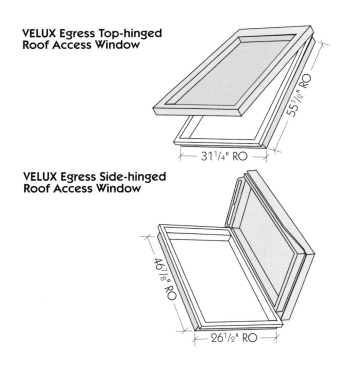

VELUX Egress Top-hinged Roof Access Window

VELUX Egress Side-hinged Roof Access Window

Natural Daylighting

Light Penetration vs. Window Height

Architects and lighting designers generally use the rule:

> Light penetration = 2–2.5 × window height

With the standard window height of 6' 8" and tiny house maximum building width of 12 feet, daylight penetration is not a problem. Increased daylighting may be achieved, however, with either skylights of light tubes.

Glare

The pupil of the human eye adjusts in response to lighting intensity. When the light striking the eye comes from a dark background *and* a small bright source (see top, left diagram), the pupil is unable to adjust to both. The resulting painful sensation is called glare.

Glare—not intensity—can be reduced by:

- increasing the area of the bright source
- increasing the reflected, diffuse light by painting the background walls a lighter color
- the combination of both steps

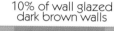

10% of wall glazed dark brown walls   25% of wall glazed tan walls

10% of wall glazed gray walls   25% of wall glazed white walls

Light From Two Directions

In addition to glare, rooms with windows on but a single wall suffer from an unnatural two-dimensional flattening of lit objects.

Providing daylit, openable windows on adjacent walls provides double benefits:

- more natural lighting
- cross ventilation with outside air.

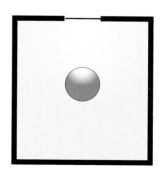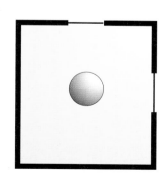

Natural Ventilation

It is only within the last 100 years—about 0.01% of human existence—that we could rely on anything but nature to keep us cool. That genetic memory no doubt accounts for the popularity of camping and sleeping porches. For that reason we find natural breezes more pleasant than any form of mechanical cooling.

The ability to utilize natural breezes is an important element in shelter design:

• Identify the direction of the prevailing summer breezes for your site.

• Make sure the windows facing that breeze are openable.

• Consider plantings such as shown in the illustration to direct or funnel the breeze into adjacent windows.

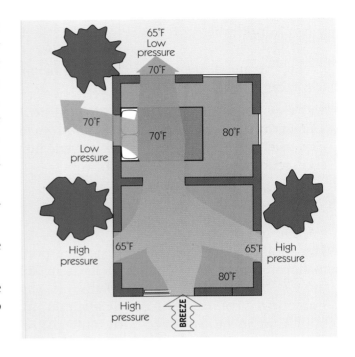

Window Fans

In the absence of a natural breeze a remarkable simulation may be created with strategically placed, inexpensive box fans.

With no natural breeze, the ambient air temperature will be uniform on all sides of the building. We are therefore free to choose any one or more windows in which to place the fan(s).

But box fans, particularly on high speed, are noisy. For a peaceful sleep bathed in what feels like a natural cooling breeze, place the window fan in a remote location blowing the stale house air out. Close all windows and doors except the ones in the bedroom that will cause the inflowing air to cross your sleeping body.

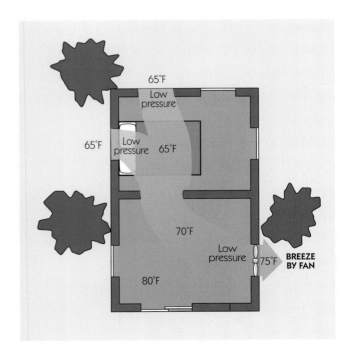

The View Looking Out

An analogy may be made between people and windows. Ask yourself, "Which is more important: how I look or how I feel?" Similarly, which is more important: how your home's windows appear to the neighbors or how they function for you from the inside?

The essential functions of providing daylight and ventilation have already been discussed. Here we consider the function of providing connection to the outside world.

The illustration below shows four figures and the height of their eyes above the floor:

- a standing man of average height
- a standing woman of average height
- a seated woman
- a person lying in bed.

At the right are four window applications:

- a patio door with safety (tempered) glass extending from 3" to 78" above the floor
- a window with the lowest non-safety glass allowed glazing height of 18" above the floor
- a bedroom window with sill height at mattress level but below sight-to-outdoors height
- a dining room window with sill height above table and chair level.

A standard, but not sacred, rule of thumb for a home's exterior appearance is for the tops of all windows and doors to be at the same height. All four examples in the illustration conform to this rule.

View and Window Sill Height

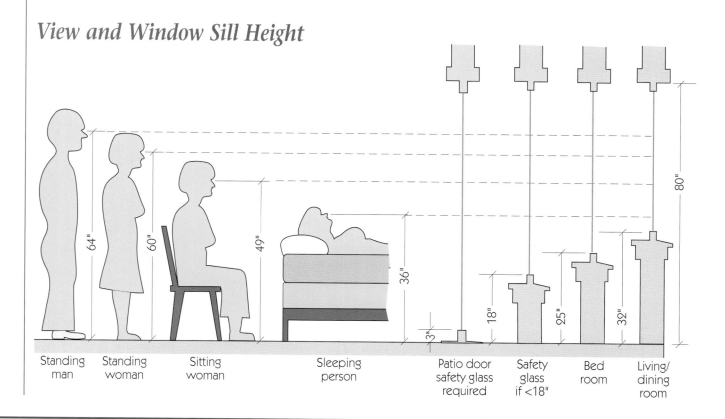

| Standing man | Standing woman | Sitting woman | Sleeping person | Patio door safety glass required | Safety glass if <18" | Bed room | Living/ dining room |

Installing Windows

The instructions illustrated are for a generic modern single- or double-hung window with attached nailing flange. These are the most common type of windows you will find at your local home center. Instructions for other window types would be similar, but would contain extra steps for multi-unit assemblies such as picture windows with flanking units. ALWAYS follow the manufacturer's directions included with the window or downloaded from the manufacturer's website.

In particular, note whether the window meets the code requirements for your location. Windows in coastal areas must meet more stringent requirements for impact resistance. If in doubt, consult your local code official.

Here is a list of the tools required for installation in a common wood-framed wall with previously applied house wrap over structural sheathing:

- tape measure
- 2-foot bubble level
- framing square
- hammer
- drill/driver
- caulking gun
- utility knife
- staple gun
- putty knife

Installing Single- and Double-Hung Windows

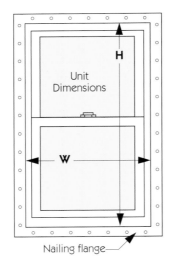

1. Measure the window unit dimensions which are the width and height of the body that will fit inside the framing rough opening.

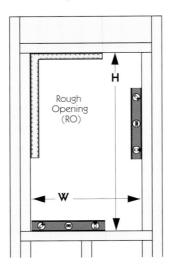

2. Confirm that the rough opening is at least 1/2" wider and taller than the window's unit dimensions and that the opening is level and square.

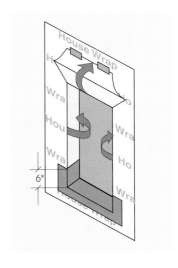

3. Slit the house wrap and fold it into the framed opening. Apply formable flashing over the sill and 6" up the jambs in a single piece.

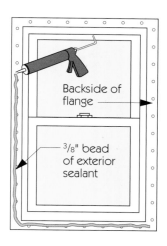

4. Apply a ³/₈" bead of exterior caulk to the back (against the house wrap) side of the nailing fin along and over the line of holes.

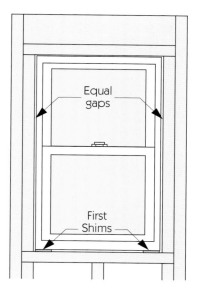

5. Place shims at the bottom corners, and set the window into the opening. Center the window so the side gaps are equal.

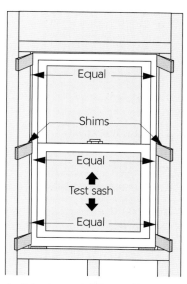

6. Shim top, middle, and bottom of both sides loosely. Test the sash to make sure it moves up and down easily.

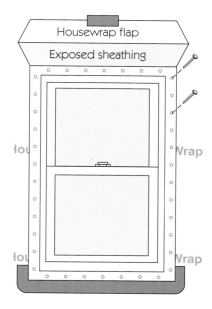

7. Fasten the nailing fin to the sheathing through the house wrap. Check to make sure the sash still moves freely.

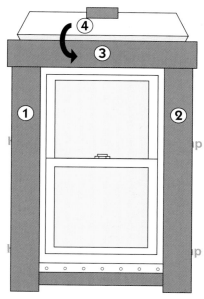

8. Apply self-adhering flashing in the order shown. Release the top flap and tape it down with house wrap tape.

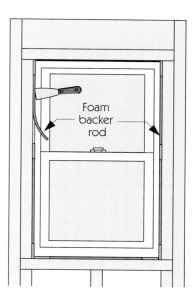

9. Pack foam backer rod into the gaps between the window unit and framing. Check sash operation against overpacking.

About Doors

"Swing" Definition

LEFT-HAND DOOR **RIGHT-HAND DOOR**

Parts Terminology

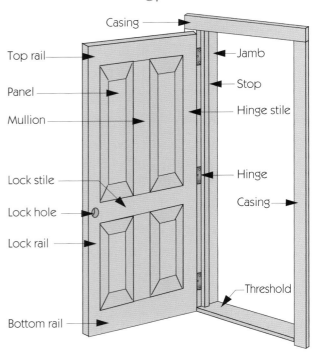

Casing
Top rail
Panel
Mullion
Lock stile
Lock hole
Lock rail
Bottom rail
Jamb
Stop
Hinge stile
Hinge
Casing
Threshold

Construction: Four Types

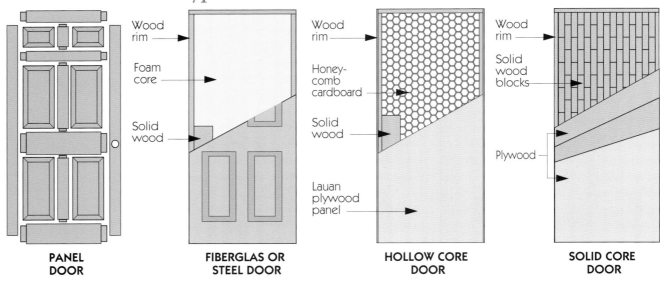

Wood rim
Foam core
Solid wood

Wood rim
Honey-comb cardboard
Solid wood
Lauan plywood panel

Wood rim
Solid wood blocks
Plywood

PANEL DOOR   **FIBERGLAS OR STEEL DOOR**   **HOLLOW CORE DOOR**   **SOLID CORE DOOR**

Energy Efficiency of Doors

Door Performance Rating Label

We tend to overlook the energy performance of doors because their performance in other regards is so important. However, the insulation factors of the old standby wood panel door are no better than those of an ordinary double-glazed window, and air leakage, particularly as the door ages, can be extreme.

Modern prehung entrance doors are designed to be energy efficient. Instead of solid or panelized wood, they consist of fiberglass, vinyl, or metal shells filled with insulating foam. And instead of weatherstrips installed as an afterthought, the new doors include integral weatherstripping designed as part of the door.

Still, energy performance varies. For this reason doors, like windows, now carry performance rating labels like the one shown. The meanings of the three important energy factors are illustrated below.

World's Best Door Company

Exterior Doors
Fiberglass Door
Clear Glazing

ENERGY PERFORMANCE RAINGS

Product Description	U-Factor/Solar Heat Gain Coefficient (SHGC)			
Default Frame Wood	Individual Option			
	1/4 Lite	1/2 Lite	3/4 Lite	Full Lite
Dual/Clear/Air/.75	0.20 / 0.05	0.28 / 0.20	0.32 / 0.27	0.36 / 0.35
Dual/Clear/Air/.75 With Grids	0.20 / 0.04	0.28 / 0.17	0.32 / 0.24	0.36 / 0.31
Dual/Clear/Air/.29	0.20 / 0.05	0.29 / 0.20	0.34 / 0.27	0.38 / 0.35
Dual/Clear/Air/.29 With Grids	0.20 / 0.04	0.28 / 0.20	0.34 / 0.24	0.38 / 0.31
Flush	**U-Factor** 0.16		SHGC 0.01	
Embossed	**U-Factor** 0.17		SHGC 0.01	
Air Leakage 0.30 cfm/ft²				

Manufacturer stipulates that these ratings conform to applicable NFRC procedures for determining whole product performance. NFRC ratings are determined for a fixed set of environmental conditions and specific product size. Consult manufacturer's literature for other product performance information.
www.nfrc.org

Three Performance Factors

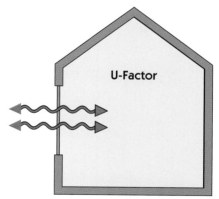

U-Factor measures the rate of heat conduction through the window due to a temperature difference between the inside and outside.

Solar Heat Gain Coefficient is the fraction of solar energy striking the window glazing that passes through to heat the house.

Air leakage is the infiltration of hot or cold air through or around the window in cubic feet per minute per square foot.

14 Installing Prehung Doors

Installing an entrance door used to require the skills of an experienced finish carpenter. The wood door had to be planed to an exact fit, the hinges mortised with chisel or router into the door edge, and the locking hardware bored and mortised. Now entrance doors are purchased already assembled with casings, threshold, and exterior trim. Installing a prehung door is no more complicated than the similar process for windows.

As with windows, the door itself is more likely a shell of fiberglass or plastic filled with insulating foam. Trimming the door in either height or width is impossible, so make sure the rough opening (R.O.) in the frame is perfectly vertical, level, square, and of the recommended width and height before you begin.

The door instructions below are, as with those for a window, for a generic prehung door. Different manufacturers have different preferences for a few of the details, so make sure you read and follow the installation instructions for your particular door. If you lose the instructions they can always be downloaded from the manufacturer's website.

The two areas most subject to variation are the installation of a pan under the threshold and the flashing on the exterior.

The tools required for installation are the same as those for windows on page 172.

Installing Prehung Exterior Doors

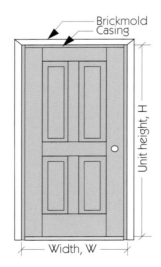

1. Measure the door unit dimensions which are the width and height of the body that will fit inside the framing opening.

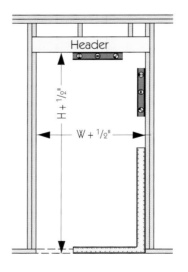

2. Confirm that the rough opening is at least $1/2$" wider and taller than the door unit dimensions and that the opening is both level and square.

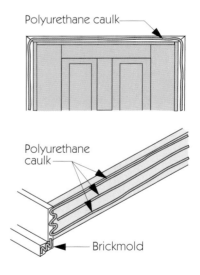

3. Apply $3/8$" beads of polyurethane caulk to the backside of the attached brickmold and to the bottom of the threshold.

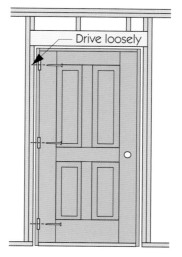

4. Predrill ⅛" holes through all three hinge center holes and jamb and install #8 x 3" screws loosely to hold the door in place.

5. Insert shims above each screw. Using a 6' level, adjust the shims to plumb the hinge-side jamb while maintaining equal spaces between the door and both jambs.

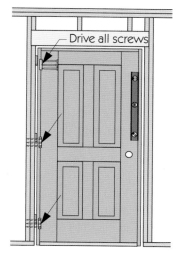

6. Drive #8 x 3" screws through all hinge holes tight through the casing and into the framing.

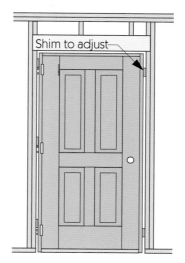

7. Drill ⅛" holes through the lock-side casing near the top and bottom and install single #8 x 3" screws loosely. Shim to maintain an even space between casing and stud.

8. Drive pairs of #8 x 3" screws through top and bottom shims. Install a shim behind the strike plate and fasten with #8 x 3" screws through the strike plate holes.

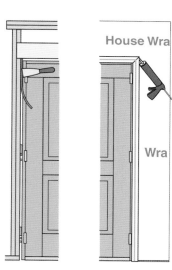

9. Pack foam backer rod into gaps between the jambs and the framing. On the outside, caulk around the brickmold and between brickmold and siding.

Notes

15 INSULATION

Insulation. Everyone knows it's a good thing. It keeps you warmer in winter and cooler in summer. But few know how much the devil is in the details. Installing carelessly, installing improperly, or installing the wrong material in the wrong place will result in poor performance. It may even result in damage to the building.

For those reasons we explain how and why each of four options for the three building heat loss surfaces (foundation or floor. walls, and roofs/ceilings) work. And we show only insulation options considered "best practice" by building scientists.

Heads Up! Chances are great your building code official is charged with enforcing the state residential energy code. Because the code expects houses of 2,000+ square feet, the prescribed floor/wall/ceiling R-values for new residential construction are very high: for example R49 to R60 for ceilings in northernmost states. That's 16 to 20 inches of fiberglass! Requiring that for a 200 to 400 square foot tiny house is akin to requiring your refrigerator to have 6-inch foam walls.

The code official has latitude to grant exemptions. Show him or her the annual heat load calculation (pages 224–226) for your design. The result for the tiny house example used throughout this book in cold Detroit, MI, is just 16,000,000 Btu, equivalent to 2/3 cord of hardwood, 145 gallons of fuel oil, or 1,880 kWh electricity in a heat pump.

15 Insulation and R-Value

Choosing Your Insulation

Heat losses in winter and gains in summer through a building's roof, walls, and floor are inversely proportional to their thermal resistances (R-values). Insulations—materials having especially high R-values per inch of thickness—are placed inside roof, wall, and floor cavities or over building surfaces to increase their total R-values. All of the insulation materials in the table below are available at lumberyards or through insulation contractors.

When choosing the insulation(s) for your home, consider all of the product's characteristics, not just their R-values. Some insulations require a cover of fire-resistant material. Others may absorb condensed moisture, reducing their R-values. And unfaced foams disintegrate when exposed for long periods to direct sunlight.

For this reason four options, each combining high R-value, appropriate product, and proper installation, are described for each building surface on the following pages. In every case the thicknesses and corresponding R-values of the insulations can be adjusted to reflect the local climate.

Insulation Materials Compared

Type of Insulation	R/in.	Maximum Temp., °F	Vapor Barrier	Water Absorption	Moisture Damage	Direct Sunlight	Fire
Roll, Blanket, or Batt							
Fiberglass	3.2 (2.9–3.8)	180	unfaced: P	G	E	E	G
Fiberglass, high density	4.0 (3.8–4.2)	180	unfaced: P	G	E	E	G
Rock wool	3.2 (2.9–3.8)	>500	unfaced: P	G	E	E	E
Loose Fill							
Cellulose	3.5 (3.2–3.8)	180	P	P	P	G	F
Fiberglass	2.5 (2.2–2.7)	180	P	G	E	E	G
Rock wool	3.1 (3.0–3.3)	>500	P	G	E	G	G
Rigid Board							
Expanded polystyrene	3.8 (3.6–4.0)	165	P	P	G	P	P
Extruded polystyrene	4.8 (4.5–5.0)	165	G	E	E	P	P
Polyurethane	6.2 (5.5–6.5)	165	G	E	E	P	P
Polyisocyanurate, foil-faced	7.0	180	F	G	E	E	G
Polyisocyanurate, unfaced	5.6	200	G	G	E	P	P
Sprayed or Foamed in Place							
Fiberglass, high-density	4.2	180	P	G	E	E	G
Polyurethane, closed cell	6	165	G	E	E	P	P
Polyurethane, open cell	3.6	165	P	P	E	P	P

Key: E = excellent; G = good; F = fair; P = poor

Effective R-Values

As stated before, insulation is placed inside cavities and over surfaces in order to increase roof, wall, and floor R-values. However, placing an R-19 fiberglass batt inside a wall does not make the wall an "R-19 wall." The overall, or effective, R-value of a roof, wall, or floor is determined by the materials and thicknesses of the framing, sheathing, siding, interior finish, even the surface air films.

See below for the effective R-values of the most common wood frame applications.

2 x 4, 16 in. o.c. WOOD FRAME WALLS, ¹/₂ in. SHEATHING, SIDING, ¹/₂ in. DRYWALL

R-11 batt

R-11 batt + 1 in. extruded polystyrene sheathing

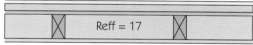

R-11 batt + 1 in. polyisocyanurate sheathing

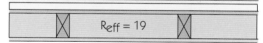

2 x 6, 24 in. o.c. WOOD FRAME WALLS, ¹/₂ in. SHEATHING, SIDING, ¹/₂ in. DRYWALL

R-19 batt, no insulating sheathing

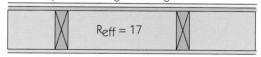

R-19 batt + 1 in. extruded polystyrene sheathing

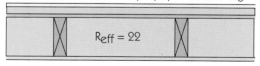

R-19 bat + 1 in. polyisocyanurate sheathing

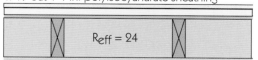

2 x 6, 24 in. o.c. WOOD FRAME ROOF/FLOOR, ¹/₂ in. SHEATHING, ¹/₂ in. DRYWALL

No insulation

R-11 batt

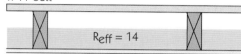

R-19 batt

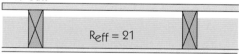

R-11 batt+ 2 in. polyisocyanurate

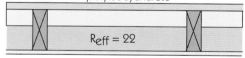

3 in. polyisocyanurate on top

R-19 batt + 1 in. polyisocyanurate inside

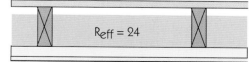

Floor Insulation Options

On a Trailer

Tiny houses on trailers pose several insulation challenges. First, being on a trailer intended for highway travel exposes the floor to water, snow, and ice. Second, the highway height restriction of 13' 6" over the ground requires the floor to be as low and thin as possible.

In the generic plan below, the first requirement is satisfied by a galvanized or stainless sheet metal pan attached to the bottom of the trailer

frame. While tempting, placing the floor insulation between the frame members ignores the thermal short circuit of the highly heat-conductive steel beams, so it is better to leave this space as a chase for wiring.

The combination of fiberglass or rock wool over rigid or sprayed foam between the wood floor joists provides both a decent R-value and a freeze-proof space for water supply pipes.

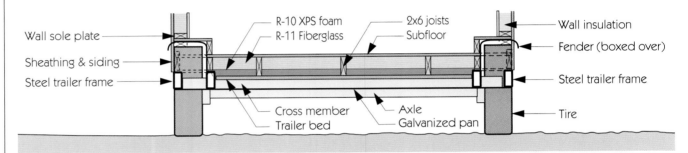

On Skids

A tiny house built and delivered to a site on skids needn't be protected against road hazards but is usually sited on blocking and so exposed at least to temperature extremes and critters.

The ideal solution is again insulating between the floor joists with fiberglass or rock wool over a rigid foam insulation. Foil-faced isocyanurate is the foam of choice because it: a) discourages

critters and insects, and b) provides the highest R-value per inch of thickness.

Were the R-values of the foam and fiberglass equal, the temperature at their interface would be halfway between that of the building interior and the outdoors. Halfway between 70°F and 0°F is 35°F, so the fiberglass-filled joist cavities could be utilized as freeze-proof plumbing chases.

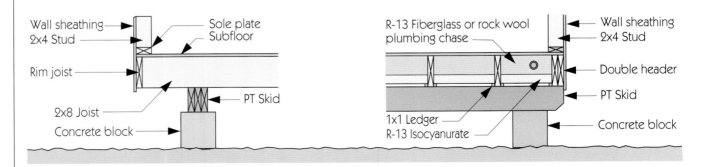

On Poles or Piers

Whether built offsite and delivered onto a foundation of poles/piers or built on site, the best insulating system is similar to that of a house built on skids.

A major difference, however, is the lack of a building height restriction, allowing the floor joist depths and insulation to be greater. While the joists of a trailer- or skid-built floor might be 2 × 6 or even 2 × 4, those of a floor constructed on a pole or pier foundation could be 2 × 10 or 2 × 12.

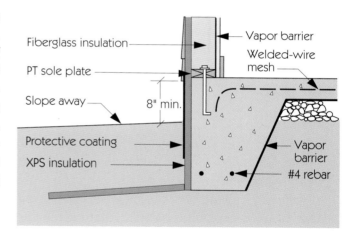

R-13 Fiberglass or rock wool plumbing chase

2 × 8 Joists, 16" oc

2" R-13 Foil-faced Isocyanurate

Dbl. 2 × 10 sill   Ledger strip

PT telephone pole

Concrete collar

Footing below frost line

On a Slab on Grade

As an approximation, the temperature deep beneath the ground surface, say 10 feet or more, is 90°F minus the site latitude. At a latitude of 40°N, the earth beneath NYC is thus about 50°F year-round. Since heat loss is directly proportional to temperature difference, most of the heat loss from a slab is through its perimeter. Place 1½- or 2-inch (R-7.5 or R-10) extruded polystyrene down and out around a slab as shown. Don't omit the protective coating which prevents degradation by the sun.

Fiberglass insulation

PT sole plate

Slope away

Protective coating

XPS insulation

Vapor barrier

Welded-wire mesh

8" min.

Vapor barrier

#4 rebar

On a Crawl Space

The floor over a closed crawl space can be insulated the same way as a floor over skids or poles provided ground moisture is capped by a complete vapor-retarding polyethylene ground cover.

Alternatively the floor can be left uninsulated, but the crawl space walls insulated (not shown). This prevents the crawl space from freezing, making it a convenient space for running plumbing lines.

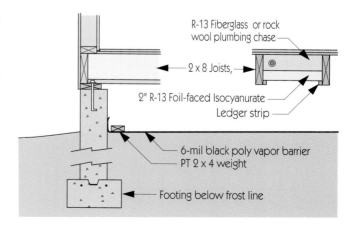

R-13 Fiberglass or rock wool plumbing chase

2 × 8 Joists,

2" R-13 Foil-faced Isocyanurate

Ledger strip

6-mil black poly vapor barrier

PT 2 × 4 weight

Footing below frost line

Fiberglass Batt Between Studs

This is the wall long favored by builders because it is both simple and inexpensive. Unfortunately the effective R-value is reduced by 25% by conduction through the wood framing. Also, fiberglass insulation is neither air- nor water-vapor-tight.

If you choose to go this route, make sure the fiberglass batts fill the wall cavity completely with zero gaps, and use housewrap over the outside of the sheathing to reduce air leakage.

Walls in northern heating zones require an additional caution. If warmed interior air finds its way into a cold wall, the moisture in the air can condense (like the moisture appearing on a glass of ice water) in the fiberglass, reducing the R-value and posing a danger of mildew and rot. Keep the moist air out of the wall with two coats of interior vapor-barrier paint.

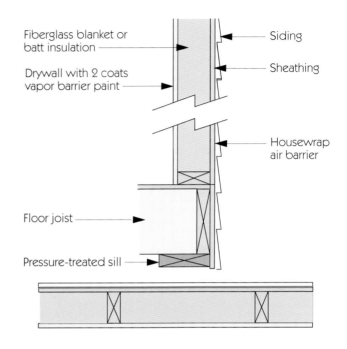

Fiberglass in Cavity + Foam Sheathing

When the wall framing doesn't provide a thick enough cavity for the desired amount of insulation, rigid insulation panels can be added on the outside of the frame. In the example shown, extruded polystyrene at R-5 per inch is nailed to the studs. Vertical furring strips nailed to each stud through the foam provide points of attachment for horizontal siding and a rain screen at the same time.

Bracing of the wall can be accomplished by either diagonal metal bracing straps or by an intermediate structural sheathing panel between the studs and the layer of foam.

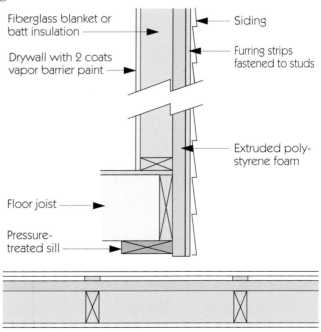

Spray Urethane + Fiberglass Between Studs

Although sprayed closed cell foam is a far better performer than fiberglass batts, it is also much more expensive. The wall illustrated here is a cost-effective compromise between the two insulations. A 2" layer of foam sprayed on the inside of the wall sheathing provides an R-value of 12 and seals the cavities against air infiltration. The high R-value also keeps the wall cavity warm enough to prevent condensation in winter.

Filling the remaining cavity space of a 2 × 6 wall with fitted R-11 fiberglass batts would increase the total effective wall R-value to about 22.

Even with 2" of sprayed foam in the cavities, it is a wise precaution to provide two coats of vapor barrier paint as a warm-side vapor barrier.

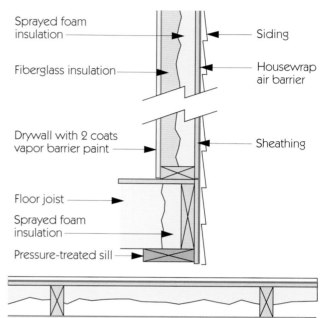

Spray Urethane Between Studs

The R-value of sprayed-in-place, closed-cell foam is 6.0 per inch as opposed to fiberglass's 3.2 per inch. In addition the closed-cell nature of the foam prevents the harmful condensation of moisture within the insulation. Best of all, the foam is sprayed onto the sheathing and frame as a liquid, which then expands and seals the cavity against infiltration of air.

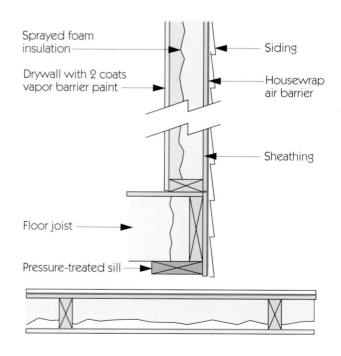

Roof Insulation Options

Vented Fiberglass Between Rafters (Cold Roof)

With typically small slopes and minimal over-hangs, tiny house roofs in heating climates could be prone to ice dams. An ice dam is a buildup of ice at the edge of the roof, causing meltwater to back up under the roofing and damage the walls and ceilings below. An ice dam occurs when snow on the roof, acting as insulation, raises the roof surface temperature above freezing, melting the bottom layer of snow. The meltwater runs down under the snow to where it again freezes at the roof's edge.

Ice dams can be prevented with vent baffles which allow cold outside air to flow from eave to ridge under the roof sheathing, keeping the temperatures of the surface and edge the same.

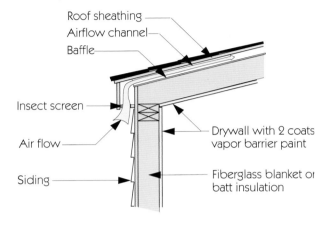

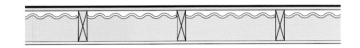

Vented Fiberglass Between Rafters + Interior Foam (Cold Roof)

When the standard "Vented Fiberglass Between Rafters" system shown in the first illustration fails to provide sufficient R-value, a layer of rigid foam may be added to the interior of the roof.

In new construction the better solution is simply increasing the depth of the rafters and fiberglass insulation. Where it is useful is in retrofitting (upgrading) an existing structure for better energy efficiency.

Note that most foams require a 15-minute fire-rated interior covering such as the ½" gypsum drywall in the illustration.

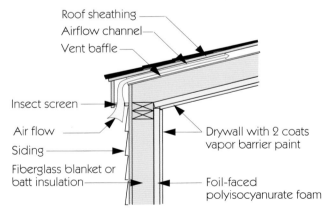

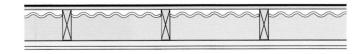

Rigid Foam Over Rafters (Hot Roof)

The purest form of the cold roof consists of several staggered layers of rigid foam insulation between a cathedral ceiling and the roof sheathing. As seen in the illustration, wood nailers of the same depth as the insulation panels alternate in direction and, nailed together and to the rafter below at their intersections, provide a solid connection between the roof sheathing and the rafters.

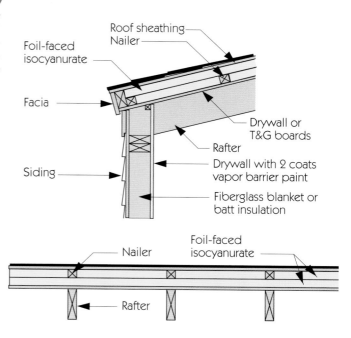

Spray Urethane + Fiberglass Between Rafters (Hot Roof)

By replacing the vent baffles in the illustration above with a thick layer of high-R spray foam, the roof surface is maintained closer to the outdoor temperature. This reduces the amount of melting while also increasing the R-value and decreasing the heat loss of the roof. In order to totally eliminate ice dam formation, any overhang at the eave must be fully insulated.

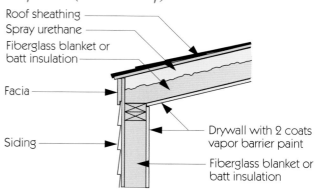

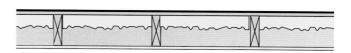

NOTES

16 WIRING

Household electrical circuits are not rocket science, but designing and installing even the simplest system in your tiny house requires a basic understanding of how electricity flows. With the assumption that you wish to at least understand what is going on inside all those wires and switches, we begin with a minicourse on the basic concept of the electrical circuit, i.e. the flow of electricity from source to load (appliance or other energy consuming device) and back.

That is followed by explanations of:

- the service drop and entrance
- types, sizes, and color codes of wires and cables
- the different circuits required by code
- what goes on inside the distribution panel
- how to physically run cables
- the details of the most common circuits

The second half of the chapter is devoted to selling you on the idea of going solar. Solar panels continue to drop in price while utility pcharges continue their rise. A complete off-the-grid solar electric system, including storage batteries, already pays for itself within half its lifetime.

Whether your tiny home is mobile or fixed, in the city or country, never again pay a utility bill or suffer a power outage.

And never again contribute needlessly to global warming!

16 The AC Electrical Circuit

Electrical Circuit Concept

A *circuit* is the path taken in a round trip. In an electrical circuit the things taking the trip are not people but electrons. Since electrons are invisible, it helps to think of the electron flow as the flow of water in a hose.

In the illustration at right the utility is a pump, the black wire is a black hose under pressure, and the white wire is a white hose under no pressure but returning the used water to the pump. The items in the box (television, light bulb, toaster) extract energy from the water flow, dropping the water pressure to zero.

The illustration below builds on the simplest concept, adding the utility pole and transformer (the pump), a utility meter (to measure the energy provided by the pump), a breaker panel to split the flow into multiple circuits, and a switch to turn the flow on and off. The black and white hoses become black and white insulated conductors (wires) through which the electrons flow.

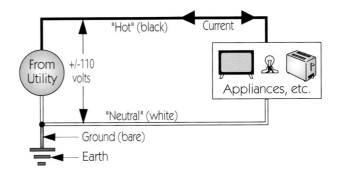

Basic Elements of a Household Electrical System

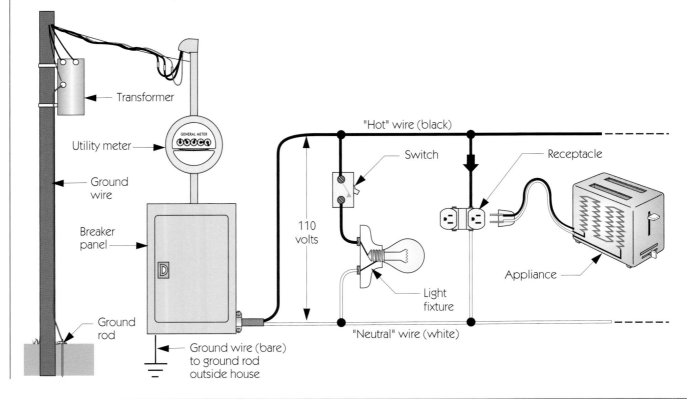

110 VAC & 220 VAC Circuits

Why Two Hot Conductors?

Most electrical items in a house run on 110 VAC (Volts Alternating Current), but a few, such as electric ranges and electric clothes dryers, run on 220 VAC. The voltages of the two live or "hot" conductors coming into the home from the utility transformer are both 110 VAC, so where does the 220 VAC come from?

In the graph at right, the voltages of the two charged conductors are 180° out of phase. When one is at +110 volts, the other is at -110 volts. If, instead of black (hot) and white (neutral) conductors, we use both black conductors, the voltage across the circuit is 220 VAC. Note: in a 3-conductor 220 VAC circuit (see below), one of the live conductors becomes red.

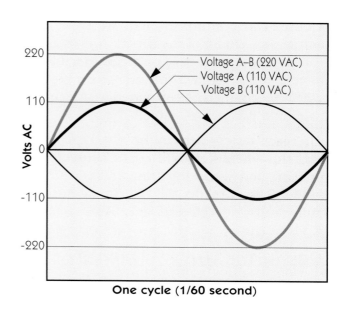

A 3-Conductor Circuit Provides Both 110 VAC and 220 VAC

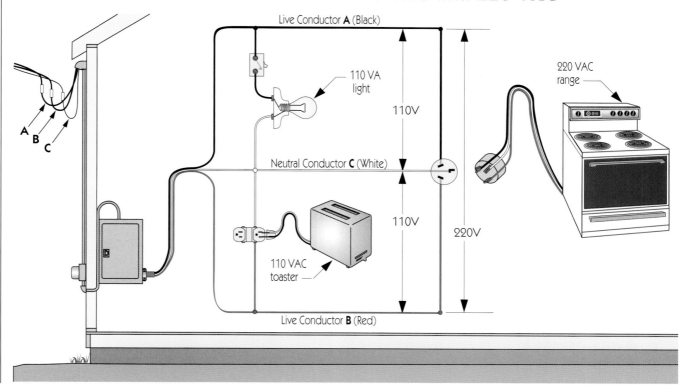

Electrical Wire & Cable

Cables

Houses can contain a *lot* of wiring. To keep things straight all of the conductors in a circuit (black, white, and bare or green in a 110 VAC circuit; black, red, white, and bare or green in a 220 VAC circuit) are contained in a jacket. The assembly is called a "cable."

The application determines the type of jacket: Non-Metallic (NM) for protected dry conditions, Service Entrance (SE), Armored, Underground Feeder (UF) for single buried circuits, and Underground SE cables.

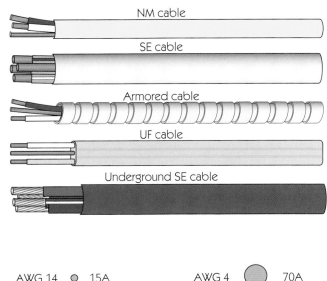

Conductor Size vs. Ampacity

Resistance to current flow generates heat in a conductor. The smaller the conductor and the greater the current, the greater the heat. For fire safety, conductors are rated for their *ampacity* (ampere capacity).

Shown at right are the actual cross-sections of conductors of standard AWG (American Wire Gauge) and their ampacities when sheathed in NM cable. Different cables types allow different ampacities.

AWG 14	15A		AWG 4	70A
AWG 12	20A		AWG 3	85A
AWG 10	30A		AWG 2	95A
AWG 8	40A		AWG 1	110A
AWG 6	55A		AWG 0	125A

The Color Code

As we have seen, each conductor in a cable serves a different purpose, so they must be properly identified when wiring devices and circuits.

At right are the standard insulation colors for all of the AC conductors used in residential wiring. Note to electronic and automotive hobbyists: the colors in DC wiring are different. While red is positive ("hot"), black is negative (ground in a "negative ground circuit").

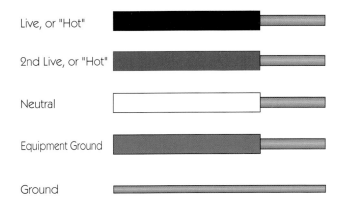

Live, or "Hot"

2nd Live, or "Hot"

Neutral

Equipment Ground

Ground

Service Drops & Entrances

The *service drop* is the wiring from the utility transformer on the street to the service head attached to the building where the utility conductors are spliced to the *service entrance* cable in a drip loop. The building owner is responsible for the service entrance cable, installation of the utility-supplied meter box, and the service entrance box (also known as the circuit breaker box).

When the utility is satisfied the service entrance wiring meets the electrical code, the utility's meter is installed and the electricity turned on.

Often a temporary service is erected on a pole or tree on site to provide power during the construction process. Specifications for temporary power and for underground service can be obtained from the utility line department.

Cable Service

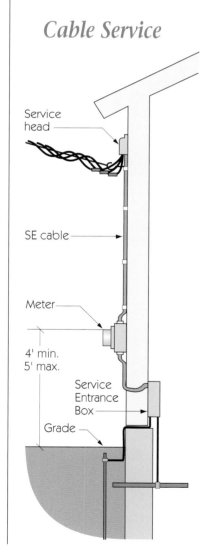

Service head

SE cable

Meter

4' min.
5' max.

Service Entrance Box

Grade

Rigid Steel Mast

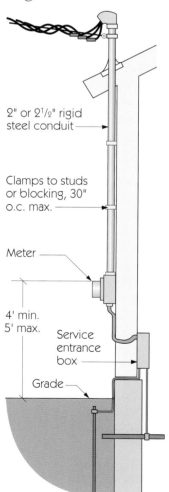

2" or 2½" rigid steel conduit

Clamps to studs or blocking, 30" o.c. max.

Meter

4' min.
5' max.

Service entrance box

Grade

Mobile Home

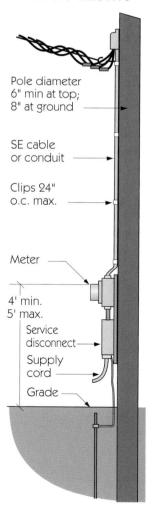

Pole diameter 6" min at top; 8" at ground

SE cable or conduit

Clips 24" o.c. max.

Meter

4' min.
5' max.

Service disconnect

Supply cord

Grade

Circuits Required by Code

GFCIs and AFCIs

Code specifies *GFCIs* (Ground Fault Circuit Interrupters) for the following: counters within 6' of a sink, bathrooms, garages, unfinished basements, crawl spaces, around swimming pools, outdoor decks, patios, porches, and at both front and rear of the house.

As protection against fire all receptacles in sleeping areas (bedrooms) must be protected by Arc-Fault Circuit Breakers, *AFCIs*.

Receptacles

Small Appliances. The Code requires two 20A circuits in the area of kitchen, pantry, and dining room. Although the circuits are rated 20A, receptacles may be rated either 15A or 20A.

Receptacles located 6–10" above counters with no point more distant than 24", except peninsulas and islands require just one receptacle each.

At least one of the kitchen small-appliance circuits must also appear in an adjacent dining room, breakfast area, or pantry.

Large Appliances. Large appliances should be served by separate circuits. These include: clothes washer, clothes dryer, dishwasher, waste disposer, water heater, water pump, electric range, electric wall oven, electric cooktop, oil burner, furnace blower, any permanently connected appliance over 1,000 watts, and any permanently connected motor over $1/8$ horsepower.

General. The "no more than 6 feet from a receptacle" rule applies here. But a little planning will ensure that receptacles don't fall behind heavy or large furnishings where they can't be accessed and that there will always be a convenient receptacle for vacuuming.

Lighting

Kitchen. Lighting should be both general (one or more overhead fixtures) and task (under wall cabinets or spots from ceiling) to illuminate work surfaces. If there are two entrances to the kitchen the overhead lights should be controlled by three-way switches at each entrance.

Bathroom. A switch-operated ceiling fixture and lights to either side of each lavatory are required. Prohibited are ceiling fixtures and ceiling fans within 3' horizontally and 8' vertically of tubs and showers.

Living Room and Bedrooms. Because lighting can be by lamps plugged into receptacles, "lighting circuits" may also include the general-purpose receptacles in a room. In any habitable room, no point along a wall may be further than 6' horizontally from a receptacle. This includes any wall 24" or more in width. If the room has more than one entrance, use 3-way switches so the lights can be switched as you pass through the room.

Closets. Light fixtures must be separated from clothes and other objects by a minimum of 12" inches horizontally and vertically. Separation may be reduced to 6" for recessed fixtures.

Garages. At least one switch-controlled light should be provided, preferably by 3-way switches controlled from both the house and the entrance door to the garage.

Stairways. Every area of a stairway should be illuminated. All stairway lights should be controlled by 3-way switches at the top and bottom landings.

Basements. Treat finished basements as living rooms, unfinished basements as garages including the requirement for GFCIs.

An Example Wiring Plan

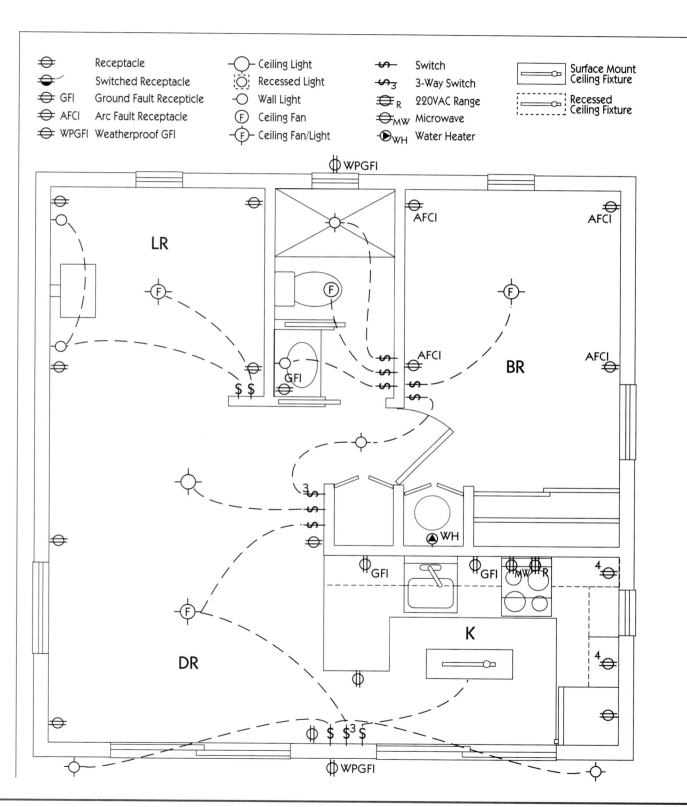

The Distribution Panel

Heart of the System

The heart of a home's electrical system is its distribution panel, also known as the *circuit breaker panel*. A 220 VAC main breaker at the top serves as the total shutoff for the entire building. The minimum size panel for a tiny home is 60 amps.

The main breaker feeds two strips of live conductor of opposite phases: bus A and bus B. Individual 110 VAC circuit breakers plug into opposite strips, so while single breakers control 110 VAC circuits, double breakers control 220 VAC circuits.

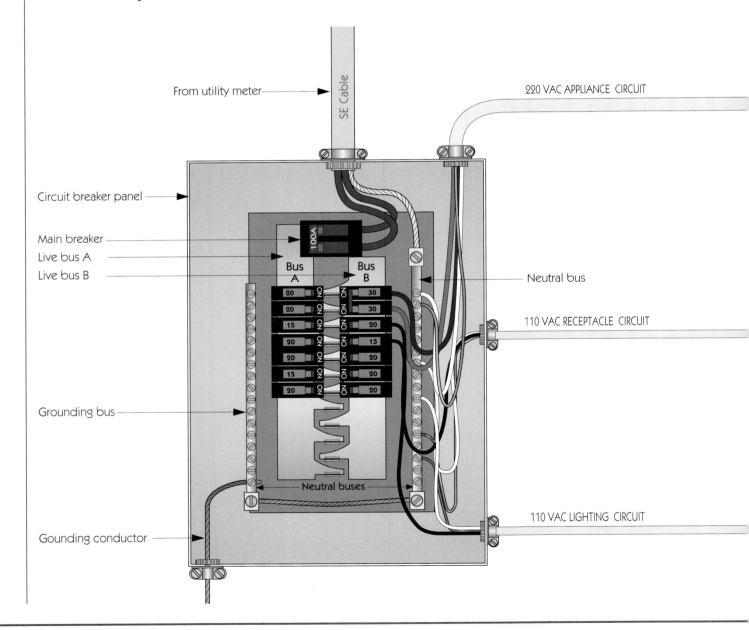

From utility meter

SE Cable

220 VAC APPLIANCE CIRCUIT

Circuit breaker panel

Main breaker

Live bus A

Live bus B

100A

Bus A

Bus B

20 · 30
20 · 30
15 · 20
20 · 15
20 · 20
15 · 20
20 · 20

Neutral bus

110 VAC RECEPTACLE CIRCUIT

Grounding bus

Neutral buses

110 VAC LIGHTING CIRCUIT

Gounding conductor

Individual Circuits

Each individual circuit begins at either its own single breaker (110 VAC circuits) or its own double breaker (220 VAC circuits). Both the breaker(s) and the cables are rated for the intended maximum amperages of the circuit loads: 15A, 20A, 30A, 50A, etc.

Ground-Fault and/or Arc-Fault protection for an entire circuit can be provided by special GFCI or AFCI circuit breakers in the main panel. Alternatively, a GFCI or AFCI receptacle can provide protection for all receptacle further downstream.

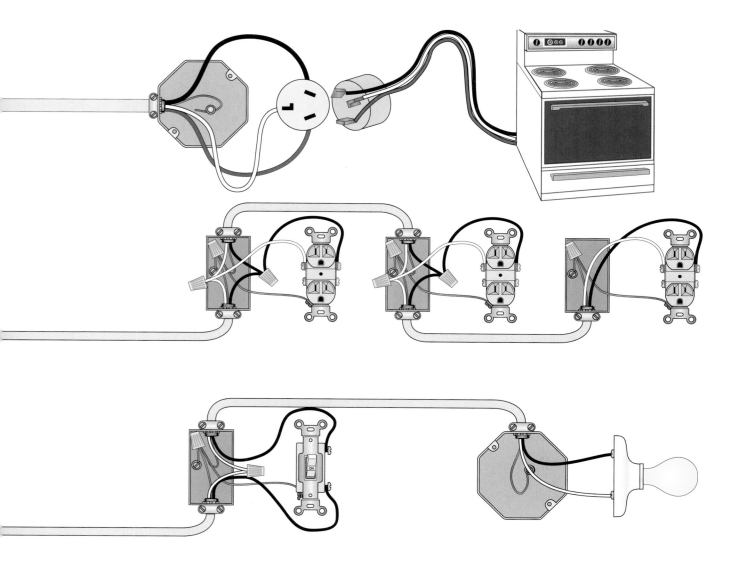

16 WIRING
Accessory Dwelling Feeds

Subpanels

Where a number of circuits serve a remote area, wing, or even smaller building remote from the main panel, a subpanel fed with Service Entrance (SE) Cable from a large breaker in the main panel reduces the amount and complexity of the wiring.

In particular, a tiny accessory dwelling unit such as a "Granny pod" is well served by its own subpanel, allowing the occupants total control over all of the electricity in the smaller dwelling.

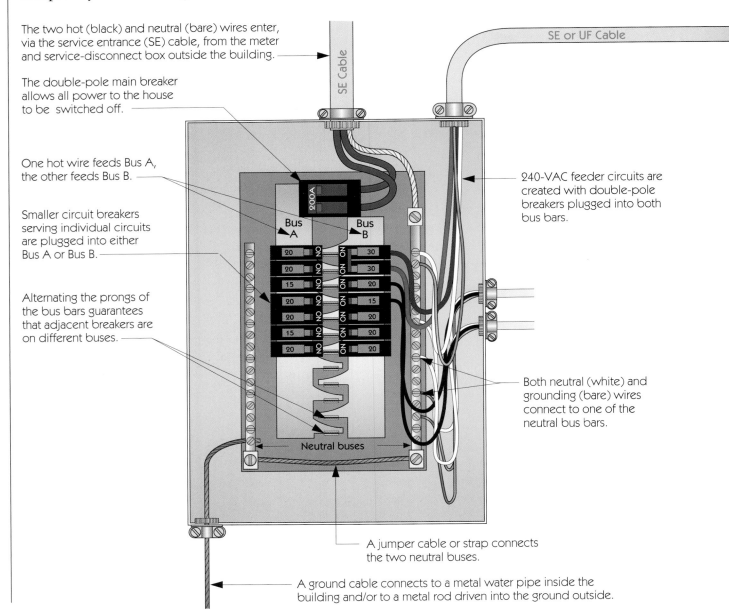

The two hot (black) and neutral (bare) wires enter, via the service entrance (SE) cable, from the meter and service-disconnect box outside the building.

The double-pole main breaker allows all power to the house to be switched off.

One hot wire feeds Bus A, the other feeds Bus B.

Smaller circuit breakers serving individual circuits are plugged into either Bus A or Bus B.

Alternating the prongs of the bus bars guarantees that adjacent breakers are on different buses.

SE Cable

SE or UF Cable

Bus A

Bus B

Neutral buses

240-VAC feeder circuits are created with double-pole breakers plugged into both bus bars.

Both neutral (white) and grounding (bare) wires connect to one of the neutral bus bars.

A jumper cable or strap connects the two neutral buses.

A ground cable connects to a metal water pipe inside the building and/or to a metal rod driven into the ground outside.

The subpanel operates just like a the main panel. A main breaker at the top matches the Amp rating of the SE feeder cable and allows all power to be shut off at a single location.

Note the difference in grounding between the main panel and the subpanel. In the main panel the neutral bus bar (where white and bare conductors connect) is jumpered to the ground bus bar. In the subpanel it is not. In both main and subpanel, both the ground bus and the metal enclosure are connected to a ground rod or a metal underground pipe.

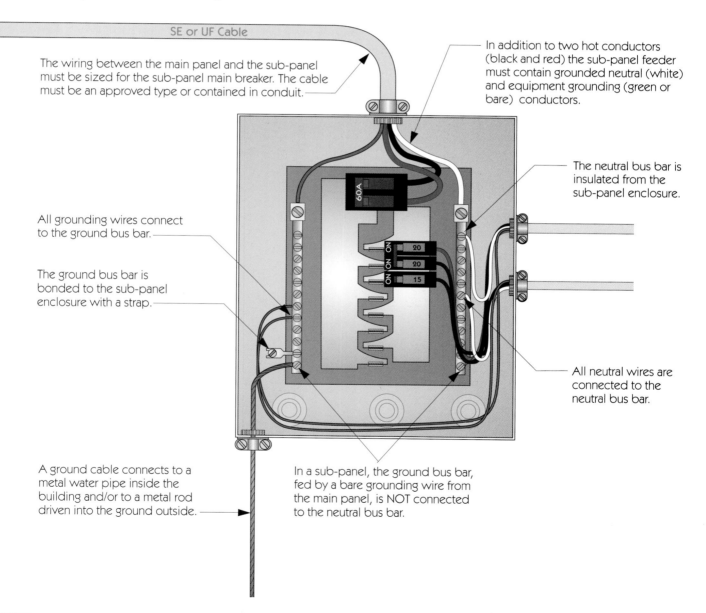

SE or UF Cable

The wiring between the main panel and the sub-panel must be sized for the sub-panel main breaker. The cable must be an approved type or contained in conduit.

In addition to two hot conductors (black and red) the sub-panel feeder must contain grounded neutral (white) and equipment grounding (green or bare) conductors.

The neutral bus bar is insulated from the sub-panel enclosure.

All grounding wires connect to the ground bus bar.

The ground bus bar is bonded to the sub-panel enclosure with a strap.

All neutral wires are connected to the neutral bus bar.

A ground cable connects to a metal water pipe inside the building and/or to a metal rod driven into the ground outside.

In a sub-panel, the ground bus bar, fed by a bare grounding wire from the main panel, is NOT connected to the neutral bus bar.

Running Cables

Nearly all residential wiring is done using plastic sheathed NM cable. The sheathing is thin and soft, so the code requires numerous protective precautions. Of particular importance is the protection of cable running through a stud. Where the hole is within 1¼ inch of the stud's inner edge an 18 ga. steel plate must be applied to the stud as protection against fasteners penetrating the cable and causing an electrical short circuit (and fire).

Be sure to follow all of the code requirements shown, as an electrical inspector will surely require reworking any mistakes.

Basic Elements of a Household Electrical System

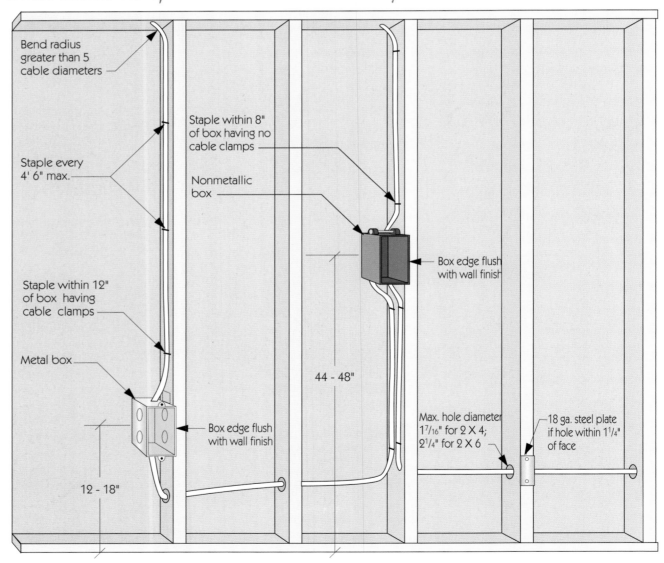

Bend radius greater than 5 cable diameters

Staple within 8" of box having no cable clamps

Nonmetallic box

Staple every 4' 6" max.

Staple within 12" of box having cable clamps

Metal box

Box edge flush with wall finish

Box edge flush with wall finish

44 - 48"

12 - 18"

Max. hole diameter 1⁷⁄₁₆" for 2 X 4; 2¼" for 2 X 6

18 ga. steel plate if hole within 1¹⁄₄" of face

The Most Common Circuits

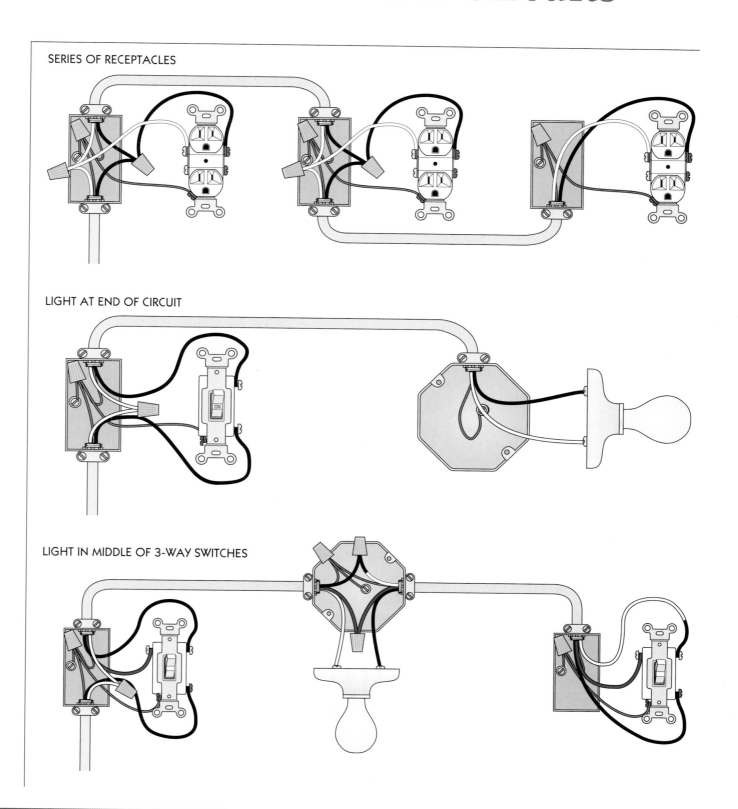

SERIES OF RECEPTACLES

LIGHT AT END OF CIRCUIT

LIGHT IN MIDDLE OF 3-WAY SWITCHES

Going Off the Grid

Path of the Sun

Shown below are the paths of the sun on the shortest day of the year, December 21, and the longest day, June 21. The sun's position at any time is defined by its altitude (degrees above the horizon) and azimuth (direction in degrees clockwise from true north).

A solar panel produces maximum power when the sun's rays strike it perpendicularly. Panel orientation is defined by its tilt above level, and azimuth (direction it faces). As a rule of thumb, for maximum annual output the ideal orientation is:

- Tilt equal to latitude in degrees
- Azimuth (facing) true south (180°).

Fortunately output degradation vs. orientation is not as severe as one might expect. The table below shows the losses in annual output vs. orientation for a panel at 30° N.

Annual Output Fraction at 30° N

Azimuth	Tilt, degrees					
	0	15	30	45	60	90
S (180°)	0.91	0.94	1.00	0.97	0.88	0.59
SSE, SSW	0.91	0.98	0.99	0.96	0.86	0.60
SE, SW	0.91	0.96	0.96	0.92	0.84	0.61
ESE, WSW	0.91	0.93	0.92	0.87	0.79	0.58
E, W	0.91	0.90	0.86	0.80	0.72	0.53

Solar Geometry

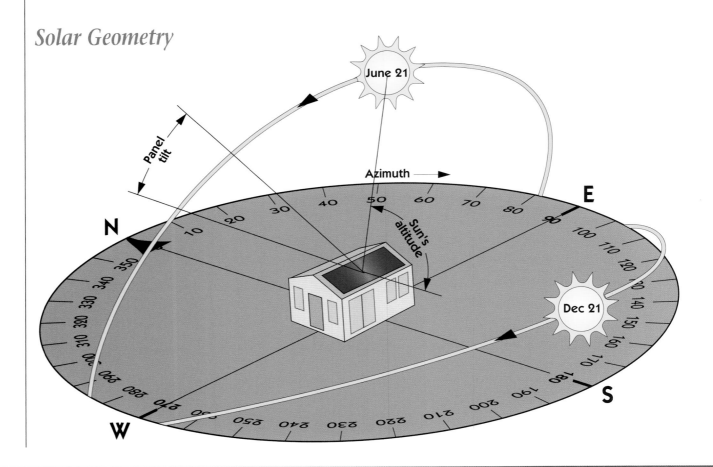

Insolation Across the US

Of course we know it is always sunny in California, and it rains constantly in Seattle, but in reality all parts of the US receive enough sunshine to power a tiny home. The map below shows, averaged over the entire year, just how much electrical power a PV panel can be expected to generate. The numbers are per rated panel Watt per day. Thus, the numbers are independent of panel size and panel type.

The figures assume a realistic system loss of 14 percent. Not considered are the additional potential losses due to less-than-optimal panel orientation and tilt, and to panel shading. Tilt and orientation loss factors are shown in the table on the previous page. Shading losses are explained on the following page. The map figure less losses, divided into your average daily electricity use, indicates the size system you need in total rated panel watts.

Average Watt-hours per Day per Panel Watt

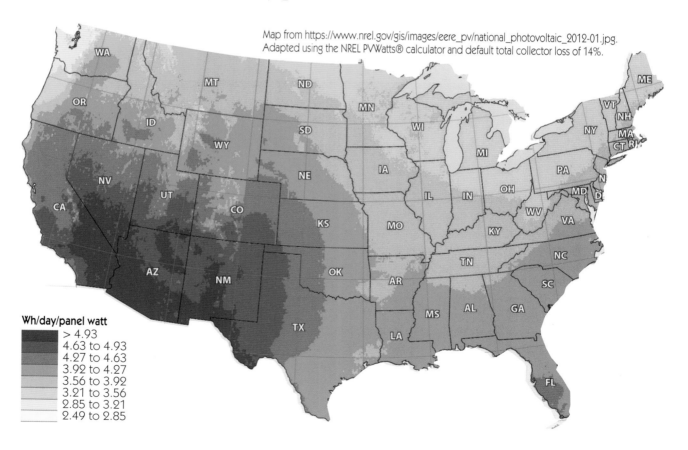

Map from https://www.nrel.gov/gis/images/eere_pv/national_photovoltaic_2012-01.jpg. Adapted using the NREL PVWatts® calculator and default total collector loss of 14%.

Wh/day/panel watt
> 4.93
4.63 to 4.93
4.27 to 4.63
3.92 to 4.27
3.56 to 3.92
3.21 to 3.56
2.85 to 3.21
2.49 to 2.85

PV Panel Shading

Losses Due to Panel Shading

Photovoltaic panels produce maximum power when struck by direct radiation. *Any* degree of shading results in a disproportionate loss in output. Thus it is imperative to determine the amount of panel shading throughout the year.

A rough percentage of annual shading can be determined using a sunpath diagram such as the one for 44° N latitude shown below. Sunpath charts for north latitudes between 24 and 60° N can be found in *The Visual Handbook of Building and Remodeling,* 4th edition.

Standing or sitting at the center of the proposed panel array, plot the outlines of all obstructions, such as buildings and trees above the southern horizon.

The most productive area of the southern sky is shown in light yellow. Roughly 90 percent of direct solar radiation comes from this area between 9AM and 3PM Standard Time. The area of sky shaded is the green area, here caused by trees. In this example we can predict an annual loss of about 15 percent (the percentage of yellow area overlapped by green). Further, we see most of the losses occur in winter. The rationale for mounting solar arrays high on roofs is obvious.

Basic Elements of a Household Electrical System

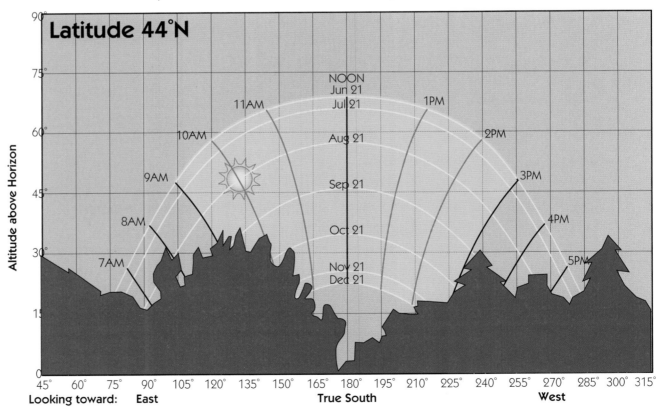

Estimating Your Usage

With Electricity, Less Is More

To size an off-the-grid solar system you need to estimate daily electricity use. Since you are planning a tiny house, let's assume you are also conservation minded and will use only Energy Star-rated appliances where possible.

With a tiny house the area of roof available for solar panels is limited. For this reason we will substitute gas for all of the really big energy hogs: space heating, clothes drying, range and oven cooking, and water heating.

The table below lists the appliances and daily usages I estimate for my own tiny house. You can make up your own table, or use the empty spaces at right to enter your own values.

Remember, the bottom line, kWh/day, is an average daily usage over the entire year. You may wish to adjust your figures to reflect different habits in the different seasons.

Table for Calculating Electrical Usage, Kilowatt-Hours/Day

Item	Watts	Hours/day	kWh/day	Hours/day	kWh/day
Ceiling fan	35	4.0	0.14	_____	_____
Clothes washer	255	1.0	0.26	_____	_____
Coffee maker	1,000	0.2	0.20	_____	_____
Computer, lap top	25	2.0	0.05	_____	_____
DVD player	17	2.0	0.03	_____	_____
Hair dryer	710	0.1	0.07	_____	_____
Lighting, six 9 Watt LEDs	54	4.0	0.22	_____	_____
Microwave oven	1,500	0.25	0.38	_____	_____
Printer, inkjet	151	0.1	0.02	_____	_____
Refrigerator, 15 cu.ft.	225	4.0	0.90	_____	_____
Router/modem, internet	6	24.0	0.14	_____	_____
Slow cooker	200	1.0	0.20	_____	_____
Television, 40" LED	150	4.0	0.60	_____	_____
Toaster	1,100	0.1	0.11	_____	_____
Vacuum	542	0.1	0.05	_____	_____
Videogame system	36	2.0	0.07	_____	_____
TOTAL kWh/day			3.44		

WIRING
Sizing the System

After estimating our usage at 3.44 kWh/day, we select a PV panel. For example we'll use the *Kyocera KD145*, rated at 145 W peak power. Two simple methods for determining the required system size in kW and the number of panels are: a) the insolation map on page 203, and b) an interactive online application, *PVWatts*.

System Size Using Insolation Map

Let our tiny home be in Greensboro, NC. From the map we find an average daily insolation of between 3.92 and 4.10 Wh per panel W. To be conservative, use 3.92 Wh/W. Dividing daily use by insolation, we find the system size in kW:

$$(3.44 \text{ kWh/day})/(3.92 \text{ Wh/Wday}) = 0.878 \text{ kW}$$

Dividing this system size by the panel rating:

$$0.878 \text{ kW}/145 \text{ W/panel} = 6 \text{ panels}$$

System Size Using PVWatts

Logging onto the *PVWatts* online calculator, *pvwatts.nrel.gov*, we are first asked for our location. Enter Greensboro, NC. *PVWatts* shows a solar data site in Greensboro, so we go on to the next page, "System Info." We are asked to modify the default values shown. We wish to verify our earlier system size result of 0.878 kW, so we enter 0.878. All other default values seem ideal, so we leave them unchanged and go to the results page. There we are presented with a table of monthly and annual radiation and AC energy output in kWh. Dividing the annual output of 1,233 kWh by 365 days we get 3.38 kWh/day. Great! Our two results agree within 2%!

However, note that the monthly results show a December output of only 76/30 = 2.53 kWh/day. In order that the system meet our daily demand of 3.44 kWh/day, we'll need more panels. We need: (3.44/2.53) × 6 panels = 8 panels.

Our Example System (See Right)

Panels Each of the eight 145W panels contains a diode ensuring current flow only in the charging direction.

Charge Combiner All panel output currents are added, producing a single current of 65A max.

Charge Controller Lead acid batteries require regulation of both voltage and charging current for optimum performance. The 80A controller also displays both charging Volts and Amps.

6-Volt Golf Cart Batteries Deep-cycle batteries contain much thicker plates than automotive types and can be deep-discharged hundreds of times. The 880 Ah bank has 3 days capacity, so daily discharge is just 33%, yielding a 6-year life.

3-kW Inverter/Charger Rated at 3-kW continuous, the inverter can supply 30A of 110VAC power to multiple circuits through the AC load panel. It can also provide up to 6-kW surge power for 20 seconds for starting motors. A built-in transfer switch and charger switches the AC load panel to the backup generator and recharges the battery bank at the same time.

AC Load Panel The 60A AC Load Panel distributes incoming AC power to all of the home's individual 110VAC circuits

DC Load Panel Inverters are less than 90% efficient and draw power even while on standby waiting for a load. Running 12 VDC devices from the DC load center and switching on the 110 VAC inverter only when needed can reduce losses by as much as 25%.

Backup Generator There will always be strings of days when meager solar input drains the battery bank. A small, quiet 3-kW generator can take over the load and, through the inverter/charger, recharge the battery bank at the same time.

Example Off-the-Grid System

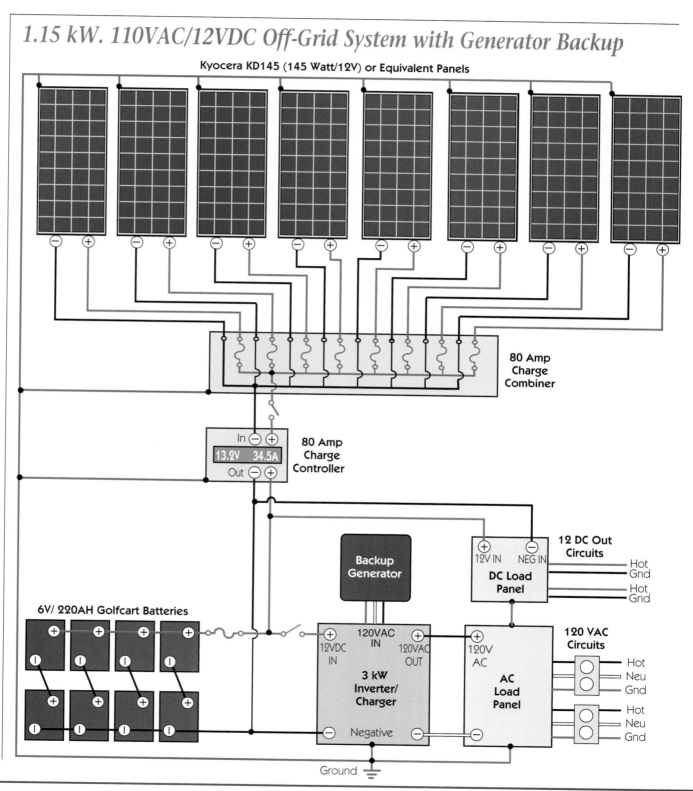

1.15 kW. 110VAC/12VDC Off-Grid System with Generator Backup

Kyocera KD145 (145 Watt/12V) or Equivalent Panels

80 Amp Charge Combiner

In ⊖ ⊕
13.2V 34.5A
Out ⊖ ⊕

80 Amp Charge Controller

Backup Generator

⊕ 12V IN   NEG IN ⊖
DC Load Panel

12 DC Out Circuits
Hot
Gnd
Hot
Gnd

6V/ 220AH Golfcart Batteries

⊕ 12VDC IN   120VAC IN   120VAC OUT ⊕
3 kW Inverter/ Charger
⊖ Negative

⊕ 120V AC
AC Load Panel
⊖

120 VAC Circuits
Hot
Neu
Gnd
Hot
Neu
Gnd

Ground

NOTES

17 PLUMBING

Like electrical wiring, plumbing is not rocket science. In spite of their high rates of pay, plumbers are as down to earth as one can get. If you get to know a plumber it won't be long before they tell you the two basic rules of plumbing:

1. Payday is Friday.
2. S*** runs downhill.

Of course it is a lot more complicated than that. We illustrate the code requirements for:

- pipe size vs. flow rates
- pipe size vs. length
- types of traps
- air venting to prevent siphoning of traps
- slopes of waste pipes

The plumbing of a tiny house is less in both extent and complexity than that of the average house with its multiple bathrooms, but measuring, cutting, sloping, and running the large and rigid drain and waste pipes can be daunting for the novice. Our intent is to have at least supplied enough guidance to allow you to plan your kitchen and bath.

Last, we discuss the difference between black (solid human) waste and gray (other) waste. Black waste requires connection to either a public sewage system or a private septic system. We consider the advantages of a toilet/gray waste system for tiny houses either on wheels or not connected to a municipal system.

Supply System

1. Water Source (see illustration)

The potable water for your tiny house may come from any of five sources:

- Utility pipes under the street or road
- Drilled or dug well on the property
- Pond or lake
- Another building (accessory dwelling)
- Delivered to a storage tank in the house.

If you pay for water and sewage, your usage is recorded by a water meter.

2. Water Heater

Most houses contain three or more bedrooms and are designed to accommodate four or more occupants, while the tiny house usually serves but one or two occupants. With its minimal demand, the tiny house water heater can be a:

- 5-gallon electric under-the-counter tank
- on-demand propane or electric wall unit
- RV 2-gallon propane/electric direct vent unit
- pot heated on the stove top.

3. Supply Pipes

Supply pipes, whether rigid copper, PVC, or flexible PEX, that serve many fixtures are called *trunk lines*, and are usually ¾″ in diameter. Pipes serving hose bibbs and other fixtures with high demands may be ¾″ as well.

Pipes serving only one or two fixtures are called *branch lines*. Because they carry less water, they are often reduced in size to ½″ and, in the case of toilets, ³/₈″. Exceptions are pipes serving both a shower and another fixture.

4. Fixtures

Fixture is the general plumbing term for any fixed device using water. The fixtures in any habitable house include a water closet (unless replaced by a composting toilet), bathroom lavatory, tub or shower, and kitchen sink.

Every fixture should have shutoff valves on both hot and cold supplies so that repairing the single fixture doesn't require shutting off the entire house supply at the meter valve.

Trunk and Branch Line Pipe Sizes

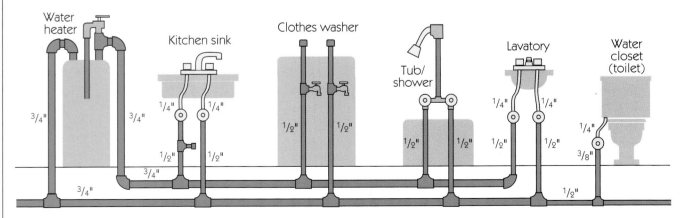

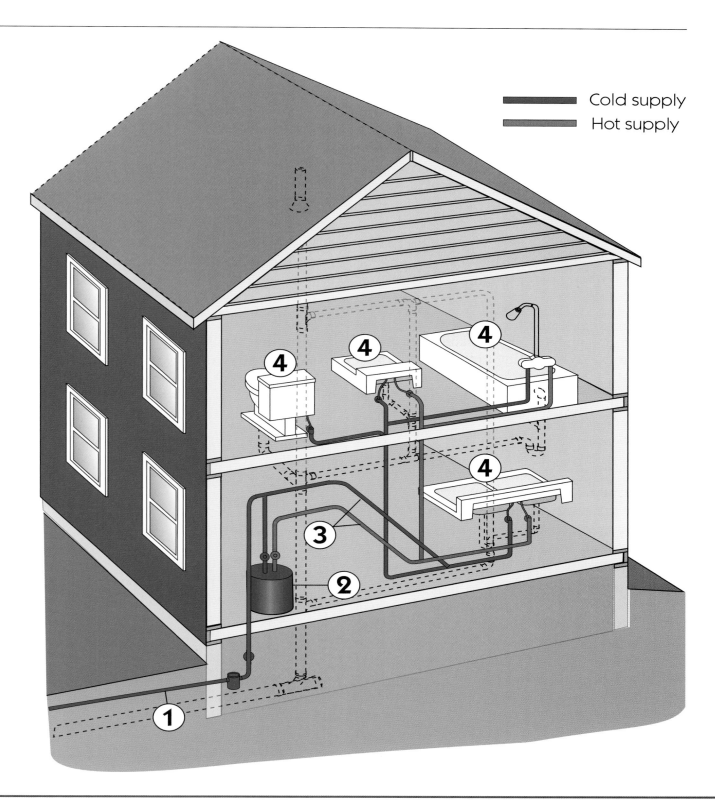

Cold supply

Hot supply

Draining the Waste

The drain and waste system is the assemblage of pipes that collect and deliver used water (*waste*) to either the municipal or private sewage system.

The minimum diameter of a *drain* is determined by the rate of discharge of the fixture(s) it serves. As with a river, the smaller tributary drain pipes that feed into the *house drain* are called *branches*.

Two types of waste are defined:

- *Black waste*, the human waste from a toilet
- *Gray waste*, all other liquid waste.

The largest vertical drain pipe, extending from the lowest point to the roof, and to which the smaller horizontal branch drains connect, is called the *soil stack*. The term *soil* implies that the drain carries black waste. If it does, and/or it serves enough fixture units, it must be at least 3" in diameter. Note that substituting a composting toilet for the standard water-flushing toilet eliminates black waste and a lot of complexity and cost.

The largest, bottom-most horizontal waste pipe is the *house drain*. In a balance between too-slow and too-rapid flow, the house drain and all other horizontal waste pipes must be sloped between $1/8$" and $1/4$" per foot.

To allow for unclogging drain pipes, Y-shaped *cleanouts* are provided. At a minimum, there will be a 4" diameter cleanout at the point where the house drain leaves the building. Additional cleanouts are required throughout the waste system for every 100' of horizontal run and every cumulative change of direction of 135°.

The waste pipe outside of the building is termed the *house sewer*. It is always at least 4" in diameter.

Function of the Vents

As you will see on pages 216 and 217, *fixture drains* must be kept at atmospheric pressure so that the water seals in their drain *traps* are not siphoned away, thereby exposing the interior of the house to sewer gases. The *vent* system consists of the pipes that relieve pressure differences within the drain system.

All plumbing fixtures (things that use and discharge waste water into the drain system) possess traps. To prevent waste water from forming a siphon during discharge, air must be introduced into the drain pipe near the outlet of the trap (maximum distance determined by the drain pipe diameter).

The primary vent is the upper part of the large-diameter vertical pipe termed the *stack*. Below the highest point of waste discharge it is the *waste stack*. Above that point it is the *vent stack*. If a waste stack also serves a water-flushing toilet (it usually does), it is called the *soil stack*. Because it provides a direct air passage to the municipal sewer pipe or private septic tank, a vent stack must be terminated in open air.

The permitted length of drain pipe from a trap to a vent (the *trap arm*) is specified by code as a function of the pipe diameter. (See page 216.) If the horizontal run of the drain is too long, another vent stack is usually provided close after the trap.

Another solution to the too-long horizontal drain is to break it into legal lengths with *revents*. Another solution, allowed only for single fixtures in locations precluding regular venting, is the *air-admittance valve* (see page 216). This is an air check valve, which allows house air into the drain.

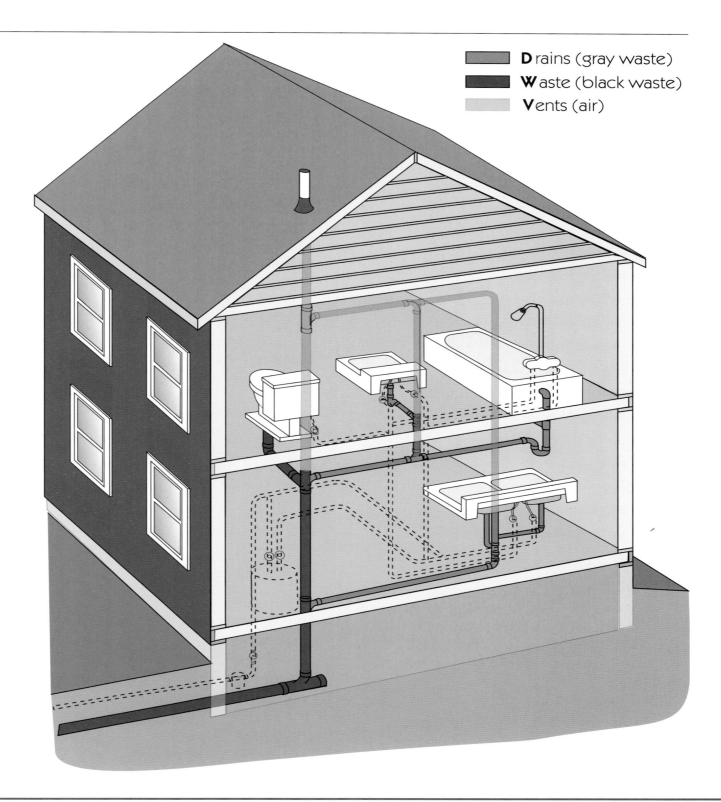

D rains (gray waste)
W aste (black waste)
V ents (air)

Roughing in the Pipes

Potable water piping, both hot and cold, can be rigid copper, chlorinated polyvinyl chloride (CPVC), or cross-linked polyethylene (PEX). Base your choice on:

- Copper is rigid, expensive, and difficult.
- CPVC is rigid, inexpensive, and simple.
- PEX is flexible, expensive, but simple.

Regardless of your choice of materials and how you run the piping, the end points—where the piping meets the fixture connections—are standardized. Unless the fixture manufacturer specifies otherwise (always read the directions!), you or your plumber will be expecting the *rough-in dimensions* shown in the illustrations.

Bathtub

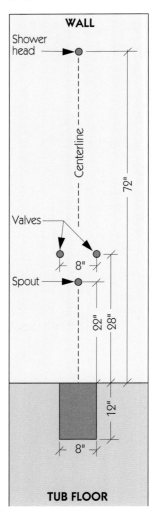

Shower

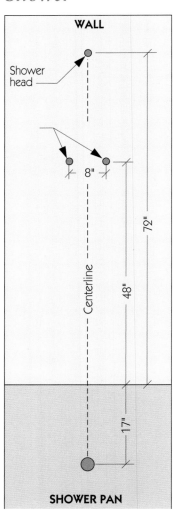

Shower Pans (Bases)

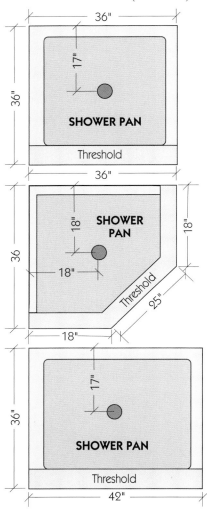

Toilet

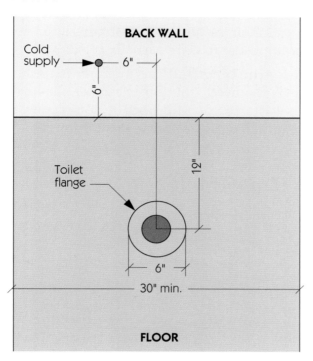

Bathroom Sink (Lavatory)

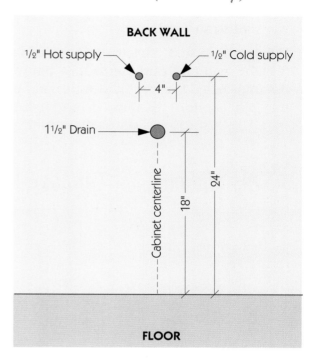

Kitchen Sink

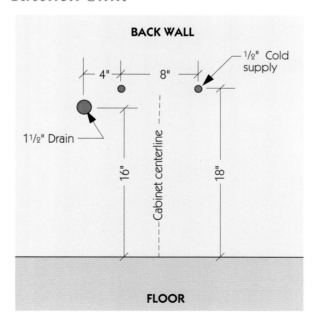

Laundry Tub

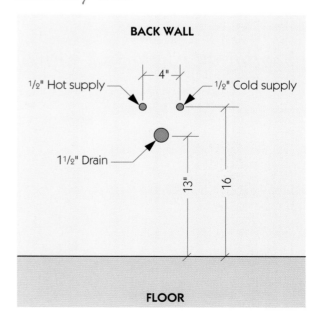

Traps & Venting

Traps are fittings that retain, or "trap," water in order to block the backflow of sewer gas. Improperly installed, they can fail in the three ways illustrated below.

S-Trap Siphon. If the wastewater completely fills the trap and outlet arm to a point below the trap outlet, the weight of water in the outlet may pull (siphon) the water behind it out of the trap. For this reason S-traps are prohibited.

Tailpiece Length. If the vertical drainpipe (the *tailpiece*) just below the fixture outlet is too long, the falling water may develop enough momentum to propel it past the outlet weir, leaving the trap only partially filled.

Trap Arm Length. If the *trap arm* is too long for its diameter, friction resistance may cause the waste to back up until it completely fills the outlet, again resulting in siphoning.

S-Trap Siphon

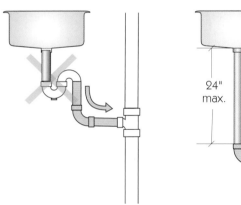

Tailpiece Length

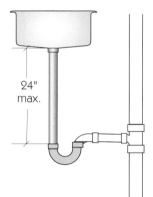

24" max.

Trap Arm Length

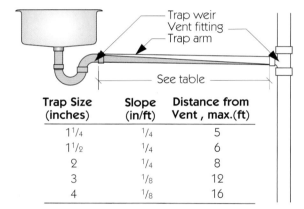

Trap weir
Vent fitting
Trap arm

See table

Trap Size (inches)	Slope (in/ft)	Distance from Vent, max.(ft)
1¼	¼	5
1½	¼	6
2	¼	8
3	⅛	12
4	⅛	16

Venting an Island Sink with an Air Admittance Valve (AAV)

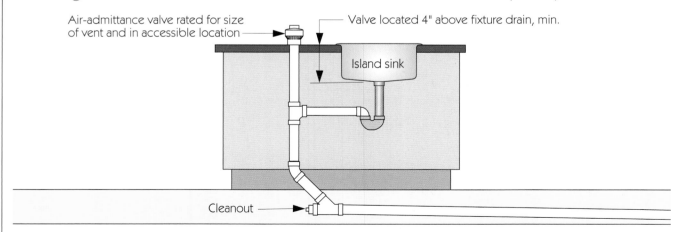

Air-admittance valve rated for size of vent and in accessible location

Valve located 4" above fixture drain, min.

Island sink

Cleanout

Integral Toilet Trap

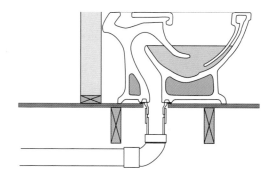

Clothes Washer Trap

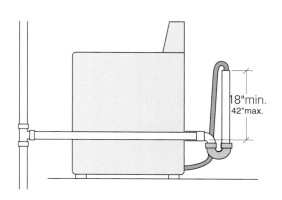

18"min.
42"max.

Below-Floor Tub Trap

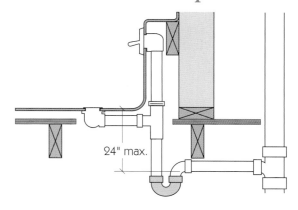

24" max.

Above-Floor Tub Trap

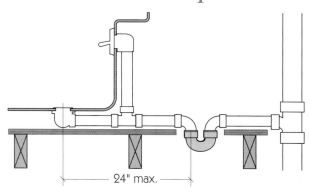

24" max.

Shower Trap

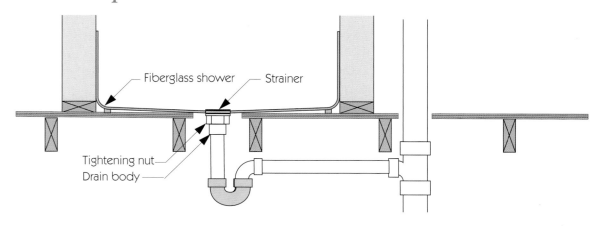

Fiberglass shower   Strainer

Tightening nut
Drain body

The Gray Waste Alternative

The Standard Solutions

Cities always, and towns often, provide potable water and sewage disposal. When available you have no choice but to connect to both where they pass in front of your property.

Homes in rural areas lacking a sewage treatment/disposal utility have their own *septic system* which treats both black and gray waste.

A typical private septic system is shown on the facing page, top. All waste, both gray waste and black (human) waste, flows by gravity through the 4-inch house drain into a large (500–2,000-gallon) *septic tank*. The tank has two chambers. In the first the raw sewage is digested by resident anaerobic bacteria. Waste that is not digestible, such as plastic-reinforced paper towels, settles to the bottom as sludge. As more water flows into the tank, the mostly digested waste flows into the second smaller chamber for further settling. Eventually the now clear waste water exits the tank and flows into a *distribution chamber* where is directed into several *leach beds*. Some of the water in the leach bed sinks into the ground; the remainder is taken up by the vegetation covering the beds.

With proper soils and with proper care, a septic tank/leach field system can last a lifetime. However, several factors make them less than ideal for tiny houses. They:

- typically cost $15,000 to $30,000.
- require pumping out every 3–5 years
- can be fouled irreversibly if the tank fills and allows untreated waste to overflow into the leach field.

A Composting Toilet Alternative

A septic tank is required because black waste contains human fecal matter. Were the waste to contain no fecal matter, the liquid effluent could be disposed of in a simple "dry well," a large pit dug in a porous soil, filled with stones, and covered by sod. Even better, the effluent could irrigate vegetation, including trees and shrubs (see illustration on the facing page, bottom).

What makes this simple, inexpensive solution possible is the modern composting toilet. The popular Nature's Head® toilet collects your "donations" in two separate containers: a 2-gallon urine bottle in front and a solids bin filled with peat moss at the rear, A microfan pulls air through the composting bin and vents it outdoors, so the unit is odorless. The urine is emptied daily, but with two people the compost requires changing just once every 2–3 weeks.

Nature's Head® Dry Toilet

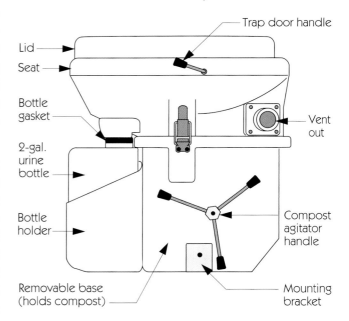

Standard Septic System

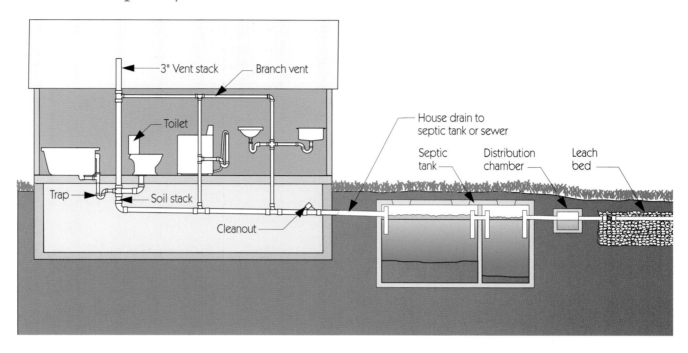

3" Vent stack — Branch vent

Toilet

House drain to septic tank or sewer

Septic tank — Distribution chamber — Leach bed

Trap — Soil stack

Cleanout

The Composting Toilet/Gray Waste Alternative

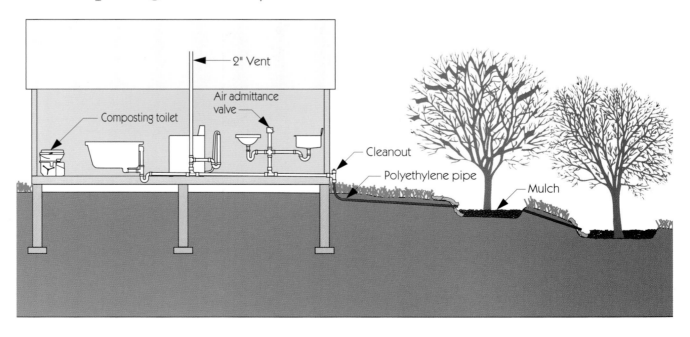

2" Vent

Air admittance valve

Composting toilet

Cleanout

Polyethylene pipe

Mulch

Notes

18 HEATING

One of the most often cited benefits of living in a tiny house—right up there with lower mortgage payments and lower taxes—is a much smaller heating bill. The annual heating bill for the average oil- or propane-heated home in northern New England is about $3,000. The heating bill for our 288-sq.ft. example tiny house is between $200 and $400.

Maximum system efficiency is achieved when the maximum heat output in Btu/hour matches the design heat load—the rate of heat loss of the house exceeded only 2.5% of the time during the heating season. Thus, the tiny home designer is faced with two tasks:

- calculating the design heat load of the little building
- finding heating systems that match tiny heat load.

This chapter enables you to do both. First we show how to calculate both the design (per hour) heat load and the annual heat load in Btu. We then show and list specifications for nine extra small systems using four different fuels.

Heat Energy: Btu

Although we buy energy in gallons of fuel oil, cords of wood, and kilowatt hours of electricity, their energy contents are all measured in the *British Thermal Unit*, the *Btu*.

And although the illustration depicts a wooden match as having an energy content of 1 Btu, the actual Btu definition is based on the energy in heated water.

> *Btu: the quantity of heat required to raise the temperature of 1 pound of water by 1F°.*

For a better perspective remember, "A pint's a pound the world around." Based on that, raising the temperature of a gallon of water by 1F° would require 8 Btu. Boiling (212°F) a gallon of water (8 lb.) starting from 72°F would require:

$$8 \times (212 - 72) = 1,120 \text{ Btu}$$

Insulation: R-Value

Heat energy can be transfered in three ways:

- *Radiation*—through space (or any other transparent medium) from warmer to cooler objects
- *Convection*—carried by fluids such as air or water
- *Conduction*—through solid materials.

In each case the transfer of heat is from warmer (higher concentration of energy) toward cooler (lower concentration of energy).

In order to simplify the calculation of heat flow through building floors, walls, roofs, windows, and doors, engineers assume all heat flow to be by conduction and may be calculated by the simple heat flow equation illustrated at right. Note that the equation can be turned around allowing the R-value of a building component

How Much Heat is 1 Btu?

Wood match = 1 Btu

The Heat Flow Equation

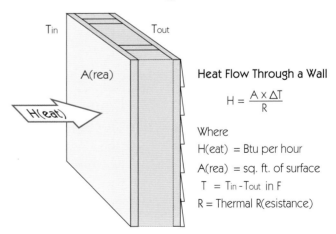

T_{in} T_{out}

A(rea)

H(eat)

Heat Flow Through a Wall

$$H = \frac{A \times \Delta T}{R}$$

Where
H(eat) = Btu per hour
A(rea) = sq. ft. of surface
T = T_{in} - T_{out} in F
R = Thermal R(esistance)

such as the wall shown to be calculated in the laboratory from the measured temperatures, area, and heat flow. This is how the R-values of insulation and other building materials are determined in the laboratory.

Heat Loss Through Building Surfaces

During the heating season the temperature inside a house is, on average, higher than outdoors. According to the heat flow equation heat will flow from inside to outside through every surface bounding the warm interior, and the rate of heat flow will be directly proportional to the temperature difference but inversely proportional to the R-values of the surfaces.

For the effective R-values of these surfaces, see the following pages:

- *Floor*—Ch 15, pages 182–183
- *Walls*—Ch 15, pages 184–185
- *Roof or ceiling*—Ch 15, pages 186–187
- *Windows*—(R = 1/U) Ch 14, page 166
- *Doors*—(R = 1/U) Ch 14, page 172

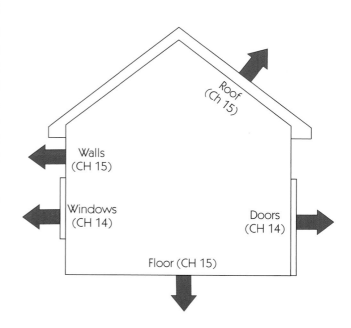

Heat Loss Through Air Leakage

The reason hot air balloons and smoke from fires rise is that warm air is less dense than the surrounding air. Like a log in water, the warm air is buoyant and floats to the top.

A heated house in winter is thus a hot air balloon. Only its great weight prevents it from floating upward. However, it is also a leaky balloon. Cracks, holes, defective weatherstrips, and plumbing and electrical penetrations allow the warmed air to escape.

A more obvious cause of air leakage is wind. The increased pressure on the upwind side and decreased pressure on the downwind side result in the air leakages into, through, and out of the building as shown.

Air leakage or "infiltration" is usually expressed as building air exchanges per hour.

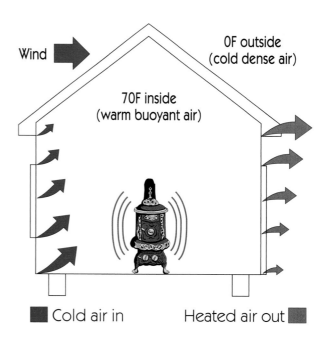

Heat Loss Design Data

In sizing a heating system for a building, we need to determine two types of heat load (rates of heat loss):

Design Heat Load is the rate at which heat is lost from the building in Btu per hour when the outside temperature is at the design minimum temperature (DMT) for the location.

Annual Heat Load is the total heat loss in Btu over the entire heating season. The quantity is used to estimate the annual heating bill.

You can the data below and the form on the facing page to estimate both loads for your tiny home. A completed example work sheet follows on page 226.

State, City	HDD$_{65}$	DMT
Alabama, Birmingham	2823	27
Alaska, Juneau	835	10
Arizona, Flagstaff	6999	-10
Arizona, Phoenix	1027	25
Arkansas, Little Rock	3084	5
California, Los Angeles	1274	35
Colorado, Denver	6128	-10
Connecticut, Hartford	6104	0
Delaware, Wilmington	4888	0
DC, Washington	4055	0
Florida, Orlando	580	33
Florida, Miami	149	35
Georgia, Atlanta	2827	10
Idaho, Boise	5727	-10
Illinois, Chicago	6498	-10
Indiana, Indianapolis	5521	-10
Iowa, Des Moines	6436	-15
Kansas, Topeka	5225	-10
Kentucky, Louisville	4352	0
Louisiana, Baton Rouge	1689	20
Maine, Portland	7318	2
Maryland, Baltimore	4720	0
Massachusetts, Boston	5630	0
Michigan, Detroit	6422	-10
Minnesota, Duluth	9724	-25
Mississippi, Jackson	2401	10

State, City	HDD$_{65}$	DMT
Missouri, St Louis	4758	0
Montana, Missoula	7622	-15
Nebraska, North Platte	6766	-20
Nevada, Las Vegas	2239	23
New Hampshire, Concord	7478	-15
New Jersey, Newark	4843	0
New Mexico, Albuquerque	4281	14
New York, New York	4754	0
North Carolina, Greensboro	3848	10
North Dakota, Bismarck	8802	-30
Ohio, Columbus	5492	-10
Oklahoma, Tulsa	3642	0
Oregon, Eugene	4786	`18
Pennsylvania, Philadelphia	4759	0
Rhode Island, Providence	5754	0
South Carolina, Columbia	2594	10
South Dakota, Rapid City	7211	-20
Tennessee, Nashville	3677	12
Texas, Austin	1648	23
Utah, Salt Lake City	5631	-10
Vermont, Burlington	7665	-10
Virginia, Norfolk	3368	15
Washington, Seattle	4615	15
West Virginia, Charleston	4644	0
Wisconsin, Madison	7493	-9
Wyoming, Casper	7571	-11

Heat Loss Form Instructions

Line 1. Floor area equals the building length x width in feet. Unless your floor will be significantly different from the four illustrated on pages 182–183, choose the R-value of the one most similar.

Line 2. Total wall area equals the total of the four rectangular wall areas (length x height) plus the gables (each 1/2 x length x height), minus the areas of windows and doors. Pick a wall R-value from those on pages 184–185.

Line 3. The roof or ceiling area is just the area warmed from below. It does not include the areas of any overhangs. Unless your roof will be significantly different from the four illustrated on pages 186–187, choose the one most similar.

Line 4. For convenience calculate the areas of windows based on their rough (framed) openings, not their glazed areas. Windows are labeled with their U-values. For the form, R-value = 1/U-value.

Line 5. It is not unusual to have two different door types, but both exterior doors are almost always 3'0" x 6'8" which equals 20 sq.ft. Doors are also labeled with U-values. For the form, again, R-value = 1/U-value.

Line 6. Standard energy-efficient construction results in an air leakage rate of about 0.5 air change per hour.

Line 7. Add all of the "result" entries above.

Line 8. Multiply the Line 7 result by the Design Minimum Temperature (DMT) in the table at left for the location most similar to your site. The result will be the hourly heat output required from your heating system or source. in Btu/hour.

Line 9. Multiply the Line 7 result by 24 and then by the Heating Degree Days (HDD_{65}) in the table at left for the location most similar to your site. The result will be the number of Btus required from your heating system over the entire heating season.

Building Heat Loss Calculation Form

Surface	Area, sq. ft.	÷	R-value	=	Result
1. Floor	_____	÷	_____	=	_____
2. Exterior walls	_____	÷	_____	=	_____
3. Roof or cathedral ceiling	_____	÷	_____	=	_____
4. Windows	_____	÷	_____	=	_____
5. Door #1	_____	÷	_____	=	_____
Door #2	_____	÷	_____	=	_____
6. Air changes/hour _____ x 0.018 x heated volume in cu.ft.			_____	=	_____
7. Sum of results of all lines above				=	_____
8. **Design heat loss:** Line 7 _____ x _____ (65°F - DMT)				=	_____ Btu/hour
9. **Annual heat loss:** Line 7 _____ x 24 x _____ HDD_{65}				=	_____ Btu/year

Example Heat Load Calculation

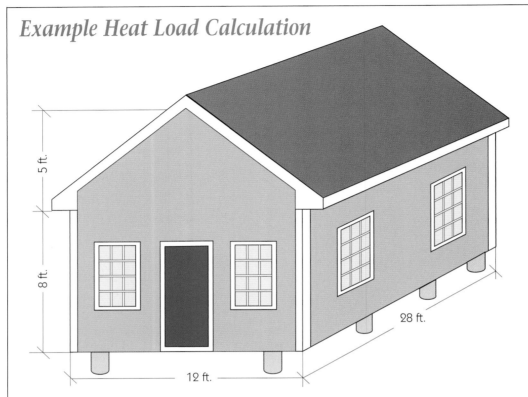

Areas & R-values

Floor: R = 22
area = 336 sq. ft.

Walls: R = 19
area = 520 sq. ft.

Roof: R = 22
area = 437 sq. ft.

Windows: R = 2.9
area = 80 sq. ft.

Door 1: R = 3.0
area = 20 sq. ft.

Door 2: R = 6.0
area = 20 sq. ft.

Vol. = 3,528 cu. ft.

Surface	Area, sq. ft.	÷	R-value	=	Result
1. Floor	336	÷	22	=	15.3
2. Exterior walls	520	÷	19	=	27.4
3. Roof or cathedral ceiling	437	÷	22	=	19.9
4. Windows	80	÷	2.9	=	27.6
5. Door #1	20	÷	3.0	=	6.7
Door #2	20	÷	6.0	=	3.3
6. Air changes/hour __0.5__ x 0.018 x heated volume in cu. ft.	3,528			=	3.8
7. Sum of results of all lines above				=	104
8. **Design heat load:** Line 7 __104__ x __75__ (65°F - DMT)				=	7,800 Btu/hour
9. **Annual heat load:** Line 7 __104__ x 24 x __6,422__ HDD$_{65}$				=	16,029,312 Btu/year

Heating Cost

Estimating Annual Heating Cost

The table at right lists the Btu contents of fuels in their usual unit quantities. The table at bottom right lists typical annual fuel utilization efficiencies (AFUEs) for heating systems applicable to tiny houses.

These figures and your building's annual heat load in Btu per year allow you to calculate the amount of fuel required for the entire heating season :

$$\text{Fuel required per year} = \frac{100 \times H}{F \times AFUE}$$

where:
- H = annual heat load, Btu/year
- F = Btu content per unit of fuel
- AFUE = annual fuel utilization efficiency, %

Example 1: How many gallons of propane would be needed to heat the example tiny house through the winter with an average new propane furnace or direct vent stove?

$$\begin{aligned}
\text{Propane per year} &= \frac{100 \times H}{F \times AFUE} \\
&= \frac{100 \times 16,029,312}{91,600 \times 80} \\
&= 219 \text{ gallons}
\end{aligned}$$

Example 2: How many kWhr of electricity would be required to heat the example tiny house through the winter with an Energy Star air-to-air heat pump?

$$\begin{aligned}
\text{Electricity per year} &= \frac{100 \times H}{F \times AFUE} \\
&= \frac{100 \times 16,029,312}{3,412 \times 250} \\
&= 1,879 \text{ kWhr}
\end{aligned}$$

Btu Content of Fuels

Fuel		Btu per	Unit
Oil	#2 (residential)	139,000	gal
Gas	Natural	103,000	ccf
	Propane	91,600	gal
Electricity		3,412	kWhr
Pellets	Ave. wood	320,000	bag
Cordwood	Beech	24,000,000	cord
	Red Oak	24,000,000	cord
	Sugar Maple	24,000,000	cord
	Red Maple	18,100,000	cord
	White Birch	20,200,000	cord
	Yellow Birch	21,800,000	cord
	Hemlock	15,900,000	cord
	Spruce	15,900,000	cord
	E. White Pine	14,300,000	cord

Heating Equipment Efficiencies

Fuel/type	AFUE
Oil furnace	
Energy Star min.	85%
Propane furnace or direct vent stove	
Average	80%
Energy Star min.	85%
Electricity	
Baseboard or central	100%
Heat pump, average	225%
Heat pump, Energy Star min.	250%
Wood pellets	
Pellet stove, min. efficiency	78%
Pellet stove, max. efficiency	85%
Wood, cord	
Air-tight stove	60%
Catalytic stove	80%

Choosing Your Heat Source

Most residential buildings in heating regions have design heat loads—the number of Btus per hour required to maintain a comfortable temperature when the outdoor temperature is at its lowest—of between 50,000 and 100,000 Btu per hour. Most whole house heating equipment is sized accordingly.

As our heat loss example on page 226 demonstrates, tiny houses typically require less than 10,000 Btu per hour. Finding heating equipment to match this tiny load can be difficult.

A second issue familiar to all homeowners in heating regions is the need for backup heat during power outages. Without a reliable and automatic second source of electricity to operate the heating system, pipes may freeze, causing great damage.

The table below and the illustration on the facing page list a variety of small heat sources and their important specifications. These are just a sampling of what is out there and are not to be taken as recommendations. Before purchase make sure the equipment fits your application in every regard. Things to consider include:

- Does the equipment operate automatically or require constant attention?
- Is the temperature control manual or by thermostat?
- Is an exhaust flue required and of what size?
- Is a backup heat source or backup electricity required during power outages?
- Will the equipment meet your local building/fire codes?
- How much floor space will the equipment require including clearances?

Small, Even Tiny, Heat Sources for Tiny Houses

Heat Source	Fuel	Output Btu/hr	Dimensions, in. H	W	D	Clearances, in. Side	Rear	Electricity Req'd Volts	Amps
1. Dwarf 3K[1]	Wood/coal	to 10,200	17	10	9	16	18	none	none
2. Jotul F602	Wood	to 28,000	25	13	21	16	18	none	none
3. Jamestown J1000	Pellets	to 25,000	24	23	14	3	1	120VAC	5.2A
4. Rinnai EX08CTP	propane	6,560	28	18	10	0	0	120VAC	.34A
5. Vermont Castings Intrepid	propane	17,500	24	22	14	4	3	120VAC[2]	—
6. Dickinson Cozy Cabin[3]	propane	to 5,000	16	8	7	0	0	none	none
7. Cadet Baseboard	electricity	3,400/2 ft.	7	24	3	0	0	240VAC	4.2A
8. Frigidaire FFRH0822R1	electricity	7,000	15	23	22	0	0	120VAC	12A
9. PioneerWYS009AMF1F1R2	electricity	9,000	12	28	8	0	0	120VAC	15A

[1] Not yet certified for residential use.   [2] Minimal, may be backed up with 4 AA batteries   [3] Marine stove

Small Heat Sources for Tiny Houses

WOOD STOVES

2. Jotul F602
5,000 - 28,000 Btuh

1. Dwarf 3K
10,200 Btuh

3. Jamestown J1000
6,000 - 38,000 Btuh

DIRECT VENT PROPANE STOVES

5. Vermont Castings Intrepid
16,000 - 17,500 Btuh

**6. Dickinson
Cozy Cabin**
5,000 Btuh

4. Rinnai EX08CTP
6,400 Btuh

ELECTRIC BASEBOARD

7. Cadet Baseboard
1,700 Btuh (per 24")

AIR-SOURCE HEAT PUMPS

8. Frigidaire FFRH0822R1
8,000 Cool/7,000 Heat Btuh

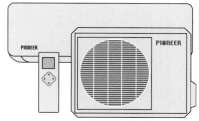

9. Pioneer WYS009AMF119RL
9,000 Cool/9,000 Heat Btuh

NOTES

19 COOLING

Ever since the taming of fire by humans we have found ways to generate *heat* in our homes. It is only recently (1902) that we found a way to generate *cold* with electricity.

Today, small window air conditioners sufficient to cool a tiny house can be had for less than $200. However, our ancestors had perfected a number of natural cooling techniques which are not only free but in many ways more healthful.

To understand and utilize these techniques, we first consider what constitutes *comfort* and its relationship to *air temperature, humidity, air movement* (breeze), and *radiation*. We then use that understanding to see how best to take advantage of:

- natural breezes
- natural ventilation
- ceiling fans
- window box fans
- evaporative coolers

Of course there are regions and times when all of the natural tricks fall short, so we end this chapter (and book) with how to determine the size of air conditioner or heat pump required to keep you and your tiny house cool.

19 COOLING
What Determines Comfort?

The Human Comfort Zone

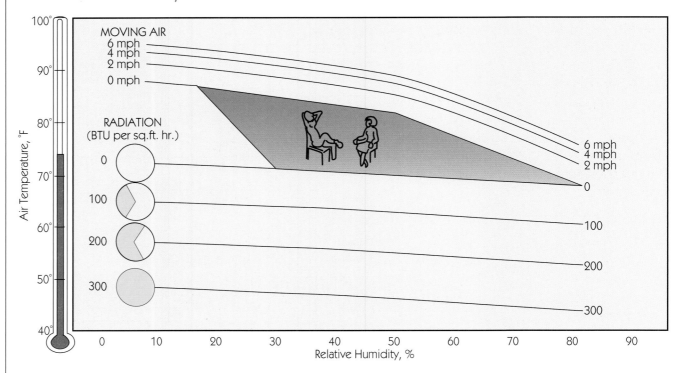

Who has not experienced the chilling effect of a breeze when emerging from a swim, the warming effect of sun on your skin, and the oppressiveness of humidity on a warm day? Air movement, thermal radiation, and relative humidity all affect our sense of comfort. The *human comfort* chart above graphically displays the effects of each on shifting the zone in which the average lightly clothed and seated person feels "comfortable."

In the absence of air movement or radiation the average person is seen to be comfortable at 50% relative humidity over a temperature range of 70°F to 83°F. Reducing the relative humidity to 20% raises the maximum comfort temperature to 87°F. In the opposite direction increasing relative humidity to 80% lowers the maximum comfort temperature to about 70°F.

The set of curves above the blue comfort zone show how air movement acts to raise the entire zone. A breeze of 6 mph is seen to shift the maximum comfort temperature upwards by about 7F°, so the upper limit at 50% relative humidity now becomes 90°F.

The curves below the comfort zone show how thermal radiation acts to lower the entire zone. Full direct sunshine on the skin, an intensity of 300 Btu per square foot per hour, can reduce the minimum comfort temperature by an incredible 24F°! Skiers can attest to feeling comfortable in shirt sleeves in the absence of wind and in full sunshine.

In the following pages we will see how to take advantage of these natural warming and cooling phenomena in the design and siting of a tiny house.

Natural Cooling

Tree Shading

Mature deciduous trees can provide 100% shade in summer while blocking just 25% of the sun in winter after dropping their leaves. So *don't*, like so many real estate developers, bulldoze those mature maple, oak, beech, etc. trees! It takes forty years for large deciduous trees to reach maturity. Site your tiny house so that its south face and roof are fully shaded from noon until 4PM June through August but bathed in sunshine throughout the heating season.

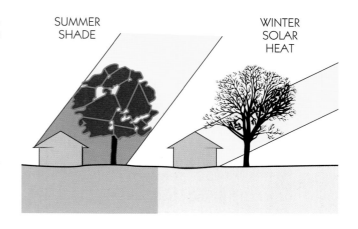

Tree Blocking & Elevation

Evergreen trees retain their foliage (needles) throughout the year. A dense stand of evergreens can block the strongest winter winds like a solid wall.

Site your house so its north side backs closely to a dense wall of evergreens. The wall of trees will nearly totally block the cold winter winds yet allow passage of a high percentage of summer breezes from other directions.

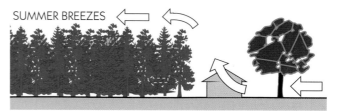

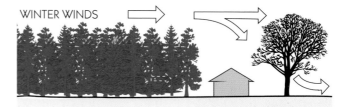

Plantings

Do you recall the front side-scoop windows in older automobiles? Driving down the road at 50 mph created a 50 mph breeze, and those little windows scooped the air and directed it right at the driver.

If your building site has a prevailing summer breeze direction, plant shrubs as in the figure to create high and low pressure areas and direct the prevailing cooling breeze through the house.

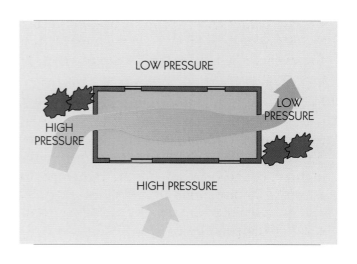

Ceiling Fans

When the breeze quits or is too warm, turn on the fans. Old-fashioned ceiling fans can't be beat for quiet efficiency. If possible, install one in every sleeping and sitting room.

Ceiling Fan Size vs. cfm

Ceiling fans range in diameter from 42 to 60 inches. The graph at right shows maximum air flow in cubic feet of air per minute (cfm) vs. diameter. As a rule match fan cfm to 2× the volume of the living space. For example, a 400 sq.ft. tiny house with average ceiling height of 10 ft. contains 4,000 cubic feet, so install fans to move 8,000 cfm. According to the graph you would need one 60" fan or two 42" fans.

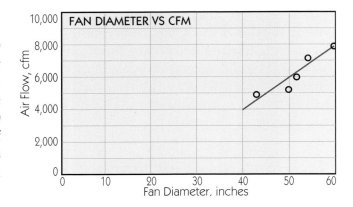

Fan Size vs. Efficiency

Compared to air conditioners, ceiling fans are remarkably efficient. The graph shows the air flow in cfm per Watt of electricity for the most efficient EnergyStar® fans at their lowest speeds. According to the graph, the 60" EnergyStar® fan can move 4,000 cfm while consuming just 10 Watts!

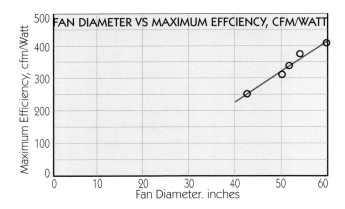

Fan Size vs. Created Breeze, mph

Recall from the human comfort chart that a breeze of 6 mph shifts the maximum comfort temperature upwards by about 7F° (making the room seem 7F° cooler). The chart at right shows the breeze directly below ceiling fans at their highest speeds are about 5 mph, so their cooling effects would be about 5F°.

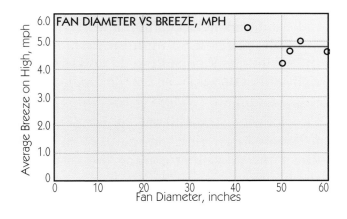

Fan Size vs. Floor Area

Usinging the data from the three previous charts, we can deduce the recommended total airflow rates and fan diameters for tiny houses ranging from less than 100 sq.ft. up to the maximum, 400 sq.ft. According to the chart a 100 sq.ft. space would be well served by a single 42" fan, while a 300 sq.ft. building could be served by a single 60" fan or several smaller fans.

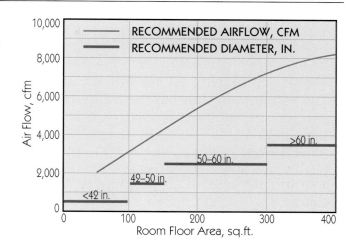

Fan Clearances, Ceiling & Wall

Fans installed less than 24" below the ceiling will be less efficient due to the friction caused by pulling the air into a constricted space. And fans whose blades come within 18" of a wall or other obstruction are likely to wobble due to turbulent air flow around the obstruction. Most important, however, is a minimum clearance above the floor of 84". Being struck in the head by a fan blade moving at its highest speed would cause serious injury, if not death!

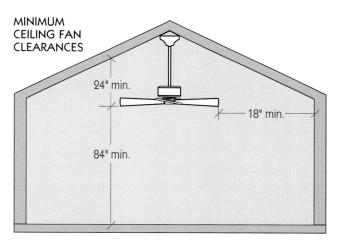

MINIMUM CEILING FAN CLEARANCES

Ceiling Fan Placement

A previous graph showed the maximum speed of vertical airflow at a fan's highest speed. This "breeze" was calculated from the fan diameter and airflow in cfm assuming all flow is in a vertical cylinder directly under the fan. Naturally, airspeed drops as the flow spreads in approaching the floor. Therefore, for maximum cooling effect, place ceiling fans directly over the locations you wish cooled.

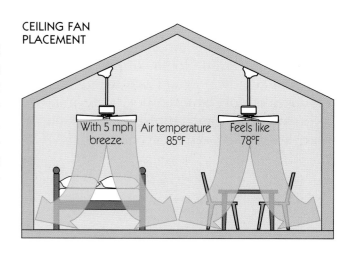

CEILING FAN PLACEMENT

Workhorse Box Fans

Ceiling fans create breezes by moving interior air *within* a building. Window fans create breezes by moving air *through* the building. The window fan thus has the ability to cool in two ways: 1) by the breeze effect of raising the maximum human comfort temperature, and 2) by forcing cooler outside air into the home.

One can purchase *window fans* designed for placement in double-hung windows, but these are generally small and move little air. Much more powerful are general-purpose, reversible, multi-speed *box fans*. With proper placement and leak-blocking filler strips (see illustration) a single box fan can replace the air in a tiny house ten to twenty times per hour.

Where to Place Box Fans

The effectiveness of a box fan depends on proper placement. First, the fan on high speed is quite loud, so for a peaceful sleep it should be located in a window far from your bedroom. Second, the fan should be used to work to *reinforce* any natural outdoor breeze, not *fight against* it. This may on occasion require either reversing the fan or moving it to another window. Third, to maximize the cooling effect, take advantage of the breeze effect on human comfort by choosing an air inlet window so the inflow is directly across your bed (see illustration).

Box Fan Window Installation

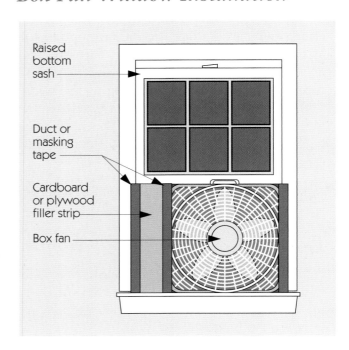

Raised bottom sash

Duct or masking tape

Cardboard or plywood filler strip

Box fan

Directing the Flow

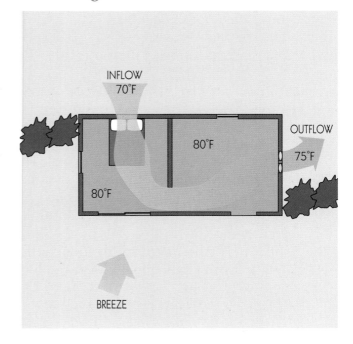

INFLOW 70°F

80°F

OUTFLOW 75°F

80°F

BREEZE

Using a Box Fan as a Heat Pump

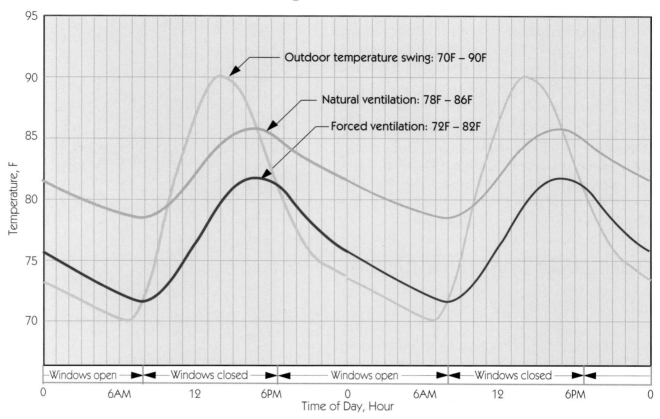

Heat Flushing to Avoid Air Conditioning

Where there is a strong diurnal swing in ambient temperature, one or more simple box fans can be used as "heat pumps" (not to be confused with heat pumps employing compressors) to maintain an average indoor temperature below the average outdoor temperature.

The idea could not be simpler but does require your participation. The yellow, red, and blue temperature plots in the graph above show how it works:

- *Yellow*—a typical outdoor temperature swing from an overnight low 70°F to a high of 90°F.

- *Red*—the interior temperature response of a well-insulated wood-framed house if windows are opened whenever the outdoor temperature is lower than that indoors.

- *Blue*—same as *Red* but with window fans augmenting the natural ventilation to cool the house nearly to the overnight low temperature.

Forced flushing of interior heat overnight is seen to lower the average maximum inside temperature by about 5F°, sometimes enough to avoid turning on the AC.

COOLING
Evaporative Coolers

How Swamp Coolers Cool the Air

Wet your hand and blow on it. Your skin feels cooler because evaporating water removes heat. An evaporative cooler's fan forces hot dry air through wet fibrous pads. As the dry air flows through the pads, its relative humidity rises, but its temperature drops.

Point A in the psychrometric chart at right represents air at 90°F and 20% RH. After passing through the evaporator, the air is at Point B, at 67°F and 80% RH. The drier the outdoor air to start, the greater the temperature drop.

The Psychrometric Chart

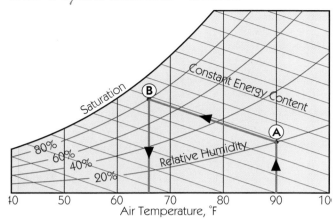

Potential for Evaporative Cooling

Evaporative coolers are economical and recommended wherever the potential temperature drop is greater than 20F° and the resulting cooled air would be below a comfortable 79°F. Unfortunately, these conditions generally obtain only in dry interior regions of the US. The table at right lists selected cities meeting both criteria. Provided your home will be in one of the qualifying areas, here is how to size an evaporative cooler:

1. Compute the interior volume of the house in cubic feet.

2. Find the recommended minutes per air change for a nearby location in the table.

3. Divide the house volume by recommended minutes to find the recommended cooler capacity in cubic feet per minute (cfm).

4. If your construction is above average in energy efficiency, divide your cubic feet per minute by 2; if your construction is poorly insulated, multiply by 2.

Location	DB °F	WB °F	Temp Drop F°	Cooled Temp °F	Minutes per Air Change
AZ, Phoenix	109	71	30	79	2
CA, Los Angeles	93	70	18	75	2
CO, Denver	93	59	27	66	4
ID, Boise	96	65	25	71	4
KS, Topeka	99	75	20	79	2
MT, Great Falls	91	60	25	66	3
NE, North Platte	97	69	22	75	3
NV, Las Vegas	108	66	34	74	3
NM, Albuquerque	96	61	28	68	3
ND, Bismarck	95	68	22	73	3
OK, Tulsa	101	74	22	79	1
SD, Rapid City	95	66	23	72	3
TX, Dallas	102	75	22	80	2
UT, Salt Lake City	97	62	28	69	4
WY, Casper	92	58	27	65	4

Air Conditioners

Window Air Conditioners

If all the previous natural and low-energy strategies prove inadequate, you will have to either suffer or install air conditioning.

Window air conditioners, designed to fit in the lower half of a doublehung window, are inexpensive and easy to install. You simply raise the bottom sash, set the AC on the window sill, spread the side filler panels, and fasten into place.

Sizing the AC is simple. For a conservative but crude estimate, simply purchase one rated for the square footage of your tiny home. They come rated for 150 sq.ft. (5,000 Btu), 250 sq.ft (6,500 Btu), 350 sq.ft (8,000 Btu), and up.

For a more accurate estimate, complete the sizing worksheet on page 241.

Split System Heat Pumps

Although inexpensive, window air conditioners have several drawbacks:

- Because they are fastened to a window sash, they are notoriously noisy in cooling mode.

- They block the view out the window.

- Unless removed in winter, they leak heat.

The more expensive split-system heat pump solves all of the above problems. Set on the ground or permanently attached to the building structure, the compressor makes little noise, and not requiring a doublehung window, it leaks no heat and blocks no view.

Best of all, however, the heat pump functions as an AC in summer and a heat source in winter. Window versions are also available but suffer all of the drawbacks of the window AC above.

Window AC Installation

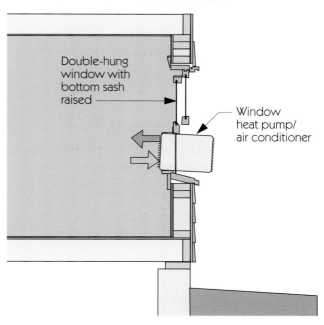

Double-hung window with bottom sash raised

Window heat pump/ air conditioner

Heat Pump Installation

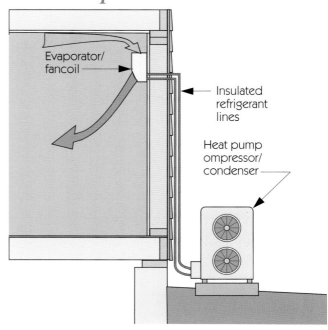

Evaporator/ fancoil

Insulated refrigerant lines

Heat pump ompressor/ condenser

AC Worksheet Instructions

Lines 1 and 2. Use line 1 if your house has a well-ventilated attic; otherwise use line 2. Find the shading factor in column 1 of Table 1. The effective R-value is 0.8 times the nominal R-value of the attic insulation. (See Chapter 15 for insulation R-values.) Use the value 2.4 if there is zero insulation present.

Line 3. Follow the same instructions as for lines 1 and 2. Enter doors as exterior walls. Do not include windows as they will be entered below.

Line 4. Interior walls are those separating cooled space from unconditioned spaces. If cooling the entire house, there will be no interior walls. The insulation factor is 0.8 times the nominal R-value of the wall insulation.

Line 5. Get the floor factor from Table 2; the insulation factor is as in line 4.

Line 6. Enter the floor area of the cooled space. Estimate air changes per hour as 0.4 for the tightest possible house to 1.3 for a drafty one.

Line 7. Window areas are height × width of the sashes. Get the glazing factors from Table 3.

Line 8. Get the shading factors from Table 1 and the glazing factors from Table 3.

Line 9. Add the results from lines 1 through 8 and multiply by the cooling factor on the map.

Line 10. Multiply your average monthly spring or fall kilowatt-hours (get these from your utility bills or by calling your electric utility) by 1.4.

Line 11. Enter the average number of people occupying the cooled space during the hot months.

Line 12. Add lines 9, 10, and 11, then multiply the result by the mass factor from Table 4.

Cooling Factors

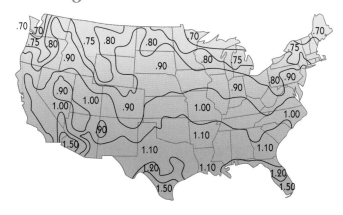

Type of Shade	Roof, Wall, Ceiling	Windows
No shade	1.00	1.00
Full shade	0.70	0.20
Partial outdoor shading	0.90	0.65
Inside window shades		0.45

Type of Floor	Factor
Open air under	1.00
Closed crawl or basement	0.00
Slab on grade	0.10

Type of Windows	Line 7	Line 8
Single-glazed	1.00	1.00
Double-glazed	0.50	0.80
Triple-glazed	0.33	0.65

Construction Factors	Factor
Light wood frame	1.00
Solid masonry or masonry veneer	0.80
Wood frame with interior masonry surfaces	0.80
Earth sheltered walls and roof	0.50

Work Sheet for Sizing Air Conditioners

Source of Heat Gain	Calculations	Results

1. Roof over ventilated attic _____ sq. ft. x 44 x _____ shading factor / _____ effective R-value = _____

2. Cathedral ceiling or roof _____ sq. ft. x 48 x _____ shading factor / _____ effective R-value = _____
   over unventilated attic

3. Exterior wall facing:
   North _____ sq. ft. x 18 x _____ shading factor / _____ effective R-value = _____

   East _____ sq. ft. x 28 x _____ shading factor / _____ effective R-value = _____

   South _____ sq. ft. x 24 x _____ shading factor / _____ effective R-value = _____

   West _____ sq. ft. x 28 x _____ shading factor / _____ effective R-value = _____

4. Interior walls facing _____ sq. ft. x 12 / _____ effective R-value = _____
   unconditioned rooms

5. Floors over unconditioned _____ sq. ft. x 20 x _____ floor factor / _____ effective R-value = _____
   spaces

6. Infiltration: living space _____ sq. ft. x _____ air changes/hour x 1.6 = _____

7. Window conduction _____ sq. ft. x 16 x _____ glazing factor = _____

8. Window solar gain:
   North _____ sq. ft. x 16 x _____ shading factor / _____ glazing factor = _____

   East, South, Southeast _____ sq. ft. x 80 x _____ shading factor / _____ glazing factor = _____

   West, Southwest, Northwest _____ sq. ft. x 140 x_____ shading factor / _____ glazing factor = _____

   Northeast _____ sq. ft. x 50 x _____ shading factor / _____ glazing factor = _____

9. Sum of lines 1 – 8 _____ x _____ cooling factor from map on page 240 = _____

10. Utility gain _____ watts being consumed in space x 3.4 = _____

11. People gain _____ number of people in space x 600 = _____

12. Peak cooling load, Btu/hour: sum of lines 9 – 11 x _____ thermal mass factor = _____

19 COOLING
AC Sizing Example

Example, Line by Line

Here is a completed example for calculating the size of an air conditioner for the tiny (336 sq.ft.) house in Detroit, MI, at right. This is the same tiny house for which we calculated the heat load and annual fuel consumption in Chapter 18, "Heating."

Line 1. There is no attic, so we skip to Line 2.

Line 2. The top of the conditioned (heated and cooled) space is a cathedral ceiling measuring 437 sq. ft. The roof is partially shaded by trees, so has a shading factor of 0.90. The effective R-value is 22.

Line 3. The north and south wall areas are each 224 sq. ft., less the window areas of 20 sq. ft., or 204 sq. ft. The east and west walls each net 86 sq. ft. by the same process. Both east and west walls are partially shaded, so their shading factors are 0.90. The north and south walls are fully shaded, giving them shading factors of 0.70. The effective R-values of all walls are 19.

Line 4. The entire house is air-conditioned, so the interior walls have no effect and are left blank.

Line 5. The house sits on posts, a vented crawl space, so the floor factor is 1.0. The floor is also insulated to the same degree as the cathedral ceiling, so its effective R-value is 22.

Line 6. The house is quite air-tight, so there are estimated to be 0.50 air changes per hour.

Line 7. The glazing factor, from column 1 of Table 3, for double-glazed windows is 0.50.

Line 8. Both east and south windows are entered on a single line. The shading factors are 0.65 and 0.20 respectively, so we enter the average value of 0.42. The glazing factor for all of the double-glazed windows is 0.80.

Line 9. The sum of the results column for all of the lines above is 6,677. Detroit's cooling factor of 0.75 is found from the map on page 240.

Example House for AC Sizing

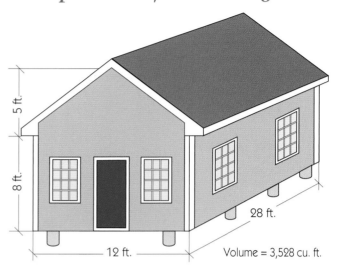

5 ft.

8 ft.

28 ft.

12 ft.

Volume = 3,528 cu. ft.

Areas & R-values

Floor: R = 22 area = 336 sq. ft.	Roof: R = 22 area = 437 sq. ft.	Door 1: R = 3.0 area = 20 sq. ft.
Walls: R = 19 area = 520 sq. ft.	Windows: R = 2.9 area = 80 sq. ft.	Door 2: R = 6.0 area = 20 sq. ft.

Line 10. The electric utility bills for the spring and fall months (minimal heating and cooling) are projected to be 350 kWh per month.

Line 1. Since this is truly a tiny house, there will most likely be either one or two occupants, so we enter an average value of 1.5.

Line 12. The thermal mass factor for a light wood frame house with no significant added mass is 1.00. The sum of lines 9 through 11 is 7,098, so the peak cooling load is 7,098 Btu/hr. It turns out that the heating and cooling loads for this tiny house are roughly equal. Moreover, both loads can be satisfied by either of the small heat pumps shown on page 229.

Work Sheet for Sizing Air Conditioners

Source of Heat Gain	Calculations	Results
1. Roof over ventilated attic	_____ sq. ft. x 44 x _____ shading factor / _____ effective R-value =	_____
2. Cathedral ceiling or roof over unventilated attic	__437__ sq. ft. x 48 x _0.90_ shading factor / _22_ effective R-value =	858
3. Exterior wall facing: North	__204__ sq. ft. x 18 x _0.70_ shading factor / _19_ effective R-value =	135
East	__86__ sq. ft. x 28 x _0.90_ shading factor / _19_ effective R-value =	141
South	__204__ sq. ft. x 24 x _0.70_ shading factor / _19_ effective R-value =	180
West	__86__ sq. ft. x 28 x _0.90_ shading factor / _19_ effective R-value =	114
4. Interior walls facing unconditioned rooms	_____ sq. ft. x 12 / _____ effective R-value =	_____
5. Floors over unconditioned spaces	__336__ sq. ft. x 20 x _1.00_ floor factor / __22__ effective R-value =	305
6. Infiltration: living space	__336__ sq. ft. x __0.5__ air changes/hour x 1.6 =	269
7. Window conduction	__80__ sq. ft. x 16 x _0.50_ glazing factor =	640
8. Window solar gain: North	__20__ sq. ft. x 16 x _0.20_ shading factor / _0.80_ glazing factor =	80
East, South, Southeast	__40__ sq. ft. x 80 x _0.42_ shading factor / _0.80_ glazing factor = 1,680-680=	
West, Southwest, Northwest	__20__ sq. ft. x 140 x _0.65_ shading factor /_0.80_ glazing factor =	2,275
Northeast	_____ sq. ft. x 50 x _____ shading factor / _____ glazing factor =	_____
9. Sum of lines 1 – 8 __6,677__	x __0.75__ cooling factor from map on page 240 =	5,008
10. Utility gain __350__ watts being consumed in space x 3.4 =		1,190
11. People gain __1.5__ number of people in space x 600 =		900
12. Peak cooling load, Btu/hour: sum of lines 9 – 11 x __1.00__ thermal mass factor =		7,098

NOTES

FURTHER INFORMATION

CH 1. Tiny Houses
Micro Living: 40 Innovative Tiny Houses Equipped for Full-Time Living, in 400 Square Feet or Less (North Adams, MA: Storey Publishing, 2018).

International Residential Code for One- and Two-Family Dwellings (Country Club Hills, IL: International Code Council, 2018).

CH 2. Tiny Aspects
International Residential Code for One- and Two-Family Dwellings (Country Club Hills, IL: International Code Council, 2018).

CH 3. Costs
Have Us Build Your Tiny House, (www. tinyhome builders.com, 2020).

CH 4. The Design Process
Designing a House (New York: The Overlook Press, 2012).

CH 5. Some Floor Plans
Tiny House Floor Plans: Over 200 Interior Designs (Amazon Createspace Independent Publishing Platform, 2012).

Micro Living: 40 Innovative Tiny Houses Equipped for Full-Time Living, in 400 Square Feet or Less (North Adams, MA: Storey Publishing, 2018).

CH 6. Drawing Plans
Architectural Drafting Simplified (Amazon Createspace Independent Publishing Platform, 2014).

CH 7. A Set of Plans
Architectural Drafting Simplified (Amazon Createspace Independent Publishing Platform, 2014).

CH 8. Foundations
Black & Decker Codes for Homeowners, 4th edition (Minneapolis, MN: Creative Publishing International, 2010).

CH 9. Framing
The Visual Handbook of Building and Remodeling, 4th edition (Newtown, CT: Taunton Press, 2017).

DEWALT Carpentry and Framing Complete Handbook (DEWALT Series), 2nd edition (Boston, MA: Cengage, 2018).

CH 10. Sheathing
Engineered Wood Construction Guide (Tacoma, WA: APA-The Engineered Wood Association, 2019).

Zip System R-Sheathing Installation Manual (Charlotte, NC: Huber Engineered Woods, 2015).

CH 11. Siding
Engineered Wood Construction Guide (Tacoma, WA: APA-The Engineered Wood Association, 2019).

The Visual Handbook of Building and Remodeling, 4th edition (Newtown, CT: Taunton Press, 2017).

CH 12. Roofing
Black & Decker DIY Roofing, (Minneapolis, MN: Cool Springs Press, 2018).

Moisture-Resistant Roof Construction (Tacoma, WA: APA-The Engineered Wood Association, 2017).

CH 13. Lofts & Stairs
International Residential Code, Appendix Q (Country Club Hills, IL: International Code Council, 2018).

CH 14. Windows & Doors
Black & Decker Codes for Homeowners, 4th edition (Minneapolis, MN: Creative Publishing International, 2010).

How to Choose Windows, (Efficient Windows Collaborative, www.efficientwindows.org, 2020).

Roof Windows (Velux Canada, velux.ca/ en/products/roof-windows, 2020).

CH 15. Insulation
The Visual Handbook of Building and Remodeling, 4th edition (Newtown, CT: Taunton Press, 2017).

CH 16. Electrical Wiring
Wiring a House, 5th edition (Newtown, CT: Taunton Press, 2014).

Mobile Solar Power Made Easy! (Amazon, CreateSpace Independent Publishing Platform, 2017).

CH 17. Plumbing
Ultimate Guide: Plumbing, 4th edition (Upper Saddle River, NJ: Creative Homeowner, 2017).

CH 18. Heating
The Visual Handbook of Building and Remodeling, 4th edition (Newtown, CT: Taunton Press, 2017).

CH 19. Cooling
The Visual Handbook of Energy Conservation, (Newtown, CT: Taunton Press, 2013).

Building Codes
Black & Decker Codes for Homeowners 4th edition, (Minneapolis, MN: Cool Springs Press, 2019).

DEWALT 2018 Residential Construction Codes: Complete Handbook, 3rd edition (Boston: Cengage, 2018)

International Residential Code for One- and Two-Family Dwellings (Country Club Hills, IL: International Code Council, 2018).

Tiny House Associations
American Tiny House Association, (*https://americantinyhouseassociation. org,* 2020).

Tiny Home Industry Association, (*https://www.tinyhomeindustryassociation.org,* 2020).

INDEX

A

Accessory dwelling units (ADU), 7
AC electrical circuits, 190. *See also* wiring
Air conditioners, 239–243
    efficiency of fans vs., 234
    sizing, overview, 240
    sizing, work sheets, 241, 243
    sizing example, 242
    types of, 239
Air-source heat pumps, 229
Alternating-tread devices, 155, 160
Amish sheds, 5
APA
    APA Engineered Wood Construction Guide,
        Form E30, 121
    bond classification, 122
    engineered wood panels, overview, 122
    Glued Floor, 125
    grade stamp, 122
    panel roof sheathing, 127
    panel subflooring, 124
    panel wall sheathing, 126
    plywood face grades, 122
    plywood underlayment, 124
    Rated Sheathing, 123
    Rated Siding, 134
    Structural I rated sheathing, 123
    Sturd-I-Floor, 123, 125
    T&G Roof Sheathing, 128
    Underlayment, 123
Appliances, design for, 36, 39
Architect's scale rule, 74
Asphalt shingles, 127, 142, 144–147, 149
Auger anchors, 94, 95
Awning windows, 164

B

Basement foundations
    North, 100
    South, 99
Bathrooms. *See* design; drawing plans; floor plans; framing; plumbing
Beams, 104–105. *See also* framing; ridge beams
Bedrooms/sleeping areas. *See* design; drawing plans; floor plans; framing
Bond classification, 122. *See also* APA
Box/window fans, 170, 236–237

Btu.

Btu. *See* cooling; heating
Building codes
    insulation and, 179
    overview, 12–14
    plumbing, 209
    for windows, 172
    See also design
Building site
    costs of, 17, 22
    impact fees, 24
    site plan, set of drawing plans for, 78 (*See also* drawing plans)
    site service costs, 23

C

Cable, electrical, 192, 193, 196–200. *See also* wiring
Casement windows, 164
Cedar shingles
    roofing, 142, 148–149
    siding, 129–131
Ceilings
    ceiling fans, 37, 234–235
    ceiling joists, framing, 116
    design for, 35
    IRC on height of, 13
    loft headroom, 154
Circuits, electrical, 190. *See also* wiring
Clapboard siding, 129, 132–133
Cold roof insulation, 186
Construction
    cooling, 231–243 (*See also* cooling)
    foundations, 91–100 (*See also* foundations)
    framing, 101–120
    heating, 221–229 (*See also* heating)
    insulation, 179–187 (*See also* insulation)
    lofts and stairs, 153–162 (*See also* lofts and stairs)
    plumbing, 209–219 (*See also* plumbing)
    roofing, 141–152 (*See also* roofs and roofing)
    sheathing, 121–128 (*See also* sheathing)
    siding, 129–139 (*See also* siding)
    windows and doors, 163–177 (*See also* doors; windows)
    wiring, 189–308 (*See also* wiring)
    See also building codes; costs; foundations; *International Residential Code*
Cooling, 231–243
    air conditioners, 239–243
    ceiling fans, 37, 234–235